ADVENTIST PROPHETIC FABLES

An Independent Consideration of Scripture

Revised Edition

by

Ioan Logos

aSys Publishing

Contents

Preface...vii

Acknowledgement..viii

Short history of Seventh-day Adventism 1

October 22, 1844 – Prophecy or prophetic blunder?.............6

The sanctuary doctrine 10

The shut door doctrine 17

Are there sins in the heavenly sanctuary? 19

Was the French Revolution a fulfilment of Bible prophecy?........21

The beast with seven heads and ten horns...........................26

The beast with two horns like a lamb..................................67

Genesis 2:2-3 79

The Fourth Commandment 87

Isaiah 66:22-23 92

Matthew 5:17-18 97

Revelation 12:17 and 14:12 105

   A. Is the Fourth Commandment applicable in heaven? 105

   B. Is the Seventh Commandment applicable in heaven?......107

   C. Is the Sinaitic Covenant faultless? 109

   D. Are Jesus' Commandments the Ten Commandments?....116

The Sanctuary 120

Old covenant and the cross of Golgotha..............................124

Cotroversial questions 126

   A. Is the seventh-day Sabbath binding on Christians?..........127

   B. Is the old covenant law binding on Christians? 136

   C. How are people converted to Adventism? 145

The Lord's Day..149

   A. Historical evidence of early Christian worship on the first day of the week..150

B. Is the Lord's Day of pagan origin? 156

C. Are Saturday and Sunday of pagan origin? 159

The Sabbath controversy..164

A. What does the Holy Scripture teach about the seventh day of the week? 164

B. What does the Holy Scripture teach about the first day of the week? 167

C. Saturday Sabbath or Sunday Sabbath? 168

Lord's rest or seventh day rest? 174

Ellen G. White – Prophetic visions or prophetic blunders? 176

A. Ellen G. White's failed prophecies....................................176

B. Ellen G. White's visions and remarks 179

C. Ellen G. White's teachings on diet....................................182

D. Ellen G. White's diverse observations 184

E. Ellen G. White – Prophetess or plagiarist? 185

F. Ellen G. White – Visions or seizures? 186

G. Who was Ellen G. White? 195

Adventist doctrinal recipes...197

1. The sanctuary doctrine 197

2. Ellen G. White...198

3. The Sabbath 199

4. Kosher food 202

5. The tithing..206

6. Adventist Church is the remnant church. 210

7. The Clear Word Bible..211

8. Seventh-day Adventists Church and the Sola Sriptura 212

Baptism – Adventist doctrines exposed! 213

1. Belief 17(18) – The gifts of prophecy 214

2. Belief 23(24) – Christ's ministry in the heavenly sanctuary.218

3. Belief 19(20) – The Sabbath...222

4. Vow 6..230

5. Belief 12(13) – The remnant and its mission 233

Conclusion...240

   Christ and the Sabbath...242

   Christ and the Law ··· 244

   Christ's Commandments......................................247

   Christians are justified before God through faith in Christ..248

   The seal of God 249

   Sanctification is the work of the Holy Spirit........................250

   Is Sabbath-keeping binding on Christians?..........................251

   The following prophetic verses cannot be attributed to the Western Roman Empire.......................................255

Bibliography...262

Preface

Some religious denominations claim prophetic inspiration and indoctrinate their subjects with the teaching that they are the chosen people, the remnant church of God. This book comes in response to such arrogant doctrinal allegations and consists of three parts, each of them conveying a specific message.

The first part analyses the three main doctrinal pillars on which Seventh-day Adventist Church was founded. These are: 1) the Sanctuary doctrine which turns out to be an attempt to give the "1844 Great Disappointment" of the Millerite movement a biblical prophetic image; 2) Ellen G. White, the alleged Lord's messenger, her prophetic visions, inspired writings and teachings; 3) the seventh-day Sabbath. Adventist doctrines and Ellen G. White's writings are analysed in the light of truth of the New Testament and alternative biblical ideology is offered to replace these myths.

The second part provides a commentary on the Book of Revelation chapters 13 and 17. It sheds new light on prophetic interpretation of the beasts of Revelation and points out that several current commentaries regarding these prophecies are erroneous or tendentious.

The third part is a brief analysis of several debatable biblical topics like: Sabbath in the New Testament, the Lord's Day, Christ and the law, similarities and differences between the Old and New Covenant. Strong biblical evidence is provided in support of this brief exegetical analysis.

Some readers may consider that the analysis of certain sensitive topics presented in this book is rather harsh, or even unacceptable. However, if they analyse and evaluate these biblical issues "*in spirit and in truth*", then their disappointment will be turned into joy.

Acknowledgement

I wish to express my sincere gratitude to all truth seekers, all who radiate and share their knowledge with others. Their devotion and zeal for the truth is an example and a source of inspiration for many believers. Despite many challenging circumstances, they took upon themselves the task of being bearers of the light of truth that shines in the darkness of this confused world of religions and doctrines.

> "[5] And the light shineth in the darkness; and the darkness [b]apprehended it not" (Jn.1:5).

Short history of Seventh-day Adventism

The word Adventist comes from the Latin, "*adventus*"[1] meaning "arrival or coming" which in turn is the translation of the Greek word "*parousia*"[1] used in reference to the Second Coming, that is, the second coming of Christ. The expression "seventh-day" is related to the seventh day Sabbath of the fourth commandment of the covenant between Yahweh and Israel established on Mount Sinai. These carefully selected words reflect doctrinal identity of the Seventh-day Adventist Church.

Adventist Church came into existence in the 19th century as a separate denomination due to its specific teachings, which had never been taught before in Christian churches. It was formed out of what we know today as the Millerite movement, and was formally established in 1863.

According to the New Testament, there will be signs in heaven and on earth before the return of Christ (Mt. 24:29-31; Mk. 13:24-27; Lk. 21:25-28; Rev. 6:12-17). Millerite leaders preached to the people about the "signs of the end time" and proclaimed the imminent advent of Christ. In their opinion, these were the signs: "the falling stars of 1833 - it was a Leonid meteor show, a phenomenon that occurs every 33 years (its manifestation seemed very intense on that date); dark day in the New England state of North America, which took place in 1780 – darkening of the sky, according to other sources, was caused by a huge forest fire combined with a weather front passing through the area; the Lisbon earthquake, which took place in 1755, presented as the worst natural cataclysm of this kind – in reality lacking the magnitude described in the Bible regarding the end times."[2]

After the "Great Disappointment of 1844" when thousands of Christians in North America having William Miller (a Baptist preacher) as their leader were expecting Christ's return on earth – without the expected event coming to pass – they realised that the calculation regarding the fulfilment of Daniel 8:14 prophecy was incorrect. Most believers involved in the Millerite movement acknowledged their mistake and reconciled. Some, however, refused to concede that the date of October 22, 1844 was a miscalculation – they were the ones who conceived new ideologies on which later was founded the Seventh-day Adventist Church.

A certain man, O. R. L. (Owen Russell Loomis) Crozier (Crosier) eventually published an article: "The Sanctuary" (*The Day-Star Extra, on February 7, 1846, pp.38-44*)[3] in which he came up with the idea that the "sanctuary" regarding Daniel 8:14 prophecy was in fact the "heavenly sanctuary", that in 1844 instead of coming to earth, as they expected, Christ had moved from the first department, the Holy Place, into the second department, the Most Holy Place of the Heavenly Sanctuar. The original idea was inspired by Hiram Edson[4].

Ellen G. White (born Harmon), after reading Crosier's article and his suggested explanation of the disappointment, had a vision: "The Lord showed me in a vision more than a year ago, that brother Crosier had the true light on the cleansing of the Sanctuary, and that it was his will that Brother C. should write out the view which he gave us in the Day-Star Extra, February 7, 1846. I feel fully authorized to recommend that Extra to every saint" (*A Word to the Little Flock, p.12, April 21, 1847*)[3], in which she said that brother Crosier had the right explanation concerning the event, and she recommended his article to the believers as the true light to follow.

Believers involved in the Millerite movement were Sunday keepers. After the "Great Disappointment", however, some of them accepted the seventh-day Sabbath, thus became Seventh-day Millerites (Sabbath keeping Millerites).

Few people know that Adventists actually borrowed the practice of Sabbath keeping from Seventh-day Baptists who called themselves Sabbatarian Baptists. Joseph Bates[5], who became the founder and developer of Sabbatarian Adventism, read a pamphlet by T. M. Preble[6], who in turn had been influenced by Rachel O. Preston [7][8], a young Seventh Day Baptist, convinced some of the Millerite leaders (James and Ellen White, Hiram Edson...) that the Bible teaches us to keep the Sabbath. It was Joseph Bates, who published his view on the Sabbath in August 1846, "The Seventh-day Sabbath. A Perpetual Sign"[5]. In his article he presented the Sabbath in a way similar to that upheld by the Seventh Day Baptist: as part of the Decalogue; a standard of Christian discipleship; a visible witness against the antichristian power that thought to change times and laws (Dan. 7:25).

"The first historical record of methodical Sabbath keeping by Christians, who stopped worshipping on the first day of the week, was two active Anabaptist leaders, Andreas Fisher and Oswald Glait, who became pioneers and promoters of the Sabbath in 1527. Both were priests who sacrificed priesthood to become first, Lutherans, and then Anabaptists. Glait and Fisher, who had been taught the false doctrines of the Catholic and Lutheran churches, that Sunday is the Sabbath, were astonished to read in the Bible that the Sabbath was indeed the 7th day. When they began to teach this, theologians were sent to persuade them to abandon what they called the "Jewish Sabbath." Both of them suffered a martyr's death, largely due to their Sabbatarian views. Sabbatarians owe a debt of gratitude to these Sabbath pioneers whose work later influenced the origin of the Seventh-day Baptist Church."[9]

As Helen Appleton stated in her book, What Seventh Day Adventists Believe, "A thoroughly indoctrinated Seventh Day Adventist believes that the denomination was raised up at a special time in history – 1844 AD with a special message, that of Revelation chapter 14, known to the Seventh Day Adventists as the "Three Angels Message" and including: 1. work of investigative judgement for the professed Christians; 2. a call for the keeping of the Seventh day Sabbath of the Old Covenant; 3. a denunciation of all other churches for rejecting these messages.

In other words, the teaching is that the 2300 "days" of Daniel

8:14 ended in 1844 AD which date marked the "cleansing of the Sanctuary" when an Investigative Judgement was to begin in heaven concerning the names of all the professed people of God. Read Great Controversy, p.480.

These "messages" are to develop a people ready to meet the Lord at His second coming. Only Seventh Day keepers will be so ready – they will have the "seal of God" upon them because of their seventh day Sabbath keeping – in other words they are accepted to God because of their "works of the law." All who reject this teaching and keep Sunday will have upon them, the "mark of the beast" and will thus incur the wrath and punishment of God. The churches that reject the "message" thus become part of the Babylon of Rev. 14:8, and as such are "fallen" and have become "the habitation of devils, and the hold of every foul spirits, and a cage of every unclean and hateful bird" as per Rev. 18."[10]

Seventh-day Adventist Church was established on these two fables: Miller's "Daniel 8:14 prophecy" and Crozier's "sanctuary doctrine" to which, in addition, was adopted Sabbath keeping. All these imaginative teachings were modelled by the so-called "prophetic visions and teachings" of Ellen G. White and subsequently incorporated into doctrines.

At first glance, such an ideological equation seems pretty attractive. In this regard, the following remarks cannot escape our attention:

1) On October 22, 1844, Christ entered into the Most Holy Place of the Heavenly Sanctuary (to the Ancient of Days).

2) On October 22, 1844, Christ entered the second and last phase of His atoning ministry, a work of investigative judgement.

3) There is sin (impurity) in the Most Holy Place of the Heavenly Sanctuary, which was brought in by the blood of Christ – the Lamb of God.

4) Ellen G. White is the Lord's messenger, a prophet, and her

writings are a continuous and authoritative source of truth in the church.

5) Seventh-day Sabbath of the old covenant is the seal of God; therefore, Sabbath keeping is essential in the salvation process of believers.

6) Sunday keeping is the mark of the beast.

7) A coalition of religious and secular authorities will enforce a Sunday law; as a consequently, Sabbath-keeping believers (Seventh-day Adventists) will be persecuted.

8) Seventh-day Adventist Church is the remnant Church of God.

Such arrogant doctrinal allegations, however, are not exempt from unexpected surprises:

- William Miller's interpretation of Daniel 8:14 prophecy proved to be erroneous – an incontestable reality;

- O. R. L. Crosier[3] later repudiated his early beliefs on the "Shut Door" and the "Sanctuary" published on February 7, 1846;

- Ellen G. White's so-called prophetic visions are very controversial and her prophecies did not come true;

- Adventist doctrinal teachings concerning Sabbath observance for believers under God's new covenant are marked by inconsistency.

It is very evident the fact that such provocative ideologies cannot be left unnoticed. Therefore, a thorough analysis of the history of Adventism and its fundamental doctrines is absolutely indispensable.

October 22, 1844 – Prophecy or prophetic blunder?

"¹⁴ He said to me, To two thousand and three hundred evenings and mornings; then shall the sanctuary be cleansed." (Dan. 8:14).

The people involved in the "Millerite movement" sincerely believed in Christ's Second Advent. However, the problem with this movement was that its leaders acted out of ignorance, for the Scripture states very clearly that only God alone knows the time of Christ's return (Mt. 24:36; Mk. 13:32). In their zeal to solve Daniel's prophecy regarding the *"cleansing of the sanctuary"* (Dan. 8:14), they thought they came up with the right answer. According to their calculation, this prophecy was to be fulfilled in 1844 AD. On this date, October 22, 1844, Christ would return to earth as prophesied; however, the great confusion that followed later confirmed a different reality.

The Millerite calculation, which leads to the fabulous date, October 22, 1844, required human imagination. These are the most probable steps of their calculation:

1) They applied the "day-year" principle, thus Daniel's 2300 prophetic days were interpreted as 2300 years.

2) The year 457 BC – the date when Artaxerxes, the king of Persia, had issued a decree for rebuilding Jerusalem (Dan. 9:24-25; Ezra 7:11-12) – marks the beginning of the 2300 year (day) prophecy; it also marks the beginning of the *"seven times seventy years"* prophecy (Dan. 9:24).

3) To 457 BC were added 2300 years, which led to 1843 AD;

however, after some adjustments, most probably based on the Jewish karaite calendar (...*on the tenth day of the seventh month?*), the final date was established – October 22, 1844.

Note: Some Millerites were expecting Christ's return in 1843.

At first impression such a calculation looks pretty attractive; however, a thorough analysis of the issue reveals contradictory facts as follows:

1) Daniel 8:14 mentions "*2300 evenings and mornings*" not 2300 days. The alleged "evening and morning-year" principle doesn't make any sense. In this case, it is common sense to suggest that "*2300 evenings and mornings*" are equal to 1150 days, as there were two sacrifices offered daily – one in the morning and another one in the evening.

   Note: Concerning Daniel 8:14, some Bible translations contains "*two thousand and three hundred days.*" Most Bible translations contain "*two thousand and three hundred mornings and evenings*" – a more accurate translation. In this respect, Daniel 8:26 gives us a clue: "*and the vision of the evenings and the mornings which was told is true...*" – this verse confirms the accuracy of Bible translation of Daniel 8:14 containing "*two thousands and three hundred evenings and mornings.*"

2) According to Daniel 8:14, "*2300 evenings and mornings*" prophecy ends in the cleansing (reconsecration) of the Sanctuary; according to Millerite calculation, "*2300 evenings and mornings*" prophecy (457 BC - 1844 AD) ends in a ruined Sanctuary (since 70 AD).

3) According to Daniel chapter 9, the decree to rebuild Jerusalem implies the Anointed One; the prophecy also predicts destruction of Jerusalem and the Temple (see: Dan. 9:25-26).

4) The "*457 BC decree*" allowed Ezra and other Israelites to return to Jerusalem for the purpose of worship (Ezra 7:11-27); the "*444 BC decree*" would be more correct, as it was directly implicated with rebuilding of Jerusalem (Neh. 2:5-8).

5) The prophecy of Daniel 8:14 involves Greek Empire (Dan. 8:8-9, 21-24), as the "*little horn*" that stopped the "*daily sacrifices*" came out of one of the four horns (Dan. 8:8-9), which represent divided Greek Empire after the prominent horn (Alexander the Great) had been broken off (Dan. 8:8-9, 21-22). Greek Empire (331 BC - 168 BC) came to power some 126 years after the 457 BC decree; Alexander the Great died in 321 BC, some 136 years after the famous decree.

6) The 457 BC decree issued by Artaxerxes, the king of Persia, involves Medo-Persian Empire (539 BC - 331 BC).

   According to the logic of William Miller, "*daily sacrifices*" had been stopped in 457 BC, as this date allegedly represents the beginning of the "*2300 mornings and evenings (or 2300 years)*" prophecy. Were the sanctuary reconsecrated and the daily sacrifices reinstated in 1844 AD?

7) The "*457 BC decree*" and the "*little horn*" imply contradiction in relation to the prophecy of Daniel 8:14, as the two are related to two different empires and different periods of time.

8) According to the logic of W. Miller, Bible prophecy concerning the "*stopping of the daily sacrifices*" and "*desecration of the Temple*" (Dan. 8:11, 14) started in 457 BC and ended in 1844 AD. Thus, daily sacrifices and religious service performed in the rebuilt Temple in Jerusalem after the return from Babylonian captivity until 70 AD are omitted. This does not concord with Daniel's prophecy.

The reasoning based on biblical and historical evidence presented above and the fact that Christ did not returned in 1844 lead to the final conclusion: the October 22, 1844 disappointment is not a prophecy but a visible manifestation of the consequence of human error of calculation regarding the fulfillment of the prophecy of Daniel 8:14.

Daniel's "*2300 evenings and mornings*" prophecy has its logical explanation in ancient history of the Jews and was fulfilled before Christ. In this case, it is suggested that the "*little horn*" (Dan. 8:9-14) represents the Syrian king, Antiochus Epiphanus (175 BC - 164 BC) of the Seleucid kingdom (one of the four horns of the divided Greek Empire), whose army invaded Jerusalem, stopped the daily sacrifices, desecrated the Temple by unclean sacrifices offered to their pagan god, the Olympian Zeus. Many Bible scholars agree with this interpretation.

The Millerite movement was founded on miscalculation of the prophecy of Daniel 8:14, therefore, it was doomed to failure from the very beginning. Many believers learned a lesson from it. However, some Millerites chose to speculate on the "Great Disappointment of 1844" thus giving it an even more controversial image.

The sanctuary doctrine

Ellen G. White wrote:

"[...] at the close of the 2300 days, in 1844, began the work of investigation and the blotting out of sins" *(The Great Controversy, p. 552).*

"[...] Instead of coming to earth at the termination of the 2300 days prophesy, in 1844, Christ entered into the Most Holy Place of the Heavenly Sanctuary to perform the closing work of the atonement preparatory to His return" *(The Great Controversy, p. 422).*

"[...] in 1844...our High Priest entered the holy of holies... to perform the work of investigation judgment. The only cases considered are those of the professed people of God" *(The Great Controversy, p. 546).*

"[...] The Proclamation, Behold the Bridegroom cometh in the summer of 1844, led thousands to expect the immediate advent of Christ. At the appointed time the Bridegroom came, not to the earth, as the people expected, but to the Ancient of Days in heaven to the marriage, the reception of His kingdom. They that were ready went in with Him to the marriage and the door was shut [...]" *(The Great Controversy, p. 487).*

"This work of examination of character, of determining who are prepared for the kingdom of God, is that of Investigative Judgment" *(The Great Controversy, p. 489).*

Sanctuary doctrine was introduced by Hiram Edson[4] (a Millerite) and published in 1846 by O. R. L. Crosier. It was conceived with the intent to explain the "Great Disappointment of 1844." Seventh-day Adventist Church was founded on this doctrine. Its teaching makes certain sense only to Adventist believers; for other, however, it is very controversial.

The Sanctuary doctrine asserts the following:

- On October 22, 1844, Christ, instead of returning to earth as some were expecting, entered into the Most Holy Place of the Heavenly Sanctuary [Ellen G. White's writings];

- On October 22, 1844, Christ entered the second and last phase of His atoning ministry. It is a work of investigative judgment, which is part of the ultimate disposition of all sin, typified by the cleansing of the ancient Hebrew sanctuary on the Day of Atonement [Ellen G. White's writings, Belief 23 (Belief 24 following the insertion of a new belief in 2005)].

The investigative judgment of the sanctuary doctrine implies that believers will be judged by their work. This judgment will determine their salvation and is called the "Investigative judgment" or "Pre-Advent Judgment" – it began on October 22, 1844.

The sanctuary doctrine, partially expressed in Belief 23 (Belief 24) and abundantly described in Ellen White's writings, implies the following allegations, not stated directly:

- Jesus Christ was not ascended to the right-hand side of the Father on the day of Ascension (40 days after the resurrection). According to this Adventist doctrinal logic, on the day of Ascension, Jesus Christ was ascended <u>into the Holy Place</u> of the Heavenly Sanctuary, where He remained until October 22, 1844. On this date, Christ moved from the Holy Place <u>into the Most Holy Place</u> of the Heavenly Sanctuary, into the presence of God the Father;

- Christ's mission of atonement was not finished on the cross of Golgotha. According to Adventist doctrinal logic, on October 22, 1844, Christ entered the second and last phase of His atoning ministry. In other words, Christ's Calvary on the cross of Golgotha was only the first phase of His atoning ministry.

Adventists might say: we don't see it that way. Well, this is the same as saying: we don't see Satan that way (we see him as an angel of light).

The Holy Scripture always provides us with answers to the provocations and extra-biblical allegations because its author is God the Creator. The Bible states the following:

1) Jesus Christ completed His work of atonement on the cross of Golgotha:

> "¹ These things spake Jesus; and lifting up his eyes to heaven, he said, _Father, the hour is come; glorify thy Son_, that the Son may glorify thee" (Jn. 17:1).

> "⁴ I glorified you on the earth. _I have accomplished the work which you have given me to do_" (Jn. 17:4 WEB).

> "³⁰ When Jesus therefore had received the vinegar, he said, _It is finished_: and he bowed his head, and gave up his spirit" (Jn. 19:30).

What do the words "_It is finished_" (Jn. 19:30) mean to Seventh-day Adventists?

2) The Bible clearly states that Jesus Christ, on the Day of Ascension, was ascended to heaven and sat at the right-hand side of God the Father as follows:

> "⁵⁰ And he led them out until they were over against Bethany: and he lifted up his hands, and blessed them. ⁵¹ And it came to pass, while he blessed them, he parted from them, ⁽ᵖ⁾and was carried up into heaven" (Lk. 24:50-51).

> "⁹ And when he had said these things, as they were looking, he was taken up; and a cloud received him out of their sight" (Acts 1:9).

> "¹⁹ So then the Lord Jesus, after he had spoken unto them, was received up into heaven, and sat down at the right hand of God" (Mk. 16:19).

> "⁶⁹ But from henceforth shall the Son of man be seated at the right hand of the power of God" (Lk. 22:69).

> "³³ Being therefore ⁽ᵐ⁾by the right hand of God exalted, and having received of the Father the promise of the Holy Spirit, he hath poured forth this, which ye see and hear" (Acts 2:33).

"55 But he, being full of the Holy Spirit, looked up stedfastly into heaven, and saw the glory of God, and Jesus standing on the right hand of God, 56 and said, Behold, I see the heavens opened, and the Son of man standing on the right hand of God" (Acts 7:55-56).

"34 who is he that condemneth? [p]It is Christ Jesus that died, yea rather, that was raised from the dead, who is at the right hand of God, who also maketh intercession for us" (Rom. 8:34).

"20 which he wrought in Christ, when he raised him from the dead, and made him to sit at his right hand in the heavenly places" (Eph. 1:20).

"1 If then ye were raised together with Christ, seek the things that are above, where Christ is, seated on the right hand of God" (Col. 3:1).

"3 who being the effulgence of his glory, and [c]the very image of his substance, and upholding all things by the word of his power, when he had made purification of sins, sat down on the right hand of the Majesty on high" (Heb. 1:3).

"1 [a]Now [b]in the things which we are saying the chief point is this: We have such a high priest, who sat down on the right hand of the throne of the Majesty in the heavens" (Heb. 8:1).

"12 but he, when he had offered one sacrifice for [e] sins for ever, sat down on the right hand of God" (Heb. 10:12).

"2 looking unto Jesus the [d]author and perfecter of our faith, who for the joy that was set before him endured the cross, despising shame, and hath sat down at the right hand of the throne of God" (Heb. 12:2).

"[22] who is on the right hand of God, having gone into heaven; angels and authorities and powers being made subject unto him" (1Pet. 3:22).

"[21] He that overcometh, I will give to him to sit down with me in my throne, as I also overcame, and sat down with my Father in his throne" (Rev 3:21).

"[5] And she was delivered of a son, a man child, who is to rule all the [a]nations with a rod of iron: and her child was caught up unto God, and unto his throne" (Rev. 12:5).

3) The Bible teaches us that those, who believe and live in union with Christ, will not be judged but have eternal life:

"[16] For God so loved the world, that he gave his only begotten Son, that whosoever believeth on him should not perish, but have eternal life. [17] For God sent not the Son into the world to judge the world; but that the world should be saved through him. [18] He that believeth on him is not judged: he that believeth not hath been judged already, because he hath not believed on the name of the only begotten Son of God" (Jn. 3:16-18).

"[24] Verily, verily, I say unto you, He that heareth my word, and believeth him that sent me, hath eternal life, and cometh not into judgment, but hath passed out of death into life" (Jn. 5:24).

"[25] Jesus said unto her, I am the resurrection, and the life: he that believeth on me, though he die, yet shall he live; [26] and whosoever liveth and believeth on me shall never die. Believest thou this?" (Jn. 11:25-26).

"[3] And this is life eternal, that they should know thee the only true God, and him whom thou didst send, even Jesus Christ" (Jn. 17:3).

> "23 For the wages of sin is death; but the free gift of God is eternal life in Christ Jesus our Lord" (Rom. 6:23).

> "1 There is therefore now no condemnation to them that are in Christ Jesus. 2 For the law of the Spirit of life in Christ Jesus made me free from the law of sin and of death" (Rom. 8:1-2).

> "11 And the witness is this, that God gave unto us eternal life, and this life is in his Son. 12 He that hath the Son hath the life; he that hath not the Son of God hath not the life" (1Jn. 5:11-12).

> "13 And one of the elders answered, saying unto me, These that are arrayed in the white robes, who are they, and whence came they? 14 And I [d]say unto him, My lord, thou knowest. And he said to me, These are they that come out of the great tribulation, and they washed their robes, and made them white in the blood of the Lamb" (Rev. 7:13-14).

4) Anyone who is the subject of this "investigative judgment" doctrine cannot have a true concept of the Gospel and enjoy its blessings. How can believers enjoy the message of salvation, if he must wait until Christ examines the books to see whether they are worthy of receiving it?

Judgment of believers is to be understood as judgment of the sinners and reward of the saved as follows:

> "27 For the Son of man shall come in the glory of his Father with his angels; and then shall he render unto every man according to his [o]deeds" (Mt. 16:27).

> "14 If any man's work shall abide which he built thereon, he shall receive a reward" (1Cor. 3:14).

> "6 and without faith it is impossible to be well-pleasing unto him; for he that cometh to God must

believe that he is, and that he is a rewarder of them that seek after him" (Heb. 11:6).

"[12] Behold, I come quickly; and my [m]reward is with me, to render to each man according as his work is" (Rev. 22:12).

According to the sanctuary doctrine, Christ's Second Advent took place on October 22, 1844 – it was manifested by Christ's entering into the Most Holy Place of the Heavenly Sanctuary. In this case, Adventists should herald Christ's Third Advent, this time on earth!

Is the sanctuary doctrine in harmony with the Holy Scripture? No! Such doctrinal allegations are blasphemous. Nevertheless, some Adventist believers will object to such remark.

The shut door doctrine

Ellen G. White wrote:
"For a time after the disappointment in 1844, I did hold, in common with the advent body, that the door of mercy was forever closed to the world...I was shown in vision, and still believe, that there was a shut door in 1844" (*Selected Messages, Book 1, p. 63*).

"I was shown that...the door was opened in the most holy place in the heavenly sanctuary, where the ark is, in which are contained the Ten Commandments. This door was not opened until the mediation of Jesus was finished in the holy place of the sanctuary in 1844. Then Jesus rose up shut the door of the holy place, and opened the door into the most holy place, and passed within the second veil, where he now is standing by the ark" (*Early Writings, p. 42*).

"[...] It was just as impossible for them (those that gave up their faith in the 1844 movement) to get on the path again and go to the city, as all the wicked world which God had rejected. They fell all the way along the path one after another", (Foregoing now deleted) "until we heard the voice of God like many waters, which gave us the day and hour of Jesus' coming. The living saints, 144.000 in number, knew and understood the voice, while the wicked thought it was thunder and an earthquake" (*A Word to the Little Flock, p. 14, edition 1847*).

There was great confusion among the followers of William Miller, when they realized that Jesus Christ did not returned to earth on October 22, 1844. Those people were in desperate need for an explanation of the "Great Disappointment." Eventually, the "sanctuary doctrine" and the "shut door doctrine" came as a response to this religious crisis to comfort the heart-broken.

The "shut door" doctrine is bases on the parable of the ten virgins of Mathew 25:

"¹ Then shall the kingdom of heaven be likened unto <u>ten virgins</u>, who took their [a]lamps, and went forth to meet the bridegroom. ² And five of them were foolish, and five were wise. ³ For the foolish, when they took their [b]lamps, took no oil with them: ⁴ but the wise took oil in their vessels with their [c]lamps. ⁵ Now while the bridegroom tarried, they all slumbered and slept. ⁶ But at midnight there is a cry, Behold, the bridegroom! Come ye forth to meet him. ⁷ Then all those virgins arose, and trimmed their [d]lamps. ⁸ And the foolish said unto the wise, Give us of your oil; for our [e]lamps are going out. ⁹ But the wise answered, saying, Peradventure there will not be enough for us and you: go ye rather to them that sell, and buy for yourselves. ¹⁰ And while they went away to buy, the bridegroom came; and they that were ready went in with him to the marriage feast: and <u>the door was shut</u>" (Mat. 25:1-10).

According to this doctrine, the five wise virgins represent believers who joined the 1844 religious event. In other words, this teaching implies that on October 22, 1844, Christ moved from the Holy Place into the Most Holy Place of the Heavenly Sanctuary. In doing so, Christ „shut the door" behind Him, that is, He shut the door of salvation to the rest of believers. Thus, the only saved ones, 144.000 believers, were those who were expecting Christ's return on October 22, 1844.

The "shut door" doctrine was abandoned as Adventist Church began to increase in number with the arrival of new members. Nowadays, Adventist leaders do not mention it anymore in their sermons – they simply "shut" the conversation when it is about the "shut door" doctrine.

Are there sins in the heavenly sanctuary?

Ellen G. White wrote:

"As the sins of the people were anciently transferred in figure, to the earthly sanctuary by the blood of the sin-of-fering, so our sins are, in fact transferred to the heavenly sanctuary by the blood of Christ" *(The Great Controversy, p. 266, edition 1886).*

"When Christ by virtue of His blood removes the sins of His people from the heavenly sanctuary at the close of His ministration, He will place them upon Satan, who in execution of the judgment, must bear the final penalty" *(The Great Controversy, p. 481, edition 1927).*

Sin, in its essence, is disobedience and rebellion against God. The original sin of man is spiritual; physical (visible) manifestation of sin is the consequence of spiritual sin.

From biblical point of view, transgression of the law is a sin. In consequence, sin leads to the death of transgressor. According to the Old Testament, life is in the blood (Gen. 9:4; Lev. 17:11, 14). Blood, for thousands of years had been used for purification and forgiveness of sins (Lev. 17:11; Heb. 9:22). Jewish Old Testament religious practice required the blood of an animal without any defects. The animal was killed outside at the entrance of the Temple, and then its blood was taken to the altar (Lev. 1:1-5). As blood contains life, its purpose in sacrificial ceremonies was to present at the altar the life it contained as redemption from sin – the quality of the blood was less relevant, as the animal was without defects.

The same thing happened on the Cross of Golgotha, where Jesus Christ – the Lamb of God – offered Himself as a perfect sacrifice to God (Heb. 9:14). He shed His blood as redemption price for the atonement of humankind. On Golgotha, Christ took upon Himself our sins and nailing them to the cross. Those who believe, the blood of Christ will purify their conscience and they will worship God *"in truth and in spirit"* – they will have eternal life.

It is unhealthy thinking to assert that the holy blood of our Lord Jesus Christ contained sin, and that sin was ascended into the heavenly sanctuary – the allegation stated by Ellen White in her book, The Great Controversy. Sin was left behind, nailed to the cross. No sin, no impurity can stand in the presence of God.

Was the French Revolution a fulfilment of Bible prophecy?

> "³ *And I will give unto my two witnesses, and they shall prophesy a thousand two hundred and three-score days, clothed in sackcloth" (Rev. 11:3).*

> "⁷ *And when they shall have finished their testimony, the beast that cometh up out of the abyss shall make war with them, and overcome them, and kill them.* ⁸ *And their* [g]*dead bodies lie in the street of the great city, which spiritually is called Sodom and Egypt, where also their Lord was crucified" (Rev. 11:7-8).*

> "¹¹ *And after the three days and a half the breath of life from God entered into them, and they stood upon their feet; and great fear fell upon them that beheld them" Rev. 11:11).*

Seventh-day Adventists have been indoctrinated with the teaching that French Revolution represents the fulfill-ment of "*two witnesses*" prophecy described in Revelation chapter 9. This allegation is based on the following reasoning:

1) The "*two witnesses*" represent the Old and the New Testament (the Bible), which allegedly was banned for "*three days and a half*", that is, for "three years and half" during the French Revolution.

2) Adventists assert that "*a thousand two hundred and threescore days*" represent 1260 years of Papal supremacy, which started in 538 AD (alleged date when the Papacy was establishment) and ended in 1798 (the date when Pope Pius VI was arrested and taken to France where he died – alleged fatal wound to the Papacy).

This, however, turns out to be either a missinterpretation of Bible prophecy or a very carefully calculated stratagem conceived for an ambitious goal – historical course of events that followed confirms this reasoning.

"Truly, the French government did make war on Christianity and the Bible... The worship of Reason began in November 26, 1793, when the Council of the Commune outlawed all religions... However, on May 9, 1794, the Convention, a superior government body, under the influence of Robespierre, decreed the worship of the Supreme Being. The government support of any worship was abolished on September 20, 1794, without much discussion. This automatically brought a considerable degree of religious liberty. It is true that the non-juring priests still suffered some persecution, but this was far more from political than from religious animosity...

On February 21, 1795, Biossy d'Anglas made a speech and a motion for complete separation of Church and State. This was passed, allowing any kind of religious worship throughout France, but with some restrictions as to place, advertising, endowments...

A new constitution was demanded to replace that of 1793. Its formation was in the hands of comparatively moderate men. Separation of Church and State and freedom of worship were incorporated in this new constitution. It was adopted on August 17, 1795. Thus we see that <u>in less than six months</u> the atheistic enactment of November 26, 1793, was abrogated; and <u>in less than two years</u> there was actually greater religious freedom guaranteed on a fundamental legal basis, than existed prior to the outbreak of atheism. The "*two witnesses*" simply did not stay "*dead*" three and a half years."[11]

The Book of Revelation, among other things, states the following prophetic clue:

> "⁷ *And when they shall have finished their testimony, <u>the beast</u> that cometh up out of the abyss <u>shall make war with them, and overcome them, and kill them</u>*" *(Rev. 11:7).*

According to Adventist doctrinal logic, the *"beast that ascends out of the <u>bottomless pit</u>"* must represent the French Revolution – a complete nonsense. The French Revolution was triggered, on the one hand, by secularism and atheism hiding behind the so-called "liberty, equality, and fraternity", and on the other hand, by anti-Catholics. The main objective of the revolution was: French monarchy and the Roman Catholic Church. Ultimately, the monarchy was overthrown and the king of France, Louis XVI – a Catholic – beheaded; property of the Catholic Church was confiscated; the clergy persecuted, forced into deportation and exile, or executed.

Who was the beast (with seven heads and ten horns) that came up out of the *"abyss"* and killed the alleged "two witnesses" of the French Revolution? Some scholars identify this prophetic beast as the revived Western Roman Empire. In this case, overthrowing the monarchy and dechristinization waged against Catholicism qualifies as self-destruction of the Roman Empire – an absurdity.

Several undeniable factors led to the French Revolution and one of them was definitely a religious one. The fact that for a short period of time religion was banned in French society is a confirmation of the existence of such a factor. Besides new philosophical concepts of life (Enlightment, Libertarianism) and scientific discoveries that evolved in the 18th century, which led to inevitable changes in France and other European countries, there was a religious factor as a result of many years of religious conflicts between Christians and non-Christians, Catholics and Protestants, which persisted in Western and Central Europe for several centuries causing, among other things, the loss of human lives. In this respect, some historians characterize this political turmoil as a revolt against religious dogmas and tyranny. On the other hand, the French Revolution gave the opportunity to certain individuals with radical convictions to interfere and impose a particular religious and political course of history in that country.

Dechristinization[12] policy carried out by the French

revolutionary government targeted Catholicism, and eventually all other forms of Christianity. Its diabolic nature reached incomprehensible proportions as follows[12][13]: imprisonment, execution or deportation of clergy; thousands of churches closed, sold, destroyed, or converted to other uses; confiscation of church property (lands); destruction of religious statues and icons, crosses, bells and other external signs of worship; forbidding the ringing of church bells, religious procession and display of the Christian cross; outlawing public and private religious worship and religious education; replacement of Christianity with the Cult of Reason (atheism) and consequently the Cult of the Supreme Being (deism); replacing Gregorian calendar with the French Republican Calendar. Repression and atrocities reached its peak during the "Reign of Terror"[13], the most violent period of the French Revolution. Representation of the "Declaration of the Rights of Man and of the Citizen"[14], a fundamental document of the French Revolution and in the history of human rights, includes "Eye of providence" symbol (eye in triangle) – this suggests the possibility of occult conspiracy behind this atrocious event in French history.

Is the French Revolution a prophetic fulfillment of Revelation chapter 11? No! Such prophetic interpretation is erroneous and misleading.

Historic and religious conflict of the French Revolution has a particular role in human history and God's plan, but is not what certain scholars and historians would expect us to believe.

The Book of Revelation gives us a clue regarding the identity of the "*two witnesses*", which were ultimately killed by the beast:

> "*7 And when they shall have finished their testimony, <u>the beast that cometh up out of the abyss</u> shall make war with them, and overcome them, and kill them. 8 And <u>their [g]dead bodies lie in the street of the great city, which spiritually is called Sodom and Egypt, where also their Lord was crucified</u>*" (Rev. 11:7-8).

It is very evident from this verse that the "*two witnesses*" of Revelation chapter 11 are to be searched in the Middle East, not in France. **Note**: The next two chapters of this book provide a clear proof that the "*beast (empire) coming up out of the abyss*", is related to the Middle East.

The beast with seven heads and ten horns

"¹ and [a]he stood upon the sand of the sea. And I saw a beast coming up out of the sea, having ten horns and seven heads, and on his horns ten diadems, and upon his heads names of blasphemy. ² And the beast which I saw was like unto a leopard, and his feet were as the feet of a bear, and his mouth as the mouth of a lion: and the dragon gave him his power, and his throne, and great authority. ³ And I saw one of his heads as though it had been [b]smitten unto death; and his death-stroke was healed: and the whole earth wondered after the beast" (Rev. 13:1-3).

"³ And he carried me away in the Spirit into a wilderness: and I saw a woman sitting upon a scarlet-colored beast, [a]full of names of blasphemy, having seven heads and ten horns" (Rev. 17:3).

"⁸ The beast that thou sawest was, and is not; and is about to come up out of the abyss, [f]and to go into perdition. And they that dwell on the earth shall wonder, they whose name hath not been written [g] in the book of life from the foundation of the world, when they behold the beast, how that he was, and is not, and [h]shall come" (Rev. 17:8).

"⁹ Here is the [i]mind that hath wisdom. The seven heads are seven mountains, on which the woman sitteth: ¹⁰ and [j]they are seven kings; the five are fallen, the one is, the other is not yet come; and when he cometh, he must continue a little while. ¹¹ And the beast that was, and is not, is himself also an eighth, and is of the seven; and he goeth into perdition" (Rev. 17:9-11).

Prophetic allegories of the Book of Revelation have always been one of the major concern for devoted believers. Wanting to unravel these prophetic mysteries, many seekers dedicated considerable time and effort studying the Bible prophecy. Consequently, certain believers came up with reasonable explanations; the work of others, however, is marked by inconsistency and tendentious interpretations.

Some Bible scholars assert that historic event of 476, when the last western Roman emperor, Romulus Augustulus, was deposed by Germanic peoples lead by Odoacer and the Western Roman Empire collapsed (a fatal wound to the Roman Empire), is the fulfillment of prophecy *"I saw one of his heads as though it had been [b]smitten unto death..."* described in Revelation 13:3. They assert that the *"ten horns"* (Rev. 13:1; Dan. 7:24) are ten European nations, which arose after the fall of Rome and the Western Roman Empire, that the *"little horn"* before whom three of the first horns were plucked up by the root (Dan. 7:8) represents the Papacy, and that the *"three horns plucked up by the root"* represent three Arian peoples (Heruli, Vandals, and Ostrogoths), which were eradicated by Rome (with significant help of the Byzantine army). This version is vehemently supported by Seventh-day Adventist Church.

According to these scholars, the allegory *"and his death-stroke was healed..."* (Rev. 13:3) represents the revived Western Roman Empire, later known as the Holy Roman Empire. At first impression, this reasoning seems to be quite plausible; however, two vital facts are being neglected:

1) The beast looked like a *"leopard, bear, and lion"* (Rev. 13:2).

2) The prophecy clearly identified the Roman Empire as the *"one is"*, not as the *"five are fallen"* (Rev. 17:10). Therefore, the so-called revived Western Roman Empire cannot be the head whose *"death-stroke was healed"*, that is, the beast described as *"was, and is not, is himself also an eighth, and is of the seven"* (Rev. 17:11).

Supporters of this prophetic interpretation have been indoctrinated with the teaching that historic event of 1798, when Pope Pius VI was arrested by Berthier (one of Napoleon's generals) and imprisoned in citadel of Valence in France where he later died, marked the fulfillment of "*42 months (1260 days) or 1260 years*" prophecy of Revelation 13:5. Therefore, historic event of 1798 marked the end of 1260 years of Papal supremacy (538-1798) – a fatal wound inflicted on Papacy. Such religious conviction, however, proves to be faulty as follows:

1) According to this interpretation, there seem to be two deadly wounds (one in 476, another in 1798).

2) Revelation 13:3 states very clearly that "*one of his heads*" (that is, one of the seven heads) seemed to have been fatally wounded – it does not say "*one of his horns*", that is, one of the ten horns, as the beast had seven heads and ten horns (Rev. 13:1). Linguistically, head and horn represent two different words with different meanings; anatomically, these have a totally different structure and function. Should head and horn, prophetically, be considered identical?

It is quite evident that such interpretation of Bible prophecy is questionable. Therefore, after a thorough analysis of this issue, inevitable remarks follow:

- The "*ten horns*" represent ten kings (kingdoms) that ascended after the fall of the Roman Empire, prophetically identified as "*legs of iron*" (Dan. 2:33, 40); the ten horns also seem to be "*ten toes*" of the prophetic statue of the Book of Daniel (Dan. 2:28-45). Feet and toes "*part of iron, and part of clay*" represent a new empire that succeeded the Roman Empire. Feet and toes "*partly of iron*" represent former Roman territories within that new empire;

- Prophetic allegory "*ten horns*" described in the Book of Daniel and the Book of Revelation seems to give an impression of discordance. The ten horns of Daniel 7:7 seem to be related to the fourth empire (Roman Empire); however, Daniel 7:24 provide an additional detail: "*ten horns*" arise after the fall of the fourth empire. The Roman Empire was ruled by many Caesars, not by ten kings (ten horns). In the Book of Revelation, the "*ten horns*" do not appear to be part of the Roman Empire. In Revelation, these horns constitute a new empire, as they receive power as kings one hour with the beast (Rev. 17:12), which is described as "*was, and is not; and is about to come up*", and which is also described as looking like a "*leopard, bear, and lion*" having "*ten crowns*" on its horns (Rev. 13:1). If "*ten horns*" also represent "*ten toes*", then the version according to which "*ten horns*" represent ten European nations that arose after the fall of the Western Roman Empire is contradictory, as the two iron legs of the Roman Empire continued with feet and five toes on each foot – the expression "Western Roman leg with a foot having ten toes", thus Eastern Roman leg with a foot without toes, is irrational. However, as, according to the Book of Revelation, the beast looked like a "*leopard, bear, and lion*", and as it "*was, and is not; and is about to come up*", it is pertinent to say that the "*ten horns*" are predominantly related to the Middle East and to what once was the Byzantine Empire (Eastern Roman leg). Therefore, ten horns or kings (kingdoms) arose after the fall of the Roman Empire, and definitive fall of the Roman Empire took place in 1453, the date when Constantinople – Christian bastion of the Eastern Roman Empire – was conquered by the Ottoman Turks. The Western Roman Empire (western iron leg) fell almost one thousand years earlier, in 476;

- It is pertinent to suggest that the "*little horn*" (Dan. 7:8, 24), which uprooted three other horns, and which is different from the earlier ones, represents the rise of Islamic Empire, and that "*three plucked up by the rooted horns*" must be three horns of the divided Greek Empire (kingdoms of Seleucus, Ptolemy, and Lysimachus), which, to some extent, were also part of the Eastern Roman Empire later being absorbed into the Islam Empire. The rise of Muslim Empire, which allegorically in Revelation chapter 9 seems to be described as "*locusts*" coming out of the smoke, which arose from the "*pit of the abyss*", was allowed to make war on Christians and Jews and defeat them;

- Regarding the verse "*I considered the horns, and behold, there came up among them <u>another horn, a little one</u>, before which three of the first horns were plucked up by the roots...*" (Dan. 7:8), the following explanation is suggested: the "*little horn*", by uprooting three of the first horns (kings), takes possession of three kingdoms and revives one of the seven heads prophetically described as „*was, and is not, is himself also an eighth, and is of the seven*" (Rev. 17:11);

- Prophetic allegory "*feet part of iron, and part of clay*" (Dan. 2:33, 40-42) is self-explanatory: iron represents the Roman Empire; clay suggests something else, from outside, not Roman. Therefore, this refers to a new empire, which consisted partly of conquered territory once belonging to the Roman Empire and partly of territory that was beyond the Roman border (new conquests in the Middle East, Central Asia, and Africa).

Some believers assert that prophetic beast with seven heads and ten horns described in the Book of Revelation chapters 13 and 17 is not the same beast. That is not quite so. These two chapters compensate each other, thus offer a more detailed picture of this mysterious beast. Revelation chapter 13 informs the reader that the beast "*coming up out of the sea*" comes up from among the peoples, kingdoms prophetically described as "*leopard, bear, and lion*" – the incipient phase of that empire. The (scarlet) beast of Revelation chapter 17 described as "*about to come up out of the abyss*" represents the final phase of that empire – a time following the prophetic event described as "*...I saw a star from heaven fallen unto the earth: and there was given to him the key of the pit of the abyss*" (Rev. 9:1), a time when the "*harlot (great city)*" becomes so spiritually depraved that she must be punished.

The central issue in Revelation chapters 13 and 17 is less the beast (empire) as such, but rather the destructive satanic power exercised through such earthly authority. However, it is essential to know the true identity of this apocalyptic beast.

The beast with seven heads and ten horns presents certain particularities:

- The red dragon having "*seven heads and ten horns, and upon his heads seven diadems*" (Rev. 12:3) represents satanic power exercised through earthly empires during the reign of the "*seven heads*", probably before Satan was cast out of heaven;

- The beast having "*ten horns and seven heads, and on his horns ten diadems*" (Rev. 13:1) represents satanic power exercised during the reign of the "*ten horns*", that is, through ten kings (kingdoms) that ruled within the new empire that arose after the fall of the Roman Empire, probably after Satan was cast out of heaven to earth (Rev. 12:7-9);

- The verse "*And he carried me away in the Spirit into a wilderness: and I saw a woman sitting upon a scarlet-colored beast,* [a] *full of names of blasphemy, having seven heads and ten horns*" (Rev. 17:3) is an extension of the prophetic picture described in Revelation 13:1. However, Revelation chapter 17 is focusing exclusively on the head (beast) whose wound is healed. Here, an extra element is added: the "*woman.*"

According to Revelation 13:1-2, if our Bible is a reliable translation of the original manuscripts, the beast was like "*unto a leopard*", and his feet were as the "*feet of a bear*", and his mouth as the "*mouth of a lion.*" This means that the beast looked like Greek, Medo-Persian, and Babylonian Empires (Dan. 2:31-45; 7:1-17) – the Roman Empire is missing. On the other hand, the beast, according to Revelation chapter 17, ascends from the bottomless pit in the wilderness (desert) and is presented as "*was, and is not, is himself also an eighth, and is of the seven*" (Rev. 17:3, 8, 11) – when John received the Revelation, the Roman Empire was not one of the "*five fallen heads (empires)*", in fact, the Roman Empire is prophetically described as "*one is*" (Rev. 17:10). In both cases, the Roman Empire has no relevance to this prophetic beast. In other words, the beast is related to the Middle East, to the wilderness (desert). This is a clear description of the new empire that ascends after the fall of the Roman Empire – the rise of Muslim Empire.

Once again, the beast (the "*eighth king*"), which "*was, and is not; and is about to come up* out of the abyss*", is one of the seven, that is, one of the "*five fallen heads (empires)*." John received the Revelation in the late first century. At this time, the Roman Empire was a prosperous empire thus could not be one of the "*five fallen heads (empires)*" – the Roman Empire identifies with the "*sixth head*" prophetically described as the "*one is*." Furthermore, the Roman Empire has never been prophetically described as "*ascending out of the earth*", that is to say, "*coming up out of the abyss*."

Let's compare the following verses:

> "*And I saw one of his heads as though it had been [b]smitten unto death; and his death-stroke was healed...*" (Rev. 13:3);

> "*The beast that thou sawest was, and is not; and is about to come up out of the abyss, [f]and to go into perdition...*" (Rev. 17:8);

> "*And the beast that was, and is not, is himself also an eighth, and is of the seven; and he goeth into perdition*" (Rev. 17:11);

Let's draw another parallelism:

1) a. "*one of his heads as though it had been [b]smitten unto death*" (Rev. 13:3);

    b. "*the beast that thou sawest was*" (Rev. 17:8);

    c. "*five are fallen*" (Rev. 17:10).

2) "*is not*" (Rev. 17:8), that is, the beast "*is not*" when John received the Revelation.

    a. "*his death-stroke was healed*" (Rev. 13:3);

    b. "*is about to come out of the abyss*" (Rev. 17:8);

    c. "*the beast that was, and is not, is himself also an eighth, and is of the seven...*" (Rev. 17:11).

It is pertinent to assert that all quotations mentioned above ("*smitten unto death*" head, his "*death-stroke was healed*", the beast "*that was, and is not*") identify one and the same head: the "*eighth king*", which "*is of the seven.*"

The following verses also confirm the identity of one and the same beast:

> "8 *And all that dwell on the earth shall* [h]*worship him, <u>every one whose name hath not been [i]written from the foundation of the world in the book of life</u> of the Lamb that hath been slain*" (Rev. 13:8).

> "8 ...*And they that dwell on the earth shall wonder, <u>they whose name hath not been written [g]in the book of life from the foundation of the world</u>, when they behold the beast, how that he was, and is not, and* [h]*shall come*" (Rev. 17:8).

According to the New Testament, it would be nonsense to say that the verse "*they whose names hath not been written in the book of life of the Lamb*" (Rev. 13:8; Rev. 17:8) refers to Christians – believers who accepted the "*word of God, and the testimony of Jesus.*" On the contrary, it is common sense to afirm that those "*whose names are not written in the book of life of the Lamb*" are the ones who do not accept "*Jesus Christ and His testimony*" – these must be the "non-Christians."

Once again, from the perspective of the New Testament, it is unbiblical to say that prophetic expression "*they whose names are not written in the book of life...*" (Rev. 13:8; Rev. 17:8), which refers to those who worship the beast that looks like a "*leopard, bear, and lion*" (Rev. 13:1-2), and that "*was, and is not; and is about to come up out of the abyss*" (Rev. 17:3, 7), applies to Christian believers. On the contrary, these verses refer to those who are not Christians. In support of this statement, it is appropriate to quote Jesus' prayer on the night of His arrest:

> "6 <u>*I manifested thy name unto the men whom thou gavest me out of the world*</u>: *thine they were, and thou gavest them to me; <u>and they have kept thy</u>*

word. [7] *Now they know that all things whatsoever thou hast given me are from thee:* [8] *for the words which thou gavest me I have given unto them; and they received them, and knew of a truth that I came forth from thee, and they believed that thou didst send me.* [9] *I* [b]*pray for them: I* [c]*pray not for the world, but for those whom thou hast given me; for they are thine:* [10] *and all things that are mine are thine, and thine are mine: and I am glorified in them"* (Jn. 17:6-10).

Prophetic allegory "*seven heads and ten horns*" as such is a mystery. However, Revelation chapter 17 provides details regarding the identity of the "*seven heads*" and "*ten horns*" as follows:

"[9] *Here is the* [i]*mind that hath wisdom. The seven heads are seven mountains, on which the woman sitteth:* [10] *and* [j]*they are seven kings; the five are fallen, the one is, the other is not yet come; and when he cometh, he must continue a little while.* [11] *And the beast that was, and is not, is himself also an eighth, and is of the seven; and he goeth into perdition"* (Rev. 17:9-11).

"[12] *And the ten horns that thou sawest are ten kings, who have received no kingdom as yet; but they receive authority as kings, with the beast, for one hour"* (Rev. 17:12).

"[15] *And he saith unto me, The waters which thou sawest, where the harlot sitteth, are peoples, and multitudes, and nations, and tongues"* (Rev. 17:15).

The beasts described in Revelation 13:1-3 and 17:3, 7-8 have in common the following characteristics:

1) Both beasts have "*seven heads and ten horns*."

2) Both beasts exclude the Roman Empire. The following verses confirm it:

"[2] And the beast which I saw was like unto a leopard, and his feet were as the feet of a bear, and his mouth as the mouth of a lion: and the dragon gave him his power, and his throne, and great authority" (Rev. 13:2).

"[9] Here is the [i]mind that hath wisdom. The seven heads are seven mountains, on which the woman sitteth: [10] and [j]they are seven kings; the five are fallen, the one is, the other is not yet come; and when he cometh, he must continue a little while. [11] And the beast that was, and is not, is himself also an eighth, and is of the seven; and he goeth into perdition" (Rev. 17:9-11).

"[12] And the ten horns that thou sawest are ten kings, who have received no kingdom as yet; but they receive authority as kings, with the beast, for one hour" (Rev. 17:12).

3) Both beasts exercise their power during the reign of the "ten horns." The following verses confirm it:

"[1] and [a]he stood upon the sand of the sea. And I saw a beast coming up out of the sea, having ten horns and seven heads, and on his horns ten diadems, and upon his heads names of blasphemy" (Rev. 13:1).

"[12] And the ten horns that thou sawest are ten kings, who have received no kingdom as yet; but they receive authority as kings, with the beast, for one hour. [13] These have one mind, and they give their power and authority unto the be" (Rev. 17:12-13).

4) There is a clear similarity in the following prophetic description: a) "And I saw one of his heads as though it had been [b]smitten unto death", and "his death-stroke was healed" (Rev. 13:3); b) "was, and is not; and is about to come up out of the abyss..." (Rev. 17:8), and "was, and is not, is

35

himself also an eighth, and is of the seven" (Rev. 17:11). Both descriptions identify one and the same head. In other words, one of the heads (empires), which in the first century was no more (when John received the Revelation), will rise again.

5) Prophetic characteristic in the verses below must be attributed to one and the same beast:

> "*8 And all that dwell on the earth shall [h]worship him, every one whose name hath not been [i]written from the foundation of the world in the book of life of the Lamb that hath been slain*" (Rev. 13:8).

> "*8 ...And they that dwell on the earth shall wonder, they whose name hath not been written [g]in the book of life from the foundation of the world, when they behold the beast, how that he was, and is not, and [h]shall come*" (Rev. 17:8).

The central issue in Revelation chapter 13 regarding the beast with "*seven heads and ten horns*" is the deadly wounded head, whose "*deadly wound was healed*" (Rev. 13:3), not the seven heads. The central issue in Revelation chapter 17 is also the head (or king) identified as the beast that "*was, and is not, is himself also an eighth, and is of the seven*" (Rev. 17:11). Therefore, both chapters (13 and 17) concentrate on one head, not seven heads – one head with ten horns (Rev. 17:11-12). According to Revelation chapter 17, seven heads represent a succession of kings, kingdom – each head had dominion at a particular time in human history.

Revelation chapters 13 and 17 describe one and the beast (empire) – the two chapters compensate each other. Revelation chapter 13 is focusing on the beast at its incipient phase, while Revelation chapter 17 describes the beast at final phase of its existence. Once again, the two chapters describe one and the same beast. Mystery and complexity of prophetic events described in the Book of Revelation is astonishing – the Holy Spirit speaks to the believers in allegorical language.

Such an approach of Bible prophecy may be regarded as inconsistent because a very important fact is missing: the "*woman (great city, Babylon the Great), which sits on seven mountains, on many waters.*" Certain believers have been indoctrinated with the teaching that the "*woman dressed in purple and scarlet*" sitting on the beast represents Rome and the Roman Catholic Church. Their logic is based on the fact that Rome was built on seven hills. These hills[15] are: *Aventinus, Caelius, Capitolinus, Esquilinus, Palatinus, Quirinalis, Viminalis*. It seems that, deliberately or out of ignorance, they neglect geographical and historical fact that *Collis (Mons) Vaticanus*[15], the hill on which Vatican city was built, is not counted among the traditional seven hills of Rome – Vatican is located across the river Tiber.

Rome has been playing a pivotal role historically, politically, and religiously for many centuries, and for a certain period of time ruled over many kings and nations. Whether or not Rome represents prophetic allegory "*woman sitting upon the beast*", one fact should not be neglected: Rome is not the only great city built on seven hills. Constantinople and Jerusalem were also built on seven hills. Some venture to say that Mecca is surrounded by seven hills (mountains). However, the Book of Revelation clearly states that the woman sits on "*seven mountains*", not on seven hills. Accurate translation of the original Greek manuscript contains the words "*seven mountains*"; yet translators of certain Bible versions permitted themselves the arrogance to replace "*seven mountains*" with seven hills.

Constantinople (New Rome), the capital of the Eastern Roman (Byzantine) Empire until 1453, was also built on seven hills[16]. The city was renamed Istanbul and became the capital of the Ottoman Empire. This city was of vital importance in both empires; however, it lacks prophetic image of the "*woman (whore)*" described in the Book of Revelation.

Jerusalem was also built on seven hills[17][18]. These are[17]: *Mount Gared, Mount Goath, Mount Acra, Mount Bezetha, Mount Moriah, Mount Ophel, and Mount Zion*. For whatever reason, Mt. Gared, Mt. Goath, Mt. Acra, and Mt. Bezetha have been deleted from nearly all maps of Jerusalem; other scholars replaced these with four other mountains: Mount of Olives, Mount of Offence, Mount of Evil Counsel, and Mount Calvary. Nowadays, many cities have the reputation of being built on seven hills[18]. Most of them, however, have no relevance to the Bible prophecy.

The "*seven heads*" on which the woman sits represent "*seven kings (kingdoms)*." But this is a succession of kings (kingdoms), as the Bible gives us a clue: "*the five are fallen, the one is, the other is not yet come*", that is to say, a fallen king (kingdom) is succeeded by another one… and so on. John's apocalyptic visions represent a description of the events to come – visions of the future. All these prophetic heads (kings, kingdoms) have one thing in common: the "*woman (great harlot)*" with whom the kings of the earth have committed fornication and the inhabitants of the earth have been made drunk with the wine of her fornication (Rev. 17:1-3, 18). This apocalyptic woman is described as:

> "⁵ and upon her forehead a name written, [d]Mystery, Babylon the Great, the Mother of the Harlots and of the Abominations of the Earth" (Rev. 17:5).

> "⁶ And I saw the woman drunken with the blood of the saints, and with the blood of the [e]martyrs of Jesus. And when I saw her, I wondered with a great wonder" (Rev. 17:6).

Several cities have the reputation of being involved in persecuting and killing God's people – all those who keep God's commandments, and have the testimony of Jesus Christ. These are: Jerusalem, Rome, and Istanbul. According to the Bible, Jerusalem is the place where initial persecution of Christians began. Pagan Rome persecuted Christians for several centuries; Christian Rome persecuted those believers whose religious views were considered by the church as heretical. Istanbul, the capital of the Ottoman Islamic Empire, is the place where for several centuries were conceived military strategies to invade and conquer Christian territories, the city where were issued orders that resulted in direct and systematic persecution and atrocities against Christians and Jews. On the other hand, one should not neglect Mecca – the holiest city in Islam [home of the greatest Islamic mosque surrounding the Kaaba[19] (a cuboid building with the "Black Stone" on its eastern corner), the holiest Islamic site], the birthplace of Muhammad, the heart of Islam (Muslims face the direction of Mecca when they pray, they face Kaaba)[19]. Islam began in Mecca. Muslim military expansion that established a huge Muslim Empire bringing along religious persecution and atrocities against those who rejected Islamic religion also commenced in Mecca. Thus, all these cities represent probable candidates for the title *"Babylon the Great, the Mother of Harlots and Abominations of the Earth."*

Again, some believers assert that prophetic allegory the *"woman sitting upon a scarlet-coloured beast"* represents Rome. Such allegation, however, is marked by inconsistency. As mentioned previously, the beast with seven heads and ten horns is described as:

> *"...was like unto a <u>leopard</u>, and his feet were as the feet of a <u>bear</u>, and his mouth as the mouth of a <u>lion</u>..." (Rev. 13:2).*

> *"...<u>was, and is not, and is about to come up</u> out of the abyss..." (Rev. 17:8).*

> *"...<u>was, and is not</u>, is himself also an eighth, <u>and is of the seven</u>..." (Rev. 17:11).*

Such prophetic description cannot be attributed to the Roman Empire in any form; therefore, prophetic allegory the *"woman (harlot)"* sitting upon the beast, which does not represent the Roman Empire, cannot be attributed to Rome.

The topic "Rome fell in 476 AD", that is, the Roman Empire received a "fatal wound in 476" is questionable. It is a fact that Rome had been sacked several times (in 410, 455...), but not in 476. Historic event of 476 refers to the deposition of the last western Roman emperor, Romulus Aurelius, who resided in Ravenna, the new capital of the Western Roman Empire at that time. Thus, year 476 marks the fall the Western Roman Empire and the end of the imperial glory of Rome. However, in 324, Emperor Constantine transferred the imperial capital from Rome to Constantinople – the New Rome. Eastern Roman Empire with its capital at Constantinople continued its dominion for almost another thousand years. Emperors of the Eastern Roman Empire (Byzantine Empire) undertook several attempts to restore the Western Roman Empire, that is, to bring back the Roman Empire to its original glory. By 1453, the date when Constantinople was conquered by the Muslim Turks, Rome has considerably recovered from its 5th century decline and fall; however, this is a different Rome – a Christian Rome. Western Europe, under the influence of Rome, fought many battles against Muslims. This includes the famous battles like: the battle of Tours (732) against the Saracens, the battle of Lepanto (1571) against the Ottoman fleet, and the battle of Vienna (1683) against the Ottomans – the three battles stopped Islamic invasion of Western Christianity. In other words, the topic regarding the fall of the Roman Empire is questionable. However, it is reasonable to assert that complete collapse of the Roman Empire took place in 1453, not in 476.

Once again, believers with radical views may argue vehemently that prophetic allegory the "_woman sitting upon a scarlet-coloured beast_, [a]_full of names of blasphemy, having seven heads and ten horns_" refers to Rome, as this city was involved in religious persecution of Jews, Christians, Muslims, and so on. Rome's variable role throughout its history is quite well known. As it was mentioned previously, the following apocalyptic verses do not identify the Western Roman Empire or Rome:

> "[2] And _the beast which I saw was like unto a leopard_, and his feet were as the feet of _a bear_, and his mouth as the mouth of _a lion_: and the dragon gave him his power, and his throne, and great authority" (Rev. 13:2).

40

"8 The beast that thou sawest was, and is not; and is about to come up out of the abyss, [f]*and to go into perdition. And they that dwell on the earth shall wonder, they whose name hath not been written* [g] *in the book of life from the foundation of the world, when they behold the beast, how that he was, and is not, and* [h]*shall come" (Rev. 17:8).*

"9 Here is the [i]*mind that hath wisdom. The seven heads are seven mountains, on which the woman sitteth:* 10 *and* [j]*they are seven kings; the five are fallen, the one is, the other is not yet come; and when he cometh, he must continue a little while.* 11 *And the beast that was, and is not, is himself also an eighth, and is of the seven; and he goeth into perdition" (Rev. 17:9-11).*

"12 And the ten horns that thou sawest are ten kings, who have received no kingdom as yet; but they receive authority as kings, with the beast, for one hour" (Rev. 17:12).

The beast with seven heads and ten horns, which "*was, and is not*" (when John received the Apocalypse), and which is also "*an eighth, and is of the seven*", that is to say, one of the "*five are fallen*", cannot be the Roman Empire. Therefore, this excludes the possibility that Rome prophetically represents the "*woman (harlot)*" sitting upon a scarlet-coloured beast (Rev. 17:3). Furthermore, Rome is not the only city built on seven hills.

Christian Rome was involved in military campaigns against Muslims. On the other hand, military interventions and judicial institutions were used to combat the spread of teachings considered by the church as heretical. It is a fact that military actions often result in the loss of human lives, which is not in harmony with Christ's two commandments of love (Mt. 22:36-40). Nevertheless, an unbiased analyst will not leave unnoticed the fact that, despite certain controversial doctrines and certain mistakes committed in the past, Rome (the Catholic Church) has been playing for many centuries a pivotal role in defending Christianity from Muslim religious militaristic ambitions, and from pseudo-Christian teachings polluting the Western Christianity. There is no doubt that, to some extent, such fundamental ecclesiastical task was susceptible to human errors. Acute religious crisis within Christianity was felt especially after the Ottoman conquest of Constantinople – the bastion and ecclesiastical centre of the Orthodox Christianity. For many Christians, Rome – the ecclesiastical centre of the Catholic Christianity – was the only hope and consolation during the centuries-long Muslim threats to the Western Christianity. On the other hand, it is pertinent to mention that alliances (official or secretive) with the Ottoman Empire were sometimes convenient for certain European leaders and influential individuals.

As mentioned earlier, certain believers will object to such prophetic interpretation. By quoting Daniel 7:7, these believers will insist that "*ten horns*" are related to the Roman Empire. At this point, it seems that Daniel 7:7 is in prophetic discordance with Revelation 17:10-12, 16. Adherents of this version, however, ought to give veritable explanation to the following remarks:

1) The beast with seven heads and ten horns looks like a "*leopard, bear, and lion*" (Rev. 13:1-2) – geographically, such description corresponds to the Middle East territory (Islamic countries); therefore, the "*ten horns*" also ought to identify with "*leopard, bear, and lion.*"

2) The beast "*that was, and is not (the eighth king)*" is one of the seven heads (empires), that is, one of the "*five fallen heads.*" The Roman Empire, when John received the Revelation, was a prosperous empire – prophetically, Roman Empire is the "*sixth head*", not one of the "*five are fallen*" (Rev. 17:9-10). The "*ten horns*" receive power as kings for an hour with the beast described as "*was, and is not, and is about to come up*" (Rev. 17:12) – this beast cannot identify with the Roman Empire.

3) The alleged ten horns rising after the fall of the Western Roman Empire make war against the Lamb of God (Rev. 17:14).

4) The ten horns (allegedly ten Western European Christian nations) and the beast (allegedly the revived Western Roman Empire, the Holy Roman Empire) hate the whore (allegedly Rome, the Catholic Church), make her desolate and destroy her with fire (Rev. 17:16) – self-destruction.

5) Why would Christians destroy each other? Why would they destroy Vatican (Rome) – the heart of over a billion Catholic Christians?

6) The prophecy states very clearly: the seven heads are "*seven mountains*", not seven hills (Rev. 17:9). The seven mountains are also seven kings/kingdoms (Rev. 17:10). The "*woman*" sits upon many waters, and these are peoples, multitudes, nations, and languages (Rev. 17:1, 15). The "*woman*" is the great city that rules over the kings of the earth (Rev. 17:18).

Nowadays, Rome stands firm and logically there isn't any potential threat of destruction of Rome by the European nations, which arose after the fall of the Western Roman Empire. The problem with prophetic interpretation based on the prophecy of Daniel chapter 7 concerning the identity of the "*ten horns*" is that there are only four empires mentioned – the rise of the new empire (Islamic Empire), which conquered a considerable territory of the fourth empire (Roman Empire), is missing. It seems that some believers have to choose between Daniel 7:7-8 and Revelation chapter 17. The Book of Revelation, however, should be a priority for believers under the new covenant. It is very evident that this apocalyptic beast represents the Islamic Empire and ten horns represent ten Muslim kings; therefore, it would be unreasonable to assert that Rome rules over Muslim kings. There was no Islam, when Rome was reigning over the kings of the earth – the Islamic Empire rose after the fall of Rome – therefore, there must be another city that identifies this prophetic allegory!

On the other hand, in the Book of Revelation are mentioned prophetic numbers that make reference to the time and duration of prophetic events:

> *"2 And the court which is without the [c]temple [d] leave without, and measure it not; for it hath been given unto the [e]nations: and <u>the holy city shall they tread under foot forty and two months</u>" (Rev. 11:2).*

> *"3 And I will give unto my two witnesses, and they shall prophesy <u>a thousand two hundred and three-score days</u>, clothed in sackcloth" (Rev. 11:3).*

> *"6 And the woman fled into the wilderness, where she hath a place prepared of God, that there they may nourish her <u>a thousand two hundred and threescore days</u>" (Rev. 12:6).*

> *"14 And there were given to the woman the two wings of the great eagle, that she might fly into the wilderness unto her place, where she is nourished <u>for a time, and times, and half a time</u>, from the face of the serpent" (Rev. 12:14).*

> *"5 and there was given to him a mouth speaking great things and blasphemies; and there was given to him authority [e]to continue <u>forty and two months</u>" (Rev. 13:5).*

If we apply "day-year" principle (see: Num. 14:34; Ezek. 4:5-6; Dan. 9:24-27), we get the following proportion: 42 months equals 1260 days, and 1260 days equals 1260 years. As to the prophecy concerning the "*holy city being tread under foot*" (Rev. 11:2), there are no historical evidence to confirm that Rome, that is, the Roman Empire (in any form) trampled on the Holy City (Jerusalem) for such a long period of time. However, the history confirms that Jerusalem was occupied and controlled by Muslims for a very long period of time – more then twelve centuries.

The Book of Revelation provides a clue regarding the identity of the "*mystery woman*":

"⁶ And I saw the woman drunken with the blood of the saints, and with the blood of the [e]martyrs of Jesus. And when I saw her, I wondered with a great wonder" (Rev. 17:6).

"²⁰ Rejoice over her, thou heaven, and ye saints, and ye apostles, and ye prophets; for God hath judged your judgment on her" (Rev. 18:20).

"²⁴ And in her was found the blood of prophets and of saints, and of all that have been slain upon the earth" (Rev. 18:24).

Biblically, one city fits this description; only one city "*killest the prophets*" – that city is Jerusalem. The following Bible verses confirm it:

"³⁷ O Jerusalem, Jerusalem, that killeth the prophets, and stoneth them that are sent unto her! how often would I have gathered thy children together, even as a hen gathereth her chickens under her wings, and ye would not! ³⁸ Behold, your house is left unto you [p]desolate" (Mat. 23:37-38).

"³³ Nevertheless I must go on my way to-day and to-morrow and the day following: for it cannot be that a prophet perish out of Jerusalem. ³⁴ O Jerusalem, Jerusalem, that killeth the prophets, and stoneth them that are sent unto her! how often would I have gathered thy children together, even as a hen gathereth her own brood under her wings, and ye would not!" (Lk. 13:33-34).

"⁴⁷ Woe unto you! for ye build the tombs of the prophets, and your fathers killed them. ⁴⁸ So ye are witnesses and consent unto the works of your fathers: for they killed them, and ye build their tombs. ⁴⁹ Therefore also said the wisdom of God, I will send unto them prophets and apostles; and some of them they shall kill and persecute; ⁵⁰ that

*the blood of all the prophets, which was shed from
the foundation of the world, may be required of
this generation; [51] from the blood of Abel unto the
blood of Zachariah, who perished between the altar
and the [x]sanctuary: yea, I say unto you, it shall be
required of this generation" (Lk. 11:47-51).*

*"[8] And their [g]dead bodies lie in the street of the
great city, which spiritually is called Sodom and
Egypt, where also their Lord was crucified" (Rev.
11:8).*

Biblical and prophetic role of Jerusalem in God's plan is indisputable – a reality confirmed in both the Old and New Testament.
However, according to the Old Testament, Jerusalem was also
called "*harlot*" by Yahweh, the God of Israel, as follows:

*"[1]The vision of Isaiah the son of Amoz, which he
saw concerning Judah and Jerusalem, in the days of
Uzziah, Jotham, Ahaz, and Hezekiah, kings of Judah.
[2] Hear, heavens, and listen, earth; for Yahweh[a] has
spoken: "I have nourished and brought up children,
and they have rebelled against me... [21] How the
faithful city has become a prostitute! She was full of
justice; righteousness righteousness lodged in her,
but now murderers murderers" (Is. 1:1-2, 21).*

*"[1] Again Yahweh's word came to me, saying, [2] Son of
man, cause Jerusalem to know her abominations
[1]Again the word of the LORD came unto me, saying,
[2]Son of man, cause Jerusalem to know her abo-mi-
nation... [35]Wherefore, O harlot, hear the word of the
LORD... [48]As I live, saith the Lord GOD, Sodom thy
sister hath not done, she nor her daughters, as thou
hast done, thou and thy daughters" (Ezek. 16:1-2,
35, 48).*

*"[4] Hear Yahweh's word, O house of Jacob, and all the
families of the house of Israel!... [20] "For long ago I
broke off your yoke, and burst your bonds. You said,*

'I will not serve;' for on every high hill and under every green tree <u>you bowed yourself, playing the prostitute</u>" (Jer. 2:4, 20).

"⁶ Moreover, Yahweh said to me in the days of Josiah the king, "<u>Have you seen that which back-sliding Israel has done</u>? She has gone up on every high mountain and under every green tree, and <u>has played the prostitute there</u>" (Jer. 3:6).

"²⁵ ⁽ʲ⁾Now this Hagar is mount Sinai in Arabia and answereth to the Jerusalem that now is: for she is in bondage with her children" (Gal. 4:25).

The Book of Revelation gives us another clue regarding the "*woman (harlot)*" sitting upon the beast with seven heads and ten horns, which clearly predicts the apocalyptic fate of this great city:

"¹⁶ And <u>the ten horns</u> which thou sawest, <u>and the beast, these shall hate the harlot</u>, and shall make her desolate and naked, and shall eat her flesh, <u>and shall burn her utterly with fire</u>" (Rev. 17:3).

This verse corresponds to the geopolitical situation in the Middle East. Muslim countries hate Israel – Jerusalem is the heart of Israel. The beast that "*looks unto a <u>leopard</u>, and his feet were as the feet of a <u>bear</u>, and his mouth as the mouth of a <u>lion</u>*" represents the Muslim Empire. The "*ten horns*" that receive authority as kings, with the beast, for an hour must represent Muslim kings (kingdoms), as they rule with the beast (Rev. 17:12). Therefore, it is pertinent to suggest that "*ten horns*" could represent ten caliphates (kingdoms) within the Islamic Empire located predominantly on the territory of the former kingdoms prophetically described as "*leopard, bear, and lion.*" The "*beast*" and the "*ten horns*" cannot possibly hate Mecca, Istanbul, or any other city of their own; otherwise, it would lead to self-destruction. Jerusalem, however, is a different case: it represents Israel – Muslims hate Israel.

Some believers may argue that the verse "_woman whom thou sawest is that great city, which reigneth over the kings of the earth_" (Rev. 17:18) does not identify Jerusalem because, for the most part of its existence, this city was under the occupation of foreign rulers. That is true! Jerusalem has always been a desired trophy for many powerful leaders. However, the expression "_reigneth over the kings of the earth_" in this case should be understood in the spiritual sense. Jerusalem is the centre of three religions: Judaism, Christianity, and Islam. Here, the verse "_And the woman... having in her hand a golden cup, [c]even the unclean things of her fornicationfull_" has spiritual significance. It symbolizes the great city that commits "_spiritual adultery_" by forsaking its spiritual purity, its allegiance to the God of Israel. Therefore, the expression "_harlot_" should be analyzed and interpreted in a spiritual sense.

Regardless of how devoted certain believers may be to Jerusalem and to the Old Testament, yet it is pertinent to affirm that after the crucifixion of the Messiah, that is to say, after the rejection of God's new covenant sealed by the blood of Jesus Christ, Jerusalem lost its divine glory. This statement is confirmed in the following Bible verses:

> "[42] _Jesus saith unto them, Did ye never read in the scriptures, [p]The stone which the builders rejected, The same was made the head of the corner; This was from the Lord, And it is marvellous in our eyes?_ [43] _Therefore say I unto you, The kingdom of God shall be taken away from you, and shall be given to a nation bringing forth the fruits thereof._ [44] [q]_And he that falleth on this stone shall be broken to pieces: but on whomsoever it shall fall, it will scatter him as dust._ [45] _And when the chief priests and the Pharisees heard his parables, they perceived that he spake of them._ [46] _And when they sought to lay hold on him, they feared the multitudes, because they took him for a prophet_" (Mt. 21:42-46).

> "[37] _O Jerusalem, Jerusalem, that killeth the prophets,_

and stoneth them that are sent unto her! how often would I have gathered thy children together, even as a hen gathereth her chickens under her wings, and ye would not! [38] _Behold, your house is left unto you_ [p]_desolate_. [39] For I say unto you, Ye shall not see me henceforth, till ye shall say, Blessed is he that cometh in the name of the Lord" (Mt. 23:37-39).

"And Jesus went out from the temple, and was going on his way; and his disciples came to him to show him the buildings of the temple. [2] But he answered and said unto them, See ye not all these things? verily I say unto you, _There shall not be left here one stone upon another, that shall not be thrown down_" (Mt. 24:1-2).

"[34] O _Jerusalem, Jerusalem, that killeth the prophets, and stoneth them that are sent unto her_! how often would I have gathered thy children together, even as a hen gathereth her own brood under her wings, and ye would not! [35] _Behold, your house is left unto you desolate_: and I say unto you, Ye shall not see me, until ye shall say, Blessed is he that cometh in the name of the Lord" (Lk. 13:34-35).

"[50] And Jesus cried again with a loud voice, and yielded up his spirit. [51] And behold, _the veil of the_ [u] _temple was rent in two from the top to the bottom_; and the earth did quake; and the rocks were rent; [52] and the tombs were opened; and many bodies of the saints that had fallen asleep were raised; [53] and coming forth out of the tombs after his resurrection they entered into the holy city and appeared unto many. [54] Now the centurion, and they that were with him watching Jesus, when they saw the earthquake, and the things that were done, feared exceedingly, saying, Truly this was [v]the Son of God" (Mt. 27:50-54).

"[37] And Jesus uttered a loud voice, and gave up the

ghost. [38] And <u>the veil of the [l]temple was rent in two</u> <u>from the top to the bottom</u>. [39] And when the centurion, who stood by over against him, saw that he [m] so gave up the ghost, he said, Truly this man was [n] the Son of God" (Mk. 15:37-39).

"[44] And it was now about the sixth hour, and a darkness came over the whole [g]land until the ninth hour, [45] [h]the sun's light failing: and <u>the veil of the [i]</u> <u>temple was rent in the midst.</u> [46] [j]And Jesus, crying with a loud voice, said, <u>Father, into thy hands I</u> <u>commend my spirit: and having said this, he gave</u> <u>up the ghost</u>. [47] And when the centurion saw what was done, he glorified God, saying, Certainly this was a righteous man" (Lk. 23:44-47).

It is said that, before the destruction of Jerusalem (in 70 AD), unusual things happened during religious services performed in the Temple, which were interpreted by some believers as a "*sign*" that the Glory of Yahweh left the Temple of Jerusalem. Indeed, God's Glory departed from the Temple! This has been confirmed by the destruction of Jerusalem and its religious edifice, and later by the Islamic mosque (with a full moon decoration on top of its dome, which evokes the crescent moon symbol of Islam) built on the place where once stood the famous Jewish Temple. Divine glory of God is revealed now to all those who accept the "*word of God and keep the testimony of Jesus Christ.*" This biblical reality is confirmed by Jesus Christ's statement in the following verses:

"[42] Jesus saith unto them, Did ye never read in the scriptures, [p]<u>The stone which the builders rejected,</u> <u>The same was made the head of the corner</u>; This was from the Lord, And it is marvellous in our eyes? [43] Therefore say I unto you, <u>The kingdom of God</u> <u>shall be taken away from you, and shall be given</u> <u>to a nation bringing forth the fruits thereof</u>" (Mt. 21:42-43).

Nowadays, Jerusalem is the center of three major monotheistic religions: 1) Judaism, religion of the Old Testament; 2) Christianity, religion of the New Testament; 3) Islam, religion observing the Quran. All three contradict each other doctrinally, thus propagate a different version of God. Such doctrinal discordance reflects deviation from the truth, compromise. The Holy Spirit is not a spirit of compromise, but of truth, peace, and holiness.

Being destroyed as prophesied, and being under Roman pagan rule for several centuries and later under Muslim occupation for over twelve hundred years, the picture of Jerusalem nowadays doesn't seem to reflect the glory it once had, or the glory of the New Jerusalem described in Revelation chapter 21. Jerusalem is a city in grief, a shadow of what once used to be – it is rather a place of religious and political intrigues. Nowadays, one can see ancient ruins of what once was the greatness of Jerusalem. The real issue is not the original glory of Jerusalem (Mount Zion) but rather what this great city has become – a venue of religious and political events, which could trigger extreme violent reaction from its neighboring Islamic countries.

Jerusalem represents the heart of Judaism. This city is also the place where Jesus Christ was condemned to death by crucifixion, the place where initial persecution of Christians began. For believers under God's new covenant, the term "Jerusalem" has a new meaning. It is perceived as the "*spiritual Jerusalem*", that is, the "*new Jerusalem, coming down out of heaven from God*" – this is pointing towards the glorious return of our Lord Jesus Christ. How should a Christian believer identify himself with a city biblically described as "...*that killeth the prophets, and stoneth them that are sent unto her!*" (Mat. 23:37-38) and where ultimately the prophesied Messiah, Jesus Christ, was sentenced to death by "*crucifixion*"? Why do we see nowadays the "*Holy City*" in ruins? Was the destruction of Jerusalem and its Temple a fulfillment of biblical prophecy or a random incident? That is, should a reasonable believer consider the destruction of Jerusalem and the Temple, where the Roman army served as an instrument, a fulfillment of Jesus' prophecy or just a random military intervention of pagan Rome? Was Babylonian destruction of Jerusalem and the first Temple a fulfillment of Jeremiah's prophecy or just another historic incident? Isn't God, who inspires the prophets, in control of all these prophecies? Extra-biblical teachings and tendentious interpretations of the Bible are very dangerous weapons – a sad reality in religion.

Some believers will argue that such exegetical analysis is unacceptable because Jerusalem is the holiest place for Jews and Christians. However, those believers should not neglect one fact: the "*holiness*" of Jerusalem was due to the Ark of the Covenant, which stood in the Most Holy Place of the Temple, where the presence of Yahweh, the God of Israel, was manifested. Nowadays, one can see the ruins of what once was the holy edifice – undoubtedly, the consequence of Israel's disobedience and unfaithfulness to Yahweh. Believers under the new covenant are longing for a new city, the "*new Jerusalem coming down out of heaven from God*", described in Revelation chapter 21.

Observing ancestral traditions and deeming certain sites of Jerusalem as holy is very honourable – it is an expression of believer's faith and devotion to God. However, God does not dwell in man-made places (Is. 66:1; Acts 7:48-50). God is Spirit; His divine presence is manifested in the heart and mind of believers. And, just as God's chosen servants (prophets, apostles) have been sanctified by the Holy Spirit, in the same way a sanctuary or a site is sanctified by the presence of the same divine power. A physical object (a stone) as such does not sanctify. Therefore, if any religion promotes excess of zeal regarding the law and tradition, this often brings about unpredictable religious, social, and political consequences. In this case, exegetical reasoning regarding Jerusalem presented above would be inconsistent without clear biblical evidence; therefore, the following verses are indispensable:

> "*[31] Behold, <u>the days come, says Yahweh, that I will make a new covenant with the house of Israel, and with the house of Judah</u>: [32] not according to the covenant that I made with their fathers in the day that I took them by the hand to bring them out of*

the land of Egypt; which my covenant they broke, although I was a husband to them, says Yahweh. ³³ But <u>this is the covenant</u> that I will make with the house of Israel after those days, says Yahweh: <u>I will put my law in their inward parts, and in their heart will I write it</u>; and I will be their God, and they shall be my people" (Jer. 31:31-33).

"²¹ Jesus saith unto her, Woman, believe me, <u>the hour cometh, when neither in this mountain, nor in Jerusalem, shall ye worship the Father</u>" (Jn. 4:21).

"²³ But <u>the hour cometh, and now is, when the true worshippers shall worship the Father in spirit and truth</u>: [g]for such doth the Father seek to be his worshippers. ²⁴ [h]<u>God is a Spirit: and they that worship him must worship in spirit and truth</u>" (Jn. 4:23-24).

"²⁰ For <u>where two or three</u> are gathered together in my name, <u>there am I in the midst of them</u>" (Mt. 18:20).

"And I saw a new heaven and a new earth: for the first heaven and the first earth are passed away; and the sea is no more. ² And <u>I saw</u> [a]<u>the holy city, new Jerusalem, coming down out of heaven from God</u>, made ready as a bride adorned for her husband" (Rev.21:1-2).

"⁹ And there came one of the seven angels who had the seven bowls, who were laden with the seven last plagues; and he spake with me, saying, Come hither, <u>I will show thee the bride, the wife of the Lamb</u>. ¹⁰ And he carried me away in the Spirit to a mountain great and high, and <u>showed me the holy city Jerusalem, coming down out of heaven from God</u>" (Rev. 21:9-10).

An honest and devout believer, being under the guidance of the Holy Spirit, cannot say: biblical evidence quoted above is irrelevant. God is Spirit. The Holy Scripture is inspired by God, therefore, must be analysed in spirit and in truth. Those who seek the truth with a sincere heart will find it, and the truth will set them free.

Despite comprehensive analysis and convincing biblical evidence, there still is uncertainty regarding the identity of the *"woman (harlot)."* In this sense, Revelation 20:9 provides a conclusive clue:

> *"7 And when the thousand years are finished, Satan shall be loosed out of his prison, 8 and shall come forth to deceive the nations which are in the four corners of the earth, Gog and Magog, to gather them together to the war: the number of whom is as the sand of the sea. 9 And <u>they</u> went up over the breadth of the earth, and <u>compassed the camp of the saints about, and the beloved city</u>: and fire came down [e]out of heaven, and devoured them. 10 And the devil that deceived them was cast into the lake of fire and brimstone, <u>where are also the beast and the false prophet</u>; and they shall be tormented day and night [f]for ever and ever" (Rev. 20:7-9).*

This verse informs the reader that, before the end time, the deceived nations will surround the *"camp of the saints, and the beloved city"* – <u>a reference to Jerusalem</u>. This is a clear confirmation of the fact that the city of Jerusalem will stand even after the destruction of the *"harlot (Babylon the Great)"*, after the destruction of the beast and the false prophet. In this regard, it is pertinent to affirm that Jerusalem cannot be the apocalyptic *"woman (harlot)"* that sits upon the scarlet-coloured beast. The initial persecution of Christians started in Jerusalem; however, the verse *"woman drunken with the blood of the saints, and with the blood of the martyrs of Jesus"* cannot prophetically identify this religious city.

Prophetically, *"seven heads"* on which the woman sits are *"seven mountains"* (Rev. 17:9); these are also *"seven kings"* (Rev. 17:10). Heads or mountains represent *"waters"*, and *"peoples,* and multitudes, and nations, and tongues" (Rev. 17:1, 15). Therefore, the "woman (great city)" sits or has dominion over many kingdoms, peoples, and nations prophetically described as seven heads (mountains). The fact that in prophetic language a "mountain" symbolizes a "kingdom" is also confirmed in the Book of Daniel (Dan. 2:34-35, 44-45). In reality, hills of Rome, Constantinople, Jerusalem, or any other city are not kings or kingdoms – one cannot attribute to a geographical "hill" such politico-administrative status. This reasoning is confirmed by the following verses:

> "And there came one of the seven angels that had the seven bowls, and spake with me, saying, Come hither, <u>I will show thee the judgment of the great harlot that sitteth upon many waters</u>" (Rev. 17:1).

> "9 Here is the [i]mind that hath wisdom. <u>The seven heads are seven mountains</u>, on which the woman sitteth: 10 and [j]<u>they are seven kings; the five are fallen, the one is</u>, the other is not yet come; and when he cometh, he must continue a little while" (Rev. 17:9-10).

> "15 And he saith unto me, <u>The waters which thou sawest, where the harlot sitteth, are peoples, and multitudes, and nations, and tongues</u>" (Rev. 17:15).

> "18 And <u>the woman</u> whom thou sawest <u>is the great city</u>, which [k]reigneth over the kings of the earth" (Rev. 17:18).

The fact that seven mountains represent seven heads, seven kings (kingdoms), and also many waters (peoples, nations...) leads to the conclusion that the version according to which the "woman (great city)" sits on seven geographical hills is biblically contradictory. In this regard, it is pertinent to affirm that the beast with seven heads and ten horns represents an empire that has dominion over seven kingdoms (former empires) and at a definite time ten kings (kingdoms) rule within that empire – this beast represents the Muslim Empire; it is pertinent to assert that the *"woman (great city)"* in the wilderness that sits on a scarlet beast with seven heads and ten horns (Rev. 17:3) has to be an Islamic city; it is pertinent to assert that only an Islamic city can rule over the vast Islamic Empire. Mecca, the spiritual center of Islam, is the place where Muslim conquest commenced, which brought along many centuries of persecution and atrocities of non-Muslims throughout the conquered territory (Rev. 17:6). It is common sense to assert that Mecca, the heart of Islam, rules over the Muslim Empire. According to some critics, however, such assertion may be regarded as absurd because in the Book of Revelation is stated that the ten horns will destroy the woman (harlot) and burn her with fire (Rev. 17:16), therefore, how can ten Islamic horns hate and destroy Mecca, the most important Islamic city? Well, religious conflict between Shia and Sunni is reaching a critical point nowadays and the establishment of Islamic caliphate is destabilizing the Muslim world thus leading to unpredictable consequences. On the other hand, the prophecy tells us that the *"ten horns"*, which will ultimately destroy the *"woman (great city)"* and burn her body with fire, fulfill God's will, and that *"ten horns"* agree and give their kingdom unto the beast until the word of God shall be fulfilled (Rev. 17:17). The following verses confirm this reasoning:

> *"³ And he carried me away in the Spirit into a wilderness: and I saw <u>a woman sitting upon a scarlet-colored beast</u>, [a]full of names of blasphemy, <u>having seven heads and ten horns</u>" (Rev. 17:3).*

> *"⁶ And I saw <u>the woman drunken with the blood of the saints, and with the blood of the [e]martyrs of Jesus</u>. And when I saw her, I wondered with a great wonder" (Rev. 17:6).*

> *"¹⁶ And <u>the ten horns</u> which thou sawest, <u>and the beast, these shall hate the harlot</u>, and shall make her desolate and naked, and shall eat her flesh, <u>and shall burn her utterly with fire</u>. ¹⁷ For <u>God did put</u>*

in their hearts to do his mind, and to come to one mind, and to give their kingdom unto the beast, until the words of God should be accomplished" (Rev. 17:16-17).

"²¹ And [q]a strong angel took up a stone as it were a great millstone and cast it into the sea, saying, Thus with a mighty fall shall Babylon, the great city, be cast down, and shall be found no more at all" (Rev. 18:21).

Once again, the Holy Scripture teaches that *"seven heads"* on which the *"woman (harlot)"* sits are *"seven mountains"*, that they are *"seven kings (kingdoms)"* (Rev. 17:9-10), and that the *"woman"* sits on many waters, which symbolize *"peoples, and multitudes, and nations, and tongues"* (Rev. 17:1, 15). The *"five fallen heads (kings)"* represent fallen empires of Babylonia, Medo-Persia, Greece, and quite probably Assyria and Egypt. According to the Book of Daniel, the third beast (Greek Empire), which extended its dominion over the territory of the previous empires (Medo-Persian and Babylonian), later was divided into four kingdoms prophetically described as *"four heads/horns"* (Dan. 7:6; 8:8). Three heads (horns) of the divided Greek Empire superposed kingdoms of Egypt, Assyria, Babylonia, and Medo-Persia.

The version according to which prophetic allegory *"his death-stroke was healed"* (Rev. 13:3) represents the revived Western Roman Empire and the *"little horn"*, before which *"three of the first horns"* were plucked up by the roots, represents the Papacy, is based on Daniel 7:7-8. It is very evident that prophetic characteristics of the beast of Revelation chapters 13 and 17 are attributed to the fourth beast of Daniel chapter 7. This seems to be a very brave attempt to solve the prophecy; however, it is inconsistent and rather contradictory as follows:

1) According to Revelation chapter 13, the beast with seven heads and ten horns was *"like unto a leopard, and his feet were as the feet of a bear, and his mouth as the mouth of a lion"* – leopard, bear, and lion represent a prophetic allegory of the

57

Greek, Medo-Persian, and Babylonian Empires. The Roman Empire is missing; therefore, the beast is not related to the Roman Empire. This beast is to be searched on the territory of kingdoms prophetically described as *"leopard, bear, and lion."*

2) The version according to which *"ten horns"* represent ten European nations arising after the fall of the Western Roman Empire makes no sense, as prophetic allegory *"leopard, bear, and lion"* cannot be attributed to the Western Roman Empire.

3) According to Revelation chapter 17, the *"ten horns"* receive power as kings for one hour with the beast (Rev. 17:12). This beast prophetically described as *"<u>was, and is not</u>; and is about to come up out of the abyss"*, and also as *"<u>was, and is not</u>, is himself also an eighth, and <u>is of the seven</u>"*, is in fact one of the *"five are fallen."* The Roman Empire, when John received prophetic visions of Revelation, was the sixth head, that is, *"one is"*, not one of the five fallen heads (empires). Therefore, the *"beast that was, and is not, and is about to come"* and the *"ten horns"* cannot be attributed to the Roman Empire – the beast must be related to one of the empires that was before the Roman Empire.

4) If the *"beast with seven heads and ten horns"* described in Revelation chapters 13 and 17 cannot be attributed to the Roman Empire, and if the *"ten horns"* that receive power as kings for one hour with the beast cannot be attributed to West European nations coming out after the fall of the Western Roman Empire, then the *"little horn"*, before which *"three of the first horns"* were plucked up by the roots (Dan. 7:8, 24), cannot be attributed to the Papacy, and the *"three uprooted horns"* cannot be three kings (kingdoms) coming out of the Western Roman Empire.

5) The following reasoning demonstrates that the beast of Revelation described as *"one of his heads as though it had been [b]smitten unto death; and his death-stroke was healed"* (Rev. 13:3), as *"was, and is not, and is about come up out of the abyss"* (Rev. 17:8), and as *"was, and is not, is himself also an eighth, and is of the seven"* (Rev. 17:11) identifies an empire geographically located in the Middle East – it refers to the rise of Muslim Empire:

- Prophetic allegory *"feet part of iron, and part of clay"* (Dan. 2:33, 42) – the last empire of Nebuchadnezzar's prophetic statue – refer to the Islamic Empire, as it consisted partly of iron, the conquered Roman territory in the Middle East and North Africa, and partly of clay (earth, desert), the new territorial conquests in the Middle East, Central Asia, and African;

- Two prophetic allegories described in Revelation chapter 9 draw particular attention: the "*pit of the abyss*" and the "*locusts*" that came out of the smoke, which arose from the pit of the abyss. These locusts were commanded that *"they should not hurt the grass of the earth, neither any green thing, neither any tree, but only such men as have not the seal of God on their foreheads"* (Rev. 9:4). This is a clear proof that these are not ordinary locusts – a locust feeds on (green) vegetation. Desert locust invasion destroying crops is a reality in the Middle East and Africa. The Book of Joel chapter 2 describes desert locust invasion – a prophetic reference to a military invasion (an army). Therefore, it is very evident that the "*locusts*" of the Book of Revelation refer to a Muslim (Arab) army. On the other hand, the scarlet-coloured beast (Rev. 17:3, 8) also comes up out of the "*abyss.*" Thus, the locusts and the beast with seven heads and ten horns have a similar prophetic characteristic – the two refer to the rise of one and the same empire;

- Muslims established their vast empire on the territory of the kingdoms prophetically described as *"leopard, bear, and lion"*, which geographically coincides with the Middle East;

- The verse *"And it was given unto him to make war with the saints, and to overcome them"* (Rev. 13:7) applies to Islamic Empire, as this is the empire that throughout its vast territory made war on Jews and Christians and defeated them. In this regard, it is pertinent to mention that similar prophetic characteristic is also attributed to the "*little horn*" described in Daniel (Dan. 7:8, 21, 24-25) – this horn (king) seems to fit the beast of Revelation (Rev. 13:5-7), as the two have in common similar prophetic characteristics. Although arguable, it is pertinent to suggest that the "*little horn (another king)*" refers to the rise of

Islamic Empire and the "*three horns plucked up by the roots*" seem to correspond territorially to the three horns of the divided Greek Empire, which to some extent were also part of the Roman Empire;

- Bible verse "*These shall war against the Lamb...*" (Rev. 17:14), where "*these*" refers to the ten horns, cannot be attributed to ten Western European <u>Christian</u> nations. However, the assertion that ten horns of the Islamic Empire make war against the Lamb of God and His followers makes sense – it is an undeniable biblical and hystorical reality.

6) It is very evident that apocalyptic beast with seven heads and ten horns represents the Islamic Empire, which at its peak stretched from the Atlantic coast of North Africa (and Iberian Peninsula) to the Middle East and beyond. Therefore, "*ten horns*" must be ten Muslim kings (kingdoms) ruling within the Islamic Empire. In this sense, it is pertinent to suggest that "*ten horns*" quite probably represent ten Islamic caliphates. History confirms that the Muslim world was often governed by more than one caliphate at the same period of time – parallel caliphates; on the other hand, smaller caliphates were conquered, engulfed by the larger and more powerful ones. The issue regarding caliphs and caliphates is debatable among Shia and Sunni Muslims.

Any attempt to identify "*ten horns*" outside the Islamic Empire does not concord with the following prophetic description: the beast looks like a "<u>*leopard, bear, and lion*</u>"; the beast "<u>*was, is not, and is about to come up*</u>"; the ten horns "<u>*...receive authority as kings, with the beast, for one hour*</u>." On the other hand, prophetic expression "*receive authority as kings <u>for one hour</u>*" is challenging. This seems to indicate a very short time. Nevertheless, the beast with seven heads and ten horns, also described as "<u>*an eighth, and is of the seven*</u>" (Rev. 17:11), exercised its imperial authority during the reign of the horns ["*...on his horns <u>ten diadems</u>*" (Rev. 13:1) and "<u>*ten horns*</u> *(ten kings)... <u>receive authiority</u> as kings, <u>with the beast</u>, for one hour*" (Rev. 17:12)], not during the reign of the heads. More than twelve centuries of Muslim imperial domination is not a short period of time. As the Islamic world is going through a severe crisis – the conflict between Shia and Sunni and the rise of Islamic Caliphate – it is reasonable to assert that ten horns of Islam, quite probably under the influence of the beast with "*two horns like unto a lamb*" (Rev 13:11) that exercises all the authority of the "*first beast in his sight*", are to rise and fulfill the prophecy of Revelation 17:16-17.

7) According to Revelation chapter 17, the scarlet beast with "*seven heads and ten horns*" ascends from the "*pit of the abyss*", not from the sea.

8) In the prophecy of Daniel is not mentioned the "<u>*woman*</u>" sitting upon the beast.

9) The verse "*And it was given unto him to <u>make war with the saints, and to overcome them</u>*" (Rev. 13:7; Dan. 7:21) seems ambiguous. Does it refer to Jews or Christians? If it only refers to the Jews – believers of the old covenant – then such interpretation reflects partiality because Christians – believers of the new covenant – are being excluded. If it refers to both Christians and Jews, to all those who honour God in spirit and in truth, then everything makes perfect sense. However, the Book of Revelation was revealed to John, a Christian, and is predominantly meant for believers under the new covenant, all those who accepted the "*word of God and the testimony of Jesus Christ*." For non-Christians, the Book of Revelation seems irrelevant! In the past, Muslims defeated Christians and Jews throughout the territory of the Islamic Empire. Even nowadays, persecution and acts of atrocity against Christian believers are still being committed in many Islamic countries.

10) Radical believers may argue that prophetic verse "*it was given unto him to <u>make war with the saints, and to overcome them</u>*" (Rev. 13:7; also Dan. 7:21) identifies imperial power of Rome manifested through destruction of Jerusalem, Crusades, Inquisition, and other military interventions of religious character. Indeed, the use of sword to solve religious conflicts is not in harmony with Christ's two commandment of (agape) love. Decision making is susceptible to human error; on the other

hand, not all those involved in a just cause are sincerely devoted to their calling. Western society has been considerably influenced by double standard ideologies regarding the circumstances, causes, and provocations that triggered religious conflicts within Christianity. Roman siege and devastation of Jerusalem, which ended with the destruction of the Temple, and persecution of Christians in the first three centuries is a typical manifestation of pagan imperial power. The Crusades were military campaigns undertaken by Western Christians to free Jerusalem and the Holy Land, to defend Christianity from Muslim religious military aggression. However, Crusades had a limited success – Jerusalem and the Holy Land were re-conquered by Muslims. The Inquisition was created to combat heresy (according to canon law) and the spread of religious sectarianism. However, Protestant Reformation – the peak of anti-Catholicism – was not defeated. On the contrary, the Reformation spread all over the world. It is a known fact that, to some extent, Crusades and Inquisition were marked by human error and even departure from its original goal. Despite many differences of opinion, however, prophetic expression "*made war with saints, and overcame them*" cannot identify Christian Rome. Human history has many faces; quite often historical evidence is distorted, obscured, and history books dictated by the winners.

Despite clear biblical evidence, some critics may still deem exegetical analysis of the beasts of Revelation presented in this book as pro-Catholic, anti-Islamic. The answer to this remark is: such prophetic interpretation is pro-biblical and is confirmed by the Book of Revelation chapters 9, 13, 17, the Book of Daniel, and other biblical evidence. The given prophetic analysis comes in response to the following observation: How could "certain" historians, scholars, and religious leaders focus their attention mainly on Christianity and neglect or speak only vaguely of the beast ascending from the Middle East – the Muslim Empire – that made war on Jews and Christians and defeated them, the power that has been threatened Christianity with annihilation for many centuries? How could they focus their attention predominantly on Rome (and the alleged revived Western Roman Empire) thus ignore dramatic reality of Christians and Jews living in the Balkans, Middle East and other territories, ignore the undeniable fact that religious identity of those believers has been trampled upon for many centuries by Muslims? It is quite evident that such erroneous, tendentious interpretation of Bible prophecy is intended to divert believers' attention away from the truth.

History and religion have often been the subject of much speculation. Freedom of expression does not guarantee the veracity and accuracy of the facts, as an individual has the freedom of choice between speaking the truth or adopting a double standard position; therefore, this so-called "freedom" quite often becomes an instrument of propaganda and disinformation. Islam, the new religion that emerged in the 7th century, is ideologically antagonistic to Christianity and Judaism and, to a considerable extent, seems to counterfeit the Bible. According to traditional sources, Muslims initially were facing Jerusalem (the Temple Mount) during prayer; later, Muslim Qibla[20] (direction of prayer) was facing the Kaaba in Mecca. There seem to be interesting similarities between the Kaaba of the Great Mosque in Mecca and the Jewish Temple that stood in Jerusalem. Some of these similarities are: both cities are declare holy; both cities shelter the holiest site; both sites contain the holy stone; direction of worship; pilgrimage; circumambulation; animal sacrifices. Despite speculations over this issue, it seems that Kaaba of Mecca, from religious point of view, is an imitation of the Temple of Jerusalem. There are people who think that Islam is a religion of peace; however, they seem to manifest ignorance of history regarding persecution and atrocities committed for many centuries by Muslims and of the fact that thousands of Christian churches were destroyed or turned into mosques.

Islamic Empire lost its imperial dominion following the collapse of the Ottoman Caliphate; therefore, it seems that the beast with seven heads and ten horns has fallen. Nowadays, Islamic Empire as such no longer exists; however, its dominion throughout the territory of its former empire is manifested in a different form – <u>a religious Islamic form</u>. This new form of dominion seems to fit the beast prophetically described as *"coming up out of the earth... exerciseth all the authority of the first beast in his sight"* (Rev. 13:11-12). The complexity of this prophetic mystery is evident and certain questions still remain unanswered:

- Who is the seventh head, which prophetically is also described as *"when he cometh, <u>he must continue a little while</u>"* (Rev. 17:10)? The Hunnic Empire seems to identify with the seventh head. In the 5th century, this empire stretched from the steppes of Central Asia to Central Europe; however, it was a short lived empire – it lasted less than a century. Hunnic expansion stimulated the Great Migration (Barbarian Invasion); Huns also invaded Roman territory in Balkans and Central Europe. These two factors undoubtedly contributed to the collapse of the Western Roman Empire. On the other hand, the Mongol Empire could also be identified with this prophecy. This empire stretched from the Sea of Japan to Central Europe (including a considerable territory of the Middle East). At the zenith of its power, the empire was divided into four khanates, three of which adopted Islam – the religion of the beast (empire) that was already in the world for about six centuries; therefore, the Mongol Empire does not correspond to this prophecy. The Ottoman Empire cannot be the *"seventh head"*, as its imperial dominion lasted 600 years (a long period of time) and was an Islamic caliphate;

- Who is the deadly wounded head whose deadly wound was healed? Was it one of the empires that preceded the Roman Empire? Was it the fatal wound of the Abbasid Caliphate in 1258, when Bagdad – the splendor of Islam at that time – was destroyed by the Mongols? According to the Book of Revelation chapter 17, the head that *"was, and is not"* is one of the *"five fallen heads."* More precisely, this head (or the deadly wounded head) is the eighth king, the beast (Rev. 17:9-11) – it revives one of the fallen empires;

- Who are the ten horns, which receive authority as kings, with the beast, for one hour? It is quite evident that these horns must represent ten Muslim kings. These "*ten horns*" and the beast will hate the "*woman (great harlot)*" and ultimately destroy her and burn her with fire, thus fulfil the final act of Bible prophecy.

As mentioned previously, it is pertinent to attribute prophetic allegory the "*beast that looks like a leopard, bear, and lion*" to the Islamic Empire, as this empire geographically was located on the territory of kingdoms prophetically described as "*leopard, bear, and lion*", which represent the former Greek, Medo-Persian, and Babylonian empires. The Muslim Empire carved its way through history for more that twelve hundred years but no longer exists as such. However, we are witnessing Muslim religious aggressive expansion in various parts of the world, which quite often is manifested in a militaristic form.

Some believers consider that prophetic events described in the Book of Revelation have already taken place in the first century. Such approach of Bible prophecy, however, does not seem to provide a very consistent explanation regarding the identity of the beast that looks like "*leopard, bear, and lion*" (Rev. 13:2), the ten horns which are "*ten kings, which have received no kingdom as yet*" (Rev. 17:12), and the beast with "*two horns like a lamb*" (Rev. 13:11). On the other hand, the rise of Muslim Empire and other subsequent events of prophetic and historic significance do not seem to be part of the Apocalypse anymore.

In summary, the following conclusive remarks regarding the identity of the beast with seven heads and ten horns deserve due consideration:

1) The allegations according to which prophetic allegory "*smitten unto death head*" refers to the historic event that took place in 476 and the prophecy regarding the "*end of the 1260 evenings and mornings*" was fulfiled in 1798 are contradictory.

2) The beast with seven heads and ten horns described as "*was like unto a leopard, and his feet were as the feet of a bear, and his mouth as the mouth of a lion*", and as "*was, and is not, and is about to come*" cannot be attributed to the Western Roman Empire in any form.

65

3) Several Protestant reformers propagated, among other things, the teaching according to which the Papacy (the Pope) was identified as the beast, the Antichrist. Therefore, it is quite evident that many Christians during the Protestant Reformation had been caught in a very aggressive religious propaganda campaign, which consequently contributed to the escalation of religious conflicts and bloodshed between Catholics and Protestants. In this regard, prophetic allegations of those reformers were inconsistent and contradictory, as the beasts of Revelation described in chapter 13 and 17 cannot be attributed to the Western Roman Empire. Therefore, no matter whether it was erroneous or tendentious, such distorted interpretation of Bible prophecy cannot be regarded as the "*Sola Scriptura (by Scripture alone)*."

Prophetic mysteries of the Book of Revelation have always been the subject of constant speculation. Therefore, brief exegetical analysis of the beasts of Revelation presented in this book will not be exempt from speculative comments. However, one thing should be very clear to the reader: the identity of this prophetic beast is to be searched on the territory where once empires prophetically described as "*leopard, bear, and lion*" were located – this is predominantly the Middle East territory, the Muslim countries. Any attempt to identify the beast with seven heads and ten horns elsewhere is futile.

> "*32 and ye shall know the truth, and the truth shall make you free*" (Jn. 8:32).

The beast with two horns like a lamb

> *"[11] And I saw another beast coming up out of the earth; and he had two horns like unto a lamb, and he spake as a dragon. [12] And he exerciseth all the authority of the first beast in his sight. And he maketh the earth and them that dwell therein to [m]worship the first beast, whose death-stroke was healed" (Rev. 13:11-12).*

Seventh-day Adventists are being indoctrinated with the teaching that the "*beast with two horns like a lamb*" represents the United States of America, and that the "*two horns*" represent two principles or freedoms (religious and political) on which this new country was established. However, the Bible states very clearly that a "*horn*" represents a "*king or kingdom*" (Dan. 7:24; Dan. 8:20-22; Rev. 17:12), not principles or freedoms.

According to Bible prophecy, the second beast exercises "*all the authority of the first beast in his sight*" and makes inhabitants of the earth to worship the "*first beast, whose death-stroke was healed*" (Rev. 13:12). The expression "*in his sight*" means that the notion of space is irrelevant, as the second beast exercises all the power of the first beast in his sight (in his presence). Therefore, it would be nonsense to assert that the "*first beast*" is in Europe and the "*second beast*" is on the other side of Atlantic Ocean, in America. In other words, this version lacks consistency thus is not in concordance with the prophecy. **Note:** Some Bible versions contain: "*...on his behalf...*" instead of "*...in his sight (or in his presence)...*" (Rev. 13:12) – a rather controversial translation.

In the U.S. Constitution, the words "God, Jesus Christ, Christianity, Bible" are not mentioned, therefore, giving the impression that it was not founded on Christianity – it seems rather a secular document. Some people may argue that this was done with the intention to maintain the so-called religious neutrality. Furthermore, in the Declaration of Independence of the United States[21] are stated, among other things, the following: "the Laws of Nature and of Nature's God" and "endowed by their Creator." Such statements, however, reflect rather a deistic viewpoint. Can the USA, allegedly the second beast, be identified as "exercising the power of the first beast" whose deadly wound was healed, allegedly the revived Western Roman Empire (a Christian empire)? No!

Adventists are also being indoctrinated with the teaching that the number of the beast "*666*" (Rev. 13:18) represents the Pope. According to such logic, the second beast is located in the USA and the number of the beast, that is, the first beast is located in Vatican (Europe); therefore, two authorities with radically different ideologies in two different locations separated by an ocean. This prophetic interpretation is erroneous – it contradicts prophetic statement "*exerciseth all the authority of the first beast in his sight*" (Rev. 13:12). It is quite evident that such a contradictory interpretation of Bible prophecy is not just faulty but also tendentious.

The second beast comes out of the earth and has certain particularities:

- "*he had two horns like a lamb*" (Rev. 13:11). Horns of a lamb are small, inoffensive. The lamb symbolizes innocence, purity, and biblically was used in religious rituals. Therefore, "*two horns like a lamb*" must refer to a religion-based empire;

- "*he spoke as a dragon*" (Rev. 13:11). This means that the beast was involved in religious wars and used arrogant religious claims;

- "*exercises all the authority of the first beast in his sight*" (Rev. 13:12). **Note:** Some Bible versions contain: "*...on his behalf...*" instead of "*...in his sight (or in his presence)...*" (Rev. 13:12) – a rather controversial translation;

- makes all, the small and the great, and the rich and the poor, and the free and the bond, that "*there be given them*

68

a mark on their right hand, or upon their forehead" (Rev. 13:16);

- no man should be able to buy or to sell unless he has the "_the mark, even the name of the beast or the number of his name_" (Rev. 13:17);

- the number of the beast is a number of a man: its number is "_Six hundred and sixty six_." The issue regarding the "_name or the number of the beast_", which identifies the first beast, is quite debatable. According to Bible scholars, the following names could identify with this mystery number (666): Nero Caesar, Vicarius Filli Dei (allegedly once a title of the Pope), and Muhammad. Nevertheless, the Bible gives us a clue: the mark represents the "_number of his name_", <u>not</u> the number of his <u>title</u>.

It is quite tempting for some believers to assert that this prophetic beast represents the divided Roman Empire – the Eastern and Western Roman Empire. The following arguments corroborate this version:

- the two horns represent two emperors ruling this divided empire: 1) the emperor of the Western Roman Empire ruling from Rome; 2) the emperor of the Eastern Roman (Byzantine) Empire ruling from Constantinople;

- horns like a lamb are small, inoffensive. The lamb symbolizes innocence, purity, and biblically was used in religious rituals. Therefore, "_two horns like a lamb_" refer to a religion based empire: 1) Eastern Byzantine (Orthodox); 2) Western Roman Catholic;

- this divided empire was involved in religious wars and persecution of believers. Despite the fact that it had been ruled by Christian emperors and Christian religion became its official religion, yet this empire (beast) exercised the vast political, military, judicial, and administrative authority of the first beast (the vast authority of the pagan Roman Empire); therefore, it spoke like a dragon.

Some skeptical believers allege that the "_mark on the right hand, or on the forehead_" has something to do with the practice in religious services, ceremonies, and prayers where right hand and forehead are involved – they seem to view the sign of the cross as a practice that has no biblical support, an idolatry. Such a provocative allegation nourishes an anti-Christian spirit, therefore, requires a categorical response: The cross – a symbol of Christianity – represents the instrument on which Jesus Christ was crucified. On the cross of Golgotha, Christ established God's new covenant with His people (Lk. 22:19-20; Mt. 26:26-28; 1Cor. 11:24-25). The cross is a symbol of our redemption in Christ, a symbol of Christ's victory over sin and death. The sign of the cross is a ritual blessing practiced in the Catholic and Orthodox Churches; it is also practiced in Anglican, Lutheran, and to some extent in Methodist and Reformed (Calvinist) Churches. The first historic evidence of use of the sign of the cross by Christians seems to date back to the 2nd century AD – at that time the Roman Empire was not divided. Therefore, it is very evident that the "*sign of the cross*" cannot be offensive to God; the cross as a symbol of Christianity – the religion of God's new covenant – cannot represent the mark of the beast.

No matter how plausible the arguments in favour of this version may be, a vital prophetic fact must not be neglected: the second beast "*exerciseth all the authority of the first beast in his sigh*" and makes inhabitants of the earth to "*worship the first beast, whose death-stroke was healed*" (Rev. 13:12). Therefore, the second beast uses the vast authority of the first beast in its presence, that is, in the presence of the beast prophetically described as "*was like unto a leopard, and his feet were as the feet of a bear, and his mouth as the mouth of a lion*" (Rev. 13:2). According to the Book of Daniel, "*leopard, bear, and lion*" represent three ancient empires (Greek, Medo-Persian, and Babylonian). Therefore, the second beast must be also searched on the territory where empires described as "*leopard, bear, and lion*" were once located, which is predominantly the territory of the Middle East – the Muslim countries nowadays. The Roman Empire has never been prophetically described as "*leopard, bear, and lion*"; therefore, the allegation that divided Eastern and Western Roman Empire exercising the authority of the beast that looked like a *"leopard, bear, and lion"*, which cannot be atributed to the Roman Empire, is absolute nonsense. The divided Roman Empire cannot identify with prophetic beast with two horns like a lamb.

Despite many conflicts and religious divergences within Christianity, it would be unreasonable to neglect the rise of the new empire in the Middle East, which, by putting an end to the Byzantine Empire, became an imminent threat to the entire Christianity. It is not right to overlook the means by which it became an empire – use of the sword (in the name of Allah). It isn't correct to neglect many Muslim attempts to conquer Western Europe (Western Christianity). It is unreasonable to concentrate only on the speck in the eye of Christianity and neglect the log in the eye of Islam. The real issue here is that prophetic message of the Book of Revelation is much more than what some of us were taught to believe, much more than what certain scholars, historians, and politicians would want us to accept.

As mentioned before, the beast with seven heads and ten horns prophetically described as *"was like unto a <u>leopard</u>, and his feet were as the feet of a <u>bear</u>, and his mouth as the mouth of a <u>lion</u>"* (Rev. 13:1-2), where the (iron) Roman Empire is missing, confirms the fact that the identity of this beast is related somehow to the former Greek, Medo-Persian, and Babylonian Empires. In other words, this empire (beast) comprises the territory of the Balkan Peninsula and the Middle East, that is to say, it stretches from the fertile Balkan territory towards the desert, towards the abyss (Rev. 13:1-2; Rev. 17:3, 8; Rev. 9:1-3, 11).

In Revelation chapter 17, the scarlet-coloured beast (in the wilderness) with seven heads and ten horns – the *"eighth king <u>(the beast)</u>"* – is described as *"is about <u>to come up out of the abyss</u>"* (Rev. 17:3, 8). In Revelation chapter 13, the second beast is described as *"<u>coming up out of the earth</u>"* (Rev. 13:11). Prophetic expressions *"earth*, abyss, *wilderness (desert)"* are synonymous, thus have a common characteristic – this implies similarity regarding the nature and origin of the beasts.

The second beast had *"<u>two horns like a lamb</u>, and he spake* *as a dragon*." How big the horns of a lamb can be? Why harm-less horns of a lamb? Perhaps, the spirit of prophecy intends to associate "*horns as a lamb*" with "*horns as a ram*"? According to the Book of Daniel, the "*ram with two horns*" represents Medo-Persian Empire (Dan. 8:1-3, 20).

What do the "*two horns like a lamb*" represent? Some believers identify the "*two horns*" with Shia and Sunni – the two major branches of Islam, which also represent two Islamic religious leaders; others consider that this prophecy is yet to be fulfilled. Despite plausible arguments and speculations, one fact is very clear: these are related to the Middle East, as the beast with two horns "<u>*exerciseth all the authority of the first beas in his sight*</u>", that is, the second beast exercises all the authority of the first beast that "*was unto a <u>leopard,</u> and his feet were as the feet of a <u>bear,</u> and his mouth as the mouth of a <u>lion</u>*" in its presence.

Once again, as the beast with seven heads and ten horns looked like "<u>a *leopard, a bear, and a lion*</u>", it is common sense to focus our search for the identity of the beast with "*two horns like a lamb*", which exercises all the power of the first beast <u>in his sight</u>, on the territory where the empires allegorically described as "*leopard, bear, and lion*" were once located.

Searching for the beast that looks like a "*leopard, bear, and lion*" in Western Europe, that is, within the Western Christianity is prophetically contradictory; searching for the beast with "*two horns like a lamb that spoke as a dragon*" on territory other than the Middle East – the Muslim countries – is futile. Can prophetic allegory "*spake as a dragon*" apply to a Christian kingdom that has accepted the "*word of God and the testimony of Jesus Christ*"? No! Nevertheless, certain scholars chose to ignore the rise of Islamic Arab Empire that made its way through with the use of the sword. Somehow, they chose to focus their search within Christianity. Is there a particular reason for that? Yes, it is quite evident!

Amazing scientific breakthroughs in last several decades are astonishing. However, the version according to which the "*mark of the beast*" is an implant of microchip "*on the right hand, or on the forehead*" is a <u>diversion</u>. Its principal scope is to hinder believers from realizing that this prophecy is unfolding now. It would be very naive on the part of Christians to uphold the idea that believers' salvation or condemnation does not depend on their faith, but on a microchip implant. Why only on the right hand or on forehead? Why not on other parts of the body as well? Note that the "*mark of the beast*" represents the "*name of the beast or the number of his name*" (Rev. 13:17). What is the logic of imposing a microchip implant (containing someone's name) on people's right hand or forehead? Prophetically, the "*mark*" represents the name of the beast or the number of its name (Rev. 13:17-18). What does the alleged microchip (mark) represent?

The "*beast*" is in total opposition and rebellion against God. Acceptance or rejection of the "*mark of the beast*" involves people's faith, their religion. Therefore, this issue is of religious nature, as the beast "<u>*makes the earth and them that dwell therein to worship the first beast*</u>, *whose death-stroke was healed*", as the first beast "*opened his mouth for blasphemies against God, to blaspheme his name, and his tabernacle*", and as it was given unto him "*to make war with the saints, and to overcome them.*" This statement is confirmed by the following Bible verses:

> "⁵ *and there was given to him <u>a mouth speaking great things and blasphemies</u>; and there was given to him authority* [e]*to continue forty and two months.* ⁶ *And <u>he opened his mouth for blasphemies against God, to blaspheme his name, and his tabernacle</u>, even them that* [f]*dwell in the heaven.* ⁷ [g]*And it was given unto him to make war with the saints, and to overcome them: and there was given to him authority over every tribe and people and tongue and nation.*" (Rev. 13:5-7)

> "¹² *And <u>he exerciseth all the authority of the first beast in his sight</u>. And he maketh the earth and them that dwell therein to* [m]*worship the first beast, whose death-stroke was healed*" (Rev. 13:12).

"[15] And it was given unto him to give breath to it, even to the image of the beast, [n]that the image of the beast should both speak, and cause that as many as should not [o]worship the image of the beast should be killed" (Rev. 13:15).

"[9] And another angel, a third, followed them, saying with a great voice, If any man [d]worshippeth the beast and his image, and receiveth a mark on his forehead, or upon his hand, [10] he also shall drink of the wine of the wrath of God, which is [e]prepared unmixed in the cup of his anger; and he shall be tormented with fire and brimstone in the presence of the holy angels, and in the presence of the Lamb: [11] and the smoke of their torment goeth up [f]for ever and ever; and they have no rest day and night, they that [g]worship the beast and his image, and whoso receiveth the mark of his name. [12] Here is the [h] patience of the saints, they that keep the commandments of God, and the faith of Jesus" (Rev. 14:9-12).

The controversy over the "*mark of the beast*" has been going on for many centuries. Adventists allege that Sunday, that is, Sunday keeping represents the mark of the beast (and Sabbath is the seal of God). This, however, demonstrates lack of logical reasoning – a typical product of spiritually abusive indoctrination – as follows:

- According to their logic, all Christians who have been keeping Sunday for almost two millenniums have the mark of the beast;

- Jesus Christ was resurrected on Sunday, the first day of the week (Mt. 28:1-7; Mk. 16:1-7; Lk. 24:1-7; Jn. 20:1-9); Jesus revealed Himself to His disciples on Sunday (Mt. 28:1-17; Mk. 16:9-14; Lk. 24:13-35; Jn. 20:11-29); the Holy Spirit descended upon the apostles and other followers of Christ on Sunday (Acts 2:1-4; Lev. 23:15-16); first-century Christians were gathering for worship, prayer, and the Holy Communion on Sunday, the first day of the week (Acts 20:7; 1Cor. 11:17-22; 1Cor. 16:1-2). Do all the above mentioned [Christ's resurrection, Pentecost (descent of the Holy Spirit), Christian gathering for worship on Sunday] imply the acceptance of the mark of the beast, that is, worshiping the beast? No! Such allegation is a blasphemous;

- Jewish religious leaders were plotting to kill Jesus for breaking the Sabbath law; therefore, the alleged Sabbath breaking was one of the three main accusations, which led to Jesus' arrest and ultimately to His death by crucifixion (Mt. 12:9-14; Mk. 3:1-6; Lk. 13:10-14; Jn. 5:17-18; Jn. 9:15-16; Mt. 12:1-2);

- Seventh-day Sabbath is never described in the Bible as the seal of God – the Sabbath represents a sign of the covenant between Yahweh and the people liberated from Egyptian slavery (Ex. 31:13, 16). On the other hand, the Bible states very clearly that the seal of God is manifested by the presence of the Holy Spirit within believer's life (Eph. 1:13; Eph. 4:30; 2Cor. 1:21-22);

- The Bible provides clear evidence that God put an end to the old covenant (Jer. 31:31-33; Heb. 8:7-13; Mt. 26:26-27; Mk. 14:22-24; Lk. 22:19-20; 1Cor. 11:23-25) and to the seventh-day Sabbath (Is. 1:13; Hos. 2:11; Col. 2:14-17; Gal. 4:9-11; Eph. 2:14-15; Mk. 2:27-28; Mt. 11:28). This has been achieved on the cross of Golgotha through Jesus Christ. Both the old covenant established on Mount Sinai and seventh-day Sabbath are interconnected; therefore, if God put an end to the old covenant, He also put an end to seventh-day Sabbath, the sign of that covenant. The law, the basis of the old covenant, was in charge of the people to lead them to Christ that they may be justified by faith (Ex. 34:27-28; Gal. 3:24-25; 2Cor. 3:6). Believers under the new covenant keep Christ's two commandments of love (agape) on which the entire law and the prophets depend (Mat. 22:36-40);

- If some believers still consider seventh-day Sabbath an everlasting sign (Ex. 31:13, 16), then they should observe all other practices and requirements declared as everlasting by the Old Testament law. They should apply within their communities the death penalty for breaking the Sabbath, as required by the law (Ex. 31:14-15). How many of them would pass this test nowadays? They should also observe the Sabbath year (Lev. 23:3-5; Ex. 23:10-11);

- We rest whenever we feel tired, exhausted. True rest (worship), that is, true Sabbath is in spirit. We have that rest in Christ and through Christ (Jn. 4:24; Mt. 11:28; Jn. 14:6).

Ultimately, what does the beast with two horns like a lamb represent? Where is it located? The answer to these questions is found in the following verse:

> "[12] And he exerciseth all the authority of the first beast in his sight. And he maketh the earth and them that dwell therein to [m]worship the first beast, whose death-stroke was healed" (Rev. 13:12).

The second beast is located on the territory of the first beast, which in prophetic language looks like a "*leopard, bear, and lion*" – the Middle East territory. As we already know, the first beast corresponds to the rise of Islamic Empire. This empire has a certain particularity: its military conquests have been motivated by its religious ambitions – in the name of Allah. However, this empire disintegrated politically and militarily after the fall of the Ottoman Caliphate (Empire).

Nowadays, the Islamic Empire as such no longer exists; however, all Islamized nations that once constituted the Islamic Empire have in common one vital characteristic: they all share Islamic religion – the nucleus of the Islamic Empire. Thus, all these countries are united in Islam, the religion of the former Islamic Empire. Nowadays, even though we do not see Muslim military expansion as in the past, yet there are various forms of Muslim religious aggression, which prophetically are described as "*spake as a dragon.*" Therefore, nowadays we see a new empire – a religious form empire – that "*exerciseth all the authority of the first beast in his sight*", that is, this new beast exercises all the power of the first beast – its power has its source in the Islamic religion of the first beast. The two horns seem to represent two religious leaders, the so-called two successors of their prophet Muhammad, which also stand for Shia and Sunni – the two major denominations of Islam. It is not a secret that, for a long time, radical Muslims have been propagating the idea of restoring the Islamic Caliphate and promoting the teaching that Islam will dominate the world. Nowadays, the world is witnessing an apocalyptic event: the reinstatement of Islamic caliphate in the Middle East.

For many centuries, transgression of Sharia law – the moral code and religious law of Islam – was punished with death penalty. From the earliest history of Islam, apostasy was punished with death penalty. Apostasy in Islam includes: abandonment of Islam by a Muslim, converting to another religion, speaking against Allah, Quran, Muhammad, and so on. Nowadays, it is no secret that some Islamic countries still practice the capital punishment for breaking certain Sharia laws. Could Sharia law represent prophetic allegory "*the image of the beast should both speak, and cause that as many as should not [o]worship the image of the beast should be killed*" (Rev. 13:14-15)? This is a very sensitive topic! However, such controversial practices are not something new to the mankind: according to the Old Testament, transgression of certain Mosaic laws was also punished with death penalty. On the other hand, besides Sharia law, Muslims also have their own Islamic calendar (Hijri calendar)[22] according to which the year AD 622 becomes the first year of the Muslim calendar. Could this be a reference to the prophecy "*He shall think to change times and laws*" (Dan. 7:25)?

As a suggestion, the moral duty of Christians is to live a holy life and be always prepared for the return of our Lord Jesus Christ – they should not be fanatically obsessed with the identity of these apocalyptic beasts. A Christian should avoid futile and spiritually unconstructive arguments.

In conclusion, this brief exegetical analysis of the beasts of Revelation, substantiated by incontestable biblical evidence, confirms the fact that the "*beast with two horns like a lamb*" is related to the Middle East, not to the North America or Europe as some scholars allege. This commentary is not intended to offend any religion or people's faith. It should not be regarded as an attack on Islam, but rather a revelation of certain prophetic truth described in the Book of Revelation, which is ignored by

Muslims. It has nothing to do with politics or the Middle East crisis. The art of compromise called politics and the true worship of God are two radically different things – God does not condone compromise. The purpose of this analytical reasoning is to shed a new light on the understanding of prophetic allegory " the *beast with two horns like a lamb*" and demonstrate that several current interpretations of this prophecy are erroneous or tendentious, thus not in harmony with the word of God.

> "*32 and ye shall know the truth, and the truth shall make you free*" *(Jn. 8:32).*

Genesis 2:2-3

"2 On the seventh day God finished his work which he had done; and he rested on the seventh day from all his work which he had done. 3 God blessed the seventh day, and made it holy, because he rested in it from all his work of creation which he had done" (Gen. 2:2-3).

Bible verses of Genesis 2:2-3 are of vital importance in Adventist ideology. To defend their doctrinal identity, Seventh-day Adventists and other Sabbath keeping believers often resort to these verses. They assert that seventh-day Sabbath was sanctified at creation, thus it has been kept by humankind ever since.

This doctrinal position is very devotional from the Old Testament perspective. However, it reflects partiality, as other Bible verses concerning this issue are being ignored:

1) The Book of Genesis provides no evidence that God the Creator made the seventh day rest a law and imposed it on human beings. There is no biblical evidence that Adam, Enoch, Noah, Melchizedek, Abraham, Isaac, Jacob were keeping the seventh-day Sabbath. On the other hand, the Book of Genesis mentions the following: "*covenant*" (Gen. 9:9-12; Gen. 17:4-6, 9-12), "*altar*" (Gen. 8:20; 22:9), "*sacrifice*" (Gen. 22:13), "*offering*" (Gen. 4:3-4), "*circumcision*" (Gen. 17:10-14, 23-27)... and so on. The word "Sabbath" is not mentioned in the Book of Genesis.

Is it possible that God the Creator forgot to mention keeping the seventh day Sabbath – the precept of such a vital importance – to the people of those days?

2) "*...because he rested in it from all his work of creation which he had done*" (Gen. 2:3). Does this mean that the Creator was exhausted thus needed to rest? To support this hypothesis mean to doubt the omnipotence of God. Such assertion is nonsense!

Biblical expression "God rested from his work" should be understood in the sense of God's completion of the work of creation. As God rested from His work on the seventh day, it is common sense to assert that God is still resting, as there is no biblical record of God creating again. According to the New Testament, however, God the Father is always at work (Jn. 5:17).

3) The law, including Sabbath, was introduced 430 years after the covenant with Abraham. It was meant to lead the people unto Christ. The following Bible verses confirm this statement:

"[17] Now this I say: A covenant confirmed beforehand by God, _the law, which came four hundred and thirty years after_, doth not disannul, so as to make the promise of none effect. [18] For if the inheritance is of the law, it is no more of promise: but God hath granted it to Abraham by promise" (Gal. 3:17-18).

"[24] So that _the law is become our tutor to bring us unto Christ_, that we might be justified by faith. [25] _But now that faith is come, we are no longer under a tutor_" (Gal. 3:24-25).

"[1] Brethren, my heart's [a]desire and my supplication to God is for them, that they may be saved. [2] For _I bear them witness that they have a zeal for God, but not according to knowledge_. [3] For being ignorant of God's righteousness, and seeking to establish their own, they did not subject themselves to the righteousness of God. [4] For _Christ is the end of the law unto righteousness to every one that believeth_" (Rom. 10:1-4).

Note: Some believers might contest Galatians 3:17 regarding 430 year. However, the central issue in this verse is that the law was given after Abraham, after the deliverance of Israelites from Egyptian slavery, not prior. Furthermore, in the Old Testament is not mentioned any moral code of laws prior to Moses.

4) To sustain that Old Testament patriarchs, from Adam to

Moses, were keeping the seventh-day Sabbath, is the same as to sustain that Adam honored his mother. The Holy Scripture declares that Adam was "*created*", not born of a woman; therefore, he had no mother.

5) According to the Jewish Talmud and Tosefta, the central texts of Rabbinic Judaism, the Seven Laws of Noah[23] which form the major part of Noahide Code are:

1. Prohibition of idolatry.
2. Prohibition of murder.
3. Prohibition of theft.
4. Prohibition of sexual immorality.
5. Prohibition of blasphemy.
6. Prohibition of eating of flesh taken from an animal while it is still alive.
7. Establishment of law courts (that is, courts of justice).

This code is a set of moral imperatives that, according to the Talmud (Oral Torah), were given by God as a binding set of laws for the children of Noah, that is, to all mankind. The seventh-day Sabbath is not mentioned in the Noahide Code.

6) According to the Old Testament, Israelites had to observe, among others, the following requirements of the law:

- To keep the seventh day of the week holy – a memorial of Creation, a memorial of deliverance from Egyptian slavery;
- To keep other days holy: fifteenth and twenty-first day of the first month; first, tenth, and fifteenth day of the seventh month;
- To offer sacrifices;
- To perform circumcision;
- To make pilgrimage to the Temple in Jerusalem.

Seventh-day Adventist should keep all the above mentioned practices – they should not be partial.

7) According to the New Testament, God's people under the new covenant are morally bound to observe the following:

- They regard every day holy – God is to be honoured every day;

- Christians have a new memorial day – the day of the "*resurrection of our Lord Jesus Christ*", a memorial of a new creation, a memorial of deliverance from sin;

- They perform "*spiritual circumcision*" of mind and heart, which is the work of the Holy Spirit;

- They have Jesus Christ – the Lamb of God – as the "*true and perfect sacrifice*" offered once and for ever;

- Their pilgrimage is directed towards the "*spiritual Jerusalem.*"

8) If Adventists consider that they are bound unto the law (seventh-day Sabbath), then they should also keep all other practices and rituals required by the old covenant law. If Adventists do not offer animal sacrifices and do not circumcise their sons because they think that Christ put an end to it, then why don't they keep all the other teachings of Jesus? Why don't they observe the following verses?

> "*13 Bring no more vain offerings. Incense is an abomination to me; new moons, Sabbaths, and convocations: I can't bear with evil assemblies*" (Is. 1:13).

> "*11 I will also cause all her celebrations to cease: her feasts, her new moons, her Sabbaths, and all her solemn assemblies*" (Hos. 2:11).

> "*31 Behold, the days come, says Yahweh, that I will make a new covenant with the house of Israel, and with the house of Judah: 32 not according to the covenant that I made with their fathers in the day that I took them by the hand to bring them out of the land of Egypt; which my covenant they broke, although I was a husband to them, says Yahweh. 33 But this is the covenant that I will make with the house of Israel after those days, says Yahweh: I will put my law in their inward parts, and in their heart will I write it; and I will be their God, and they shall be my people*" (Jer. 31:31-33).

> "*14 having blotted out [g]the bond written in*

ordinances that was against us, which was contrary to us: and he hath taken it out of the way, nailing it to the cross; ⁱ⁵ [h]having despoiled the principalities and the powers, he made a show of them openly, triumphing over them in it. ¹⁶ Let no man therefore judge you in meat, or in drink, or in respect of a feast day or a new moon or a sabbath day: ¹⁷ which are a shadow of the things to come; but the body is Christ's" (Col. 2:14-17).

"⁹ but now that ye have come to know God, or rather to be known by God, how turn ye back again to the weak and beggarly [b]rudiments, whereunto ye desire to be in bondage over again? ¹⁰ Ye observe days, and months, and seasons, and years. ¹¹ I am afraid of you, lest by any means I have bestowed labor upon you in vain" (Gal. 4:9-11).

"²⁷ And he said unto them, The sabbath was made for man, and not man for the sabbath: ²⁸ so that the Son of man is lord even of the sabbath" (Mk. 2:27-28).

"²⁸ Come unto me, all ye that labor and are heavy laden, and I will give you rest" (Mt. 11:28).

"ⁱ⁵ having abolished in his flesh the enmity, even the law of commandments contained in ordinances; that he might create in himself of the two one new man, so making peace" (Eph. 2:15).

"⁶ who also made us sufficient as ministers of a new covenant; not of the letter, but of the spirit: for the letter killeth, but the spirit giveth life" (2Cor. 3:6).

"ⁱ Brothers, my heart's desire and my prayer to God is for Israel, that they may be saved. ² For I testify about them that they have a zeal for God, but not according to knowledge. ³ For being ignorant of

God's righteousness, and seeking to establish their own righteousness, they didn't subject themselves to the righteousness of God. ⁴ For <u>Christ is the fulfillment</u>[a] <u>of the law for righteousness to everyone who believes</u>" (Rom. 10:1-4 WEB).

"¹⁹ Now we know that <u>what things soever the law saith, it speaketh to them that are under the law</u>; that every mouth may be stopped, and all the world may be brought under the judgment of God: ²⁰ because [k]<u>by</u> [l]<u>the works of the law shall no flesh be</u> [m]<u>justified in his sight; for</u> [n]<u>through the law cometh the knowledge of sin</u>. ²¹ But now apart from the law a righteousness of God hath been manifested, being witnessed by the law and the prophets; ²² <u>even the righteousness of God through faith</u> [o]<u>in Jesus Christ unto all</u> [p]<u>them that believe</u>; for there is no distinction; ²³ for all [q]have sinned, and fall short of the glory of God; ²⁴ being justified freely by his grace through the redemption that is in Christ Jesus" (Rom. 3:19-24).

"⁹ as knowing this, that <u>law is not made for a righteous man, but for the lawless and unruly, for the ungodly and sinners, for the unholy and profane</u>, for [c]murderers of fathers and [d]murderers of mothers, for manslayers, ¹⁰ for fornicators, for abusers of themselves with men, for menstealers, for liars, for false swearers, and if there be any other thing contrary to the [e]sound [f]doctrine; ¹¹ according to the [g]gospel of the glory of the blessed God, which was committed to my trust" (1Tim. 1:9-11).

"¹⁸ But <u>if ye are led by the Spirit, ye are not under the law</u>" (Gal. 5:18).

"¹⁵ We <u>being Jews by nature</u>, and not sinners of the Gentiles, ¹⁶ yet knowing that a man is not [l]justified by the works of the law but through faith in Jesus Christ, _even we believed on Christ Jesus, that we might be justified by faith in Christ, and not by the works of the law_: because by the works of the law shall no flesh be justified[6]" (Gal. 2:15-16).

"[9] So then they that are of faith are blessed with the faithful Abraham. [10] For _as many as are of the works of the law are under a curse_: for it is written, [k] Cursed is every one who continueth not in all things that are written in the book of the law, to do them. [11] Now _that no man is justified_ [l]_by the law before God, is evident: for,_ [m]_The righteous shall live by faith_" (Gal. 3:9-11).

"[17] Now this I say: A covenant confirmed beforehand by God, _the law, which came four hundred and thirty years after,_ doth not disannul, so as to make the promise of none effect. [18] For if the inheritance is of the law, it is no more of promise: but God hath granted it to Abraham by promise. [19] _What then is the law? It was added because of transgressions, till the seed should come to whom the promise hath been made_; and it was ordained through angels by the hand of a mediator" (Gal. 3:17-19).

"[24] So that _the law is become our tutor to bring us unto Christ,_ that we might be justified by faith. [25] But now that faith is come, _we are no longer under a tutor_" (Gal. 3:24-25).

"[7] For _if that first covenant had been faultless, then would no place have been sought for a second_. [8] For [f] _finding fault with them,_ he saith, [g]Behold, the days come, saith the Lord, That I will [h]make a new covenant with the house of Israel and with the house of Judah; [9] Not according to the covenant that I made with their fathers In the day that I took them by the

hand to lead them forth out of the land of Egypt;
For they continued not in my covenant, And I
regarded them not, saith the Lord" (Heb. 8:7-9).

"13 In that he saith, A new covenant, <u>he hath made</u>
<u>the first old. But that which is becoming old and</u>
<u>waxeth aged is nigh unto vanishing away</u>" (Heb.
8:7-13).

Partial compliance with the law does not reflect the will of God! According to the Old Testament, Israelites had been always severely punished by Yahweh, the God of Israel, for the very fact of disobedience and partial observance of the law.

Doctrinal polemic regarding Sabbath keeping has been going on for many centuries – a sad reality. However, the following New Testament verse gives us a very clear picture of Sabbath keeping in heaven:

"17 But Jesus answered them, <u>My Father worketh</u>
<u>even until now</u>, and I work" (Jn. 5:17).

The Fourth Commandment

"⁸ "Remember the Sabbath day, to keep it holy. ⁹ You shall labor six days, and do all your work, ¹⁰ but the seventh day is a Sabbath to Yahweh your God. You shall not do any work in it, you, nor your son, nor your daughter, your male servant, nor your female servant, nor your livestock, nor your stranger who is within your gates; ¹¹ for in six days Yahweh made heaven and earth, the sea, and all that is in them, and rested the seventh day; therefore Yahweh blessed the Sabbath day, and made it holy" (Ex. 20:8-11).

Seventh-day Adventism, doctrinally, is a very complex religion. It incorporates teachings of both the Old and New Testament. The Ten Commandments represent an emblem of the Sabbatarian Adventism and the fourth commandment Sabbath is at its center. The seventh-day Sabbath is God's perpetual sign of His eternal covenant between Him and His people, a symbol of their redemption in Christ, a sign of their sanctification [Creed 19 (Creed 20 following the insertion of a new belief in 2005)].

The statement "Sabbath is God's perpetual sign of His eternal covenant between Him and His people" has its origin in the following Bible verse:

"¹³ "Speak also to the children of Israel, saying, 'Most certainly <u>you shall keep my Sabbaths: for it is a sign between me and you throughout your generations;</u> that you may know that I am Yahweh who sanctifies you" (Ex. 31:13).

"¹⁶ Therefore the children of Israel shall keep the Sabbath, <u>to observe the Sabbath throughout their generations, for a perpetual covenant. ¹⁷ It is a sign between me and the children of Israel forever;</u> for

in six days Yahweh made heaven and earth, and on the seventh day he rested, and was refreshed" (Ex. 31:16-17).

This perpetual sign, the Sabbath, also comes with a warning:

"14 You shall keep the Sabbath therefore; for it is holy to you. Everyone who profanes it shall surely be put to death; for whoever does any work therein, that soul shall be cut off from among his people. 15 Six days shall work be done, but on the seventh day is a Sabbath of solemn rest, holy to Yahweh. Whoever does any work on the Sabbath day shall surely be put to death" (Ex. 31:14-15).

It is very evident the fact that Sabbath is a perpetual sign of the covenant between Yahweh and Israel – the people liberated from Egyptian slavery:

"17 It is a sign between me and the children of Israel forever; for in six days Yahweh made heaven and earth, and on the seventh day he rested, and was refreshed" (Ex. 31:17).

"15 You shall remember that you were a servant in the land of Egypt, and Yahweh your God brought you out of there by a mighty hand and by an outstretched arm. Therefore Yahweh your God commanded you to keep the Sabbath day" (Deut. 5:15).

Despite all these, the priests broke the Sabbath law on every Sabbath. According to the law, the priests had to offer on the Sabbath day two sacrifices: one in the morning and another one in the evening. To do this, animals had to be killed and prepared for sacrifice according to the law. On the other hand, priests throughout the Jewish community had to perform circumcision of newborn males on the eighth day after birth – this physical circumcision was also performed on the Sabbath day. The following verses confirm this practice:

88

"[9] "*On the Sabbath day, two male lambs a year old without defect, and two tenths of an ephah*[b] *of fine flour for a meal offering, mixed with oil, and its drink offering:* [10] *this is the burnt offering of every Sabbath, besides the continual burnt offering, and its drink offering*" (Num. 28:9-10).

"[11] *You shall be circumcised in the flesh of your foreskin. It will be a token of the covenant between me and you.* [12] *He who is eight days old will be circumcised among you, every male throughout your generations, he who is born in the house, or bought with money from any foreigner who is not of your offspring.*[f]"(Gen 17:11-12).

"[3] *In the eighth day the flesh of his foreskin shall be circumcised*" (Lev. 12:3).

"[23] *If a man receiveth circumcision on the sabbath, that the law of Moses may not be broken; are ye wroth with me, because I made* [c]*a man every whit whole on the sabbath?*" (Jn. 7:23).

Later, Jeremiah prophesied to the people of Israel that a day is coming when God will make a new covenant with His people. Therefore, God will put an end to the covenant made on Mount Sinai (Horeb) and to Sabbath, which is the sign of that covenant. This is confirmed by the following verses:

"[31] *Behold, the days come, says Yahweh, that I will make a new covenant with the house of Israel, and with the house of Judah:* [32] *not according to the covenant that I made with their fathers in the day that I took them by the hand to bring them out of the land of Egypt; which my covenant they broke, although I was a husband to them, says Yahweh.* [33] *But this is the covenant that I will make with the house of Israel after those days, says Yahweh: I will put my law in their inward parts, and in their heart will I write it; and I will be their God, and they shall be my people"* (Jer. 31:31-33).

"13 Bring no more vain offerings. Incense is an abomination to me; new moons, Sabbaths, and convocations: I can't bear with evil assemblies" (Is. 1:13).

"11 I will also cause all her celebrations to cease: her feasts, her new moons, her Sabbaths, and all her solemn assemblies" (Hos. 2:11).

This means that the covenant established on Mount Sinai and Sabbath, the sign of the covenant between Yahweh and Israel, were in effect until the day when God made a *"new covenant"* with His people. It means that the *"(eternal) covenant"* and the *"(eternal) sign, the Sabbath"* were in effect for generations until Jesus Christ established *"God's new covenant"* on the cross of Golgotha as prophesied. The following verses confirm this statement:

"19 And he took [d]bread, and when he had given thanks, he brake it, and gave to them, saying, This is my body [e]which is given for you: this do in remembrance of me. 20 And the cup in like manner after supper, saying, This cup is the new covenant in my blood, even that which is poured out for you" (Lk. 22:19-20).

"23 For I received of the Lord that which also I delivered unto you, that the Lord Jesus in the night in which he was [h]betrayed took bread; 24 and when he had given thanks, he brake it, and said, This is my body, which [i]is for you: this do in remembrance of me. 25 In like manner also the cup, after supper, saying, This cup is the new covenant in my blood: this do, as often as ye drink it, in remembrance of me" (1Cor. 11:23-25).

> "²⁶ And as they were eating, _Jesus took_ [o]_bread_, and
> blessed, and brake it; and he gave to the disciples,
> and said, Take, eat; this is my body. ²⁷ And _he took_
> [p]_a cup_, and gave thanks, and gave to them, saying,
> Drink ye all of it; ²⁸ for _this is my blood of the_ [q]_cove-_
> _nant, which is poured out for many unto remission_
> _of sins_" (Mt. 26:26-28).

> "²⁸ _Come unto me_, all ye that labor and are heavy
> laden, _and I will give you rest_" (Mt. 11:28).

It is quite obvious that Seventh-day Adventists are entangled in
the complexity of their own doctrinal teachings as follows: 1)
they resist the Holy Spirit speaking to them through the Old
Testament prophets; 2) they resist the Holy Spirit speaking to
them through the teachings of the New Testament; 3) they assert
to be believers under the new covenant and at the same time
keep Sabbath – the sign of the old covenant.

Sabbath keeping made sense for believers under the law of
the Sinaitic covenant. However, when the prophecy of Jeremiah
31:31-33 was fulfilled in Christ (Mt. 26:26-28; Lk. 22:19-20;
1Cor. 11:23-25) on the cross of Golgotha, God's people under
the new covenant order their life in harmony with Christ's
commandments of agape love.

> "[22] "For as the new heavens and the new earth, which I will make, shall remain before me," says Yahweh, "so your offspring[a] and your name shall remain. [23] It shall happen that from one new moon to another, and from one Sabbath to another, all flesh will come to worship before me," says Yahweh" (Is. 66:22-23).

Adventist believers are comforted by the promising verses of Isaiah 66:22-23. However, they neglect other verses that portray a different and rather polemical reality. These verses are:

> "[17] "For, behold, I create new heavens and a new earth; and the former things will not be remembered, nor come into mind" (Is. 65:17).

> "[20] "No more will there be an infant who only lives a few days, nor an old man who has not filled his days; for the child will die one hundred years old, and the sinner being one hundred years old will be accursed" (Is. 65:20).

> "[22] They will not build, and another inhabit. They will not plant, and another eat: for the days of my people will be like the days of a tree, and my chosen will long enjoy the work of their hands" (Is. 65:22).

The above verses provide hope to the reader. From the perspective of the New Testament, however, this is a paradox: in the new heavens and new earth there will be no childbirth and people will not die; on the other hand, some trees do not last longer than twenty, thirty years.

> "[24] "They will go out, and look at the dead bodies of the men who have transgressed against me; for their

*worm will not die, nor will their fire be quenched,
and they will be loathsome to all mankind""* (Is.
66:24).

Again, such a horrible sight cannot reflect divine and loving
nature of God in His new creation.

> *"23 It shall happen that <u>from one new moon to
> another</u>, and <u>from one Sabbath to another</u>, all flesh
> will come to worship before me," says Yahweh"* (Is.
> 66:23).

Isaiah 66:23 seems to imply the *"new moon"* celebration. Is
there going to be a new moon festivity in the new heaven and
new earth? For a devoted Christian, it is puzzling to imagine
burned offerings presented on the new moon festivals (Num.
10:10; Num. 28:11-15; 2Kg. 4:23; 1Cron. 23:31; 2Cron. 2:4;
8:31; 31:3; Ezra 3:5; Neh. 10:33; Ps. 81:3; Ezek. 46:1,3,6); it
is rather sad to associate new moon sacrifices with Yahweh. The
new moon festivity is not a part of the three main annual festivities appointed by Yahweh (Ex. 23:14-17).

Is there going to be Sabbath keeping and the observance of
the new moon festivals (including its sacrifices) in the new heaven
and on the new earth? In new heaven and new earth, according
to Revelation 21:23, the city coming down from heaven has no
need of the moon or the sun to shin on it.

The verse of Isaiah 66:23 made sense to the people living in the
days when the prophet Isaiah prophesied to Israel. Nevertheless,
for those who are very devoted or fanatical about this particular
matter, it is recommended that they give proper credit to Isaiah
66:22-23, that is, they should also keep the *"new moon"* festivals
holy in acconcordance with the law of the Old Testament.

The new moon festivals and the Sabbath have been abolished,
nailed to the Cross of Golgotha once and for all as follows:

> *"31 Behold, the days come, says Yahweh, that <u>I will
> make a new covenant with the house of Israel, and
> with the house of Judah</u>: 32 not according to the*

covenant that I made with their fathers in the day that I took them by the hand to bring them out of the land of Egypt; which my covenant they broke, although I was a husband to them, says Yahweh. ³³ But <u>this is the covenant</u> that I will make with the house of Israel after those days, <u>says Yahweh: I will put my law in their inward parts, and in their heart will I write it</u>; and I will be their God, and they shall be my people" (Jer. 31:31-33).

"¹³ Bring no more vain offerings. Incense is an abomination to me; new moons, <u>Sabbaths, and convocations: I can't bear with evil assemblies</u>" (Is. 1:13).

"¹¹ <u>I will also cause all her celebrations to cease</u>: her feasts, her new moons, <u>her Sabbaths, and all her solemn assemblies</u>" (Hos. 2:11).

"¹⁴ having blotted out [g]the bond written in ordinances that was against us, which was contrary to us: and <u>he hath taken it out of the way, nailing it to the cross</u>; ¹⁵ [h]having despoiled the principalities and the powers, he made a show of them openly, triumphing over them in it. ¹⁶ <u>Let no man therefore judge you in meat, or in drink, or in respect of a feast day or a new moon or a sabbath day</u>: ¹⁷ which are a shadow of the things to come; but the body is Christ's" (Col. 2:14-17).

"⁹ but now that ye have come to know God, or rather to be known by God, how turn ye back again to the weak and beggarly [b]rudiments, whereunto ye desire to be in bondage over again? ¹⁰ <u>Ye observe days, and months, and seasons, and years.</u> ¹¹ <u>I am afraid of you, lest by any means I have bestowed labor upon you in vain</u>" (Gal. 4:9-11).

"⁶ who also <u>made us sufficient as ministers of a new covenant; not of the letter, but of the spirit</u>: for the *letter killeth, but the spirit giveth life" (2Cor. 3:6).*

"17 Now this I say: A covenant confirmed before-hand by God, <u>the law, which came four hundred and thirty years after</u>, doth not disannul, so as to make the promise of none effect. 18 For if the inheritance is of the law, it is no more of promise: but God hath granted it to Abraham by promise. 19 <u>What then is the law? It was added because of transgressions, till the seed should come to whom the promise hath been made</u>; and it was ordained through angels by the hand of a mediator" (Gal. 3:17-19).

"24 So that <u>the law is become our tutor to bring us unto Christ</u>, that we might be justified by faith. 25 But now that faith is come, <u>we are no longer under a tutor</u>" (Gal. 3:24-25).

Jesus said:

"21 Jesus saith unto her, Woman, believe me, <u>the hour cometh, when neither in this mountain, nor in Jerusalem, shall ye worship the Father</u>" (Jn. 4:21).

"23 But <u>the hour cometh, and now is, when the true worshippers shall worship the Father in spirit and truth</u>: [g]for such doth the Father seek to be his worshippers. 24 [h]<u>God is a Spirit: and they that worship him must worship in spirit and truth</u>" (Jn. 4:23-24).

"27 And he said unto them, <u>The sabbath was made for man, and not man for the sabbath</u>: 28 so that the Son of man is lord even of the sabbath" (Mk 2:27-28).

"28 <u>Come unto me</u>, all ye that labor and are heavy laden, <u>and I will give you rest</u>" (Mt. 11:28).

According to Mark 2:28, Jesus Christ is Lord also of the Sabbath! If Jesus is Lord of the Sabbath, then Christians should honour the Word – Christ Jesus – not the seventh day of the week. Who should a true believer honour: the Creator or created things? For a Christian, the Old Testament is to be understood in the light of truth of the New Testament. Jesus Christ is Lord every day, not just of the seventh day!

Matthew 5:17-18

"¹⁷ Think not that I came to destroy the law or the prophets: I came not to destroy, but to fulfil. ¹⁸ For verily I say unto you, Till heaven and earth pass away, one jot or one tittle shall in no wise pass away from the law, till all things be accomplished" (Mt. 5:17-18).

These verses represent the cornerstone of Sabbatarian ideology concerning the law. Adventist believers make use of Matthew 5:17-18 to uphold the teaching according to which Christ did not abolish the law, thus seventh-day Sabbath is still in effect.

At first impression, these verses seem to be quite convincing. Nevertheless, a thorough and unbiased analysis of Mathew 5:17-18 brings to light a much more comprehensive significance of these verses, which Adventists do not see probably because they have been taught not to question certain doctrinal issues.

Long ago, the Old Testament prophets, under the inspiration of the Holy Spirit, predicted Christ's coming. Christ's Calvary on the cross of Golgotha represents the fulfillment of this prophecy – the entire New Testament is based on this prophetic fulfillment!

How did Jesus Christ fulfill the law? The law (the Ten Commandments) was given to Moses on Mount Horeb (Mount Sinai). On the basis of this law, Yahweh made a covenant with Israel – the people He brought out of Egypt. The covenant was sealed with the blood of animals (Ex. 24:8). The sign of this covenant was the seventh-day Sabbath. The old covenant law was introduced to show what sin is (Rom. 7:7; Gal. 3:19). It was meant to prevent people from sinning and to prepare them for the majestic coming of the promised Messiah – Jesus Christ (Gal. 3:17-19; Gal. 3:24-25). The law, the Tabernacle with its particularities (veil separating the two chambers, sacrifices and rituals), all these are a symbolic representation of God's divine plan of salvation of mankind through Christ. The veracity of this statement is confirmed by the following Bible verses:

"*8 Moses took the blood, and sprinkled it on the people, and said, "Look, this is the blood of the covenant, which Yahweh has made with you concerning all these words*"" (Ex. 24:8).

"*12 Yahweh said to Moses, "Come up to me on the mountain, and stay here, and I will give you the stone tablets with the law and the commands that I have written, that you may teach them*"" Ex. 24:12).

"*13 He declared to you his covenant, which he commanded you to perform, even the ten commandments. He wrote them on two stone tablets*" (Deut. 4:13).

"*9 When I had gone up onto the mountain to receive the stone tablets, even the tablets of the covenant which Yahweh made with you, then I stayed on the mountain forty days and forty nights. I neither ate bread nor drank water*" (Deut. 9:9).

"*11 It came to pass at the end of forty days and forty nights, that Yahweh gave me the two stone tablets, even the tablets of the covenant*" (Deut. 9:11).

"*15 So I turned and came down from the mountain, and the mountain was burning with fire. The two tablets of the covenant were in my two hands*" (Deut. 9:15).

"*21 There I have set a place for the ark, in which is the covenant of Yahweh, which he made with our fathers, when he brought them out of the land of Egypt*" (1Kgs. 8:21).

"*13 Speak also to the children of Israel, saying, 'Most*

certainly _you shall keep my Sabbaths: for it is a sign between me and you throughout your generations_; that you may know that I am Yahweh who sanctifies you" *(Ex. 31:13).*

"¹⁶ Therefore _the children of Israel shall keep the Sabbath, to observe the Sabbath throughout their generations, for a perpetual covenant_. ¹⁷ It is a sign between me and the children of Israel forever; for in six days Yahweh made heaven and earth, and on the seventh day he rested, and was refreshed" *(Ex. 31:16-17).*

"¹⁵ _You shall remember that you were a servant in the land of Egypt_, and Yahweh your God brought you out of there by a mighty hand and by an outstretched arm. _Therefore Yahweh your God commanded you to keep the Sabbath day_" *(Deut. 5:15).*

"¹² Moreover also _I gave them my Sabbaths, to be a sign between me and them_, that they might know that I am Yahweh who sanctifies them" *(Ezek. 20:12).*

"⁷ What shall we say then? Is the law sin? God forbid. Howbeit, _I had not known sin, except through_ [c]_the law: for I had not known_ [d]_coveting, except the law had said,_ [e]_Thou shalt not_ [f]" *(Rom. 7:7).*

"¹⁷ Now this I say: A covenant confirmed beforehand by God, _the law, which came four hundred and thirty years after_, doth not disannul, so as to make the promise of none effect. ¹⁸ For if the inheritance is of the law, it is no more of promise: but God hath granted it to Abraham by promise. ¹⁹ _What then is the law? It was added because of transgressions, till the seed should come to whom the promise hath been made_; and it was ordained through angels by the hand of a mediator" *(Gal. 3:17-19).*

"24 So that <u>the law is become our tutor to bring us unto Christ</u>, that we might be justified by faith. 25 But now that faith is come, <u>we are no longer under a tutor</u>" (Gal. 3:24-25).

Jesus Christ put an end to the Sinaitic (Mosaic) covenant. On the cross of Golgotha, God made a new covenant with His people – a covenant of the Spirits (2Cor. 3:6; Rom. 7:6; Rom. 8:2). This covenant was sealed with the blood of the Lamb of God – Jesus Christ. The basis of this new covenant is the Law of the Spirit, the two commandments of agape love. The sign (seal) of this new covenant is the Holy Spirit, as this is a covenant of the Spirit. The following Bible verses confirm this reasoning:

"31 Behold, the days come, says Yahweh, that <u>I will make a new covenant with the house of Israel, and with the house of Judah</u>: 32 not according to the covenant that I made with their fathers in the day that I took them by the hand to bring them out of the land of Egypt; which my covenant they broke, although I was a husband to them, says Yahweh. 33 But <u>this is the covenant</u> that I will make with the house of Israel after those days, <u>says Yahweh: I will put my law in their inward parts, and in their heart will I write it</u>; and I will be their God, and they shall be my people" (Jer. 31:31-33; Heb. 6:13).

"27 And <u>he took</u> [p]a cup, and gave thanks, and gave to them, saying, Drink ye all of it; 28 for <u>this is my blood of the</u> [q]covenant, which is poured out for many unto remission of sins" (Mt. 26:27-28; Mk. 14:23-24).

"20 And the cup in like manner after supper, saying, <u>This cup is the new covenant in my blood</u>, even that which is poured out for you" (Lk. 22:20).

"23 For I received of the Lord that which also I delivered unto you, that the Lord Jesus in the night in

which he was [h]betrayed took bread; 24 and when he had given thanks, he brake it, and said, This is my body, which [i]is for you: this do in remembrance of me. 25 In like manner also the cup, after supper, saying, <u>This cup is the new covenant in my blood: this do, as often as ye drink it, in remembrance of me</u>" (1Cor. 11:23-25).

"6 who also <u>made us sufficient as ministers of a new covenant; not of the letter, but of the spirit</u>: for the letter killeth, but the spirit giveth life" (2Cor. 3:6).

"6 But NOW <u>we have been discharged from the law</u>, having died to that wherein we were held; <u>so that we serve in newness of the spirit, and not in oldness of the letter</u>" (Rom. 7:6).

"There is therefore now no condemnation to them that are in Christ Jesus. 2 For <u>the law of the Spirit of life in Christ Jesus made me free from the law of sin and of death</u>. 3 For what the law could not do, [a] in that it was weak through the flesh, God, sending his own Son in the likeness of [b]sinful flesh [c]and for sin, condemned sin in the flesh" (Rom. 8:1-3).

"4 For <u>Christ is the end of the law</u> unto righteous-ness to every one that believeth" (Rom. 10:4).

"18 But <u>if ye are led by the Spirit, ye are not under the law</u>" (Gal. 5:18).

"13 in whom ye also, having heard the word of the truth, the [i]gospel of your salvation,—in whom, having also believed, <u>ye were sealed with the Holy Spirit of promise</u>" (Eph. 1:13).

"30 And grieve not <u>the Holy Spirit of God, in whom ye were sealed</u> unto the day of redemption" (Eph. 4:30).

"²¹ Now he that establisheth us with you [i]in Christ, and anointed us, is God; ²² [j]who also <u>sealed us, and gave us the earnest of the Spirit in our hearts</u>" (2Cor. 1:21-22).

According to the Old Testament, the broken law required the life of the transgressor. The Word, Christ Jesus, came into the world and became flesh. On the cross of Golgotha, He paid with His blood the supreme price required for redemption of mankind. The prophets and the law were pointing to God's plan of redemption – all these were pointing at the Messiah. Therefore, Jesus Christ fulfilled the law and the prophets. His own words confirm it: "*I came not to destroy, <u>but to **fulfill**</u>.*" However, Adventist doctrinal perception of Mathew 5:17-18 is different as follows:

1) According to Adventist belief 23 (belief 24) – Christ's Ministry in the Heavenly Sanctuary – in October 22, 1844 Christ entered the second and last phase of His atoning ministry – it is a work of investigative judgment which is part of the ultimate disposition of all sin. Doctrinal logic of this creed is that Christ's mission of atonement was not finished on the Cross of Golgotha – Christ's Calvary was only the first phase of His atoning ministry.

2) If Christ's atoning ministry was not finished on the cross of Golgotha, then He didn't fulfilled the law and the prophets. In this case, Adventists doctrinally reject the teachings of the New Testament – they herald a different Christ, a different Gospel.

3) Seventh-day Adventist should circumcise their sons, offer sacrifices, and observe all other practices required by the law because in Matthew 5:18 is stated: "*...one jot or one tittle shall in no wise pass away from the law...*"

4) According to the Gospel, Jesus had been arrested, accused, and ultimately sentenced to death by crucifixion for allegedly breaking the law – the **first** and the **fourth** commandments of the Sinaitic Decalogue (Jn. 5:17-18; Jn. 19:7; Mt.

26:63-66: Mk. 2:6-7; Mk. 14:61-64; Lk. 22:66-71; Mt. 12:9-14; Mk. 3:1-6; Lk. 6:2; Lk. 13:10-14; Jn. 9:15-16; Mt. 12:1-2; also Mk. 2:23-24; Lk. 6:1-2). What is the attitude of the Adventist Church in this respect? Is Jesus Christ regarded as an observer of the Sabbath or a transgressor of the law?

5) How do Seventh-day Adventists perceive Jesus' two commandments of love (*love the Lord thy God and love thy neighbour*)? Do they regard these commandments as "*two new commandments*" or as an "abolishment of the law"? If Christ's commandments are regarded as "*two new commandments*", then, according to Matthew 5:17-18, this is an "abolishment of the law"! If these are regarded as an abolishment of the law, then the authority of Jesus Christ is compromised – Jesus contradicts Himself. However, the key to logical explanation of Mathew 5:17-18 lies in the correct interpretation of Jesus' words: "*Think not that I came to destroy the law or the prophets: I came not to destroy, but to fulfill.*"

6) The following verses contain a different biblical message, hard to accept for Adventists: Jer. 31:31-34; Heb. 8:7-13; Gal. 3:17-19; Gal. 3:24-25; Is. 1:13; Hos. 2:11; Col. 2:14-17; Gal. 4:9-11; Mk. 2:27-28; Mt. 11:28; Eph. 2:15; 2Cor. 3:6; Rom. 7:6; Rom. 10:4; Rom. 3:19-24; Gal. 2:15-16; 1Tim. 1:9-10; Gal. 5:18.

The analogy of the following verses provides a clearer picture regarding Christ's mission – "*fulfilling the law and the prophets*":

> "*36 Teacher, which is the great commandment in the law? 37 And he said unto him, [n]Thou shalt love the Lord thy God with all thy heart, and with all thy soul, and with all thy mind. 38 This is the great and first commandment. 39 [o]And a second like unto it is this, [p]Thou shalt love thy neighbor as thyself. 40 On these two commandments the whole law hangeth, and the prophets*" (Mt. 22:36-40; also Mk. 12:28-31 and Lk. 10:25-27).

"9 For this, [e]Thou shalt not commit adultery, Thou shalt not kill, Thou shalt not steal, Thou shalt not covet, and if there be any other commandment, <u>it is summed up in this word, namely, Thou shalt love thy neighbor as thyself.</u> 10 Love worketh no ill to his neighbor: <u>love therefore is the fulfilment of the law</u>" (Rom. 13:9-10).

"17 Think not that I came to destroy the law or the prophets: <u>I came not to destroy, but to fulfil</u>" (Mt. 5:17).

Biblical truth is revealed to the believers as a result of constant prayer, study and meditation on the Scripture – this is the work of the Holy Spirit. For some believers, however, it seems easier to accept man-made doctrines than the testimony of Jesus Christ. It is a fact that erroneous or tendentious interpretation of the Bible is dangerous and spiritually offensive.

The whole law and the prophets depend on Christ's two commandments of (agape) love – the two commandments of God's new covenant. On the cross of Golgotha, Jesus Christ fulfilled the law and the prophets. Believers under the new covenant order their lives in harmony with Christ's teachings!

Revelation 12:17 and 14:12

"¹⁷ And the dragon waxed wroth with the woman, and went away to make war with the rest of her seed, that keep the commandments of God, and hold the testimony of Jesus" (Rev. 12:17);

"¹² Here is the [h]patience of the saints, they that keep the commandments of God, and the faith of Jesus" (Rev. 14:12).

The central issue in these verses is *"keeping the command-ments of God."* Inquisitive people, however, will ask themselves: which commandments? Many believers have a tendency to respond: the Ten Commandments of the Sinaitic covenant, as these represents a summary of God's law and moral standard of behavior. Other believers will point to Jesus' two commandments of (agape) love of the new cove-nant. At this point, it seems that believers are divided in two groups: supporters of Ten Commandments, on the one hand, and supporters of Christ's commandments, on the other hand. Therefore, which commandments reflect God's divine character throughout the whole universe?

Religious divergences are to be analyzed *"in spirit and in truth"* – any other way of resolving a religious debate leads to erroneous, biased interpretations. Proper understanding of the verses quoted above requires a careful analysis of other topic like: practical applicability of the Ten Commandments – the basis of the old covenant.

A. Is the Fourth Commandment applicable in heaven?

"⁸ "Remember the Sabbath day, to keep it holy. ⁹ You shall labor six days, and do all your work, ¹⁰ but the seventh day is a Sabbath to Yahweh your God. You shall not do any work in it, you, nor your son, nor

*your daughter, your male servant, nor your female
servant, nor your livestock, nor your stranger who
is within your gates;* [11] *for in six days Yahweh made
heaven and earth, the sea, and all that is in them,
and rested the seventh day; therefore Yahweh blessed
the Sabbath day, and made it holy"* (Ex. 20:8-11).

The answer to the question about practical applicability of the
seventh-day Sabbath in heaven is determined by logical analysis
of the following two situations:

1) The throne of God the Creator is located somewhere in our
solar system. Therefore, just as the rotation of our planet
(Earth) in relation to sun implies sunrise-sunset and day-
night cycle, in the same way such phenomenon would also
imply day-night, first day-seventh day cycle on the throne of
God and His angels. In other words, God and His multitude
of heavenly beings would become the subject of this celestial
phenomenon. Such hypothesis is irrational – it contradicts the
omnipotence of God! Does the sun of our solar system imply
such day-night cycle throughout the whole universe? No!

1) The throne of God the Creator is located somewhere in
the highest heavens, beyond our solar system, beyond our
human comprehension. God's dwelling place, the heavenly
sanctuary, is not the subject of any natural phenomenon
because divine glory of God cannot be the subject of His
creation. The following Bible verses confirm the veracity of
this statement:

> *"*[2] *I know a man in Christ, fourteen years ago
> (whether in the body, I know not; or whether out
> of the body, I know not; God knoweth),* <u>*such a one
> caught up even to the third heaven*</u>*.* [3] *And I know
> such a man (whether in the body, or apart from
> the body, I know not; God knoweth),* [4] <u>*how that he
> was caught up into Paradise, and heard unspeak-
> able words*</u>*, which it is not lawful for a man to utter"*
> (2Cor. 12:2-4).

"⁵ And this is the message which we have heard from him and announce unto you, that <u>God is light, and in him is no darkness at all</u>" (1Jn. 1:5).

"²³ And <u>the city hath no need of the sun, neither of the moon, to shine upon it</u>: for the glory of God did lighten it, [t]and the lamp thereof is the Lamb" (Rev. 21:23).

"²⁵ And the [v]gates thereof shall in no wise be shut by day (<u>for there shall be no night there</u>)" (Rev.21:25).

Logical reasoning based on biblical evidence presented above leads to an incontestable conclusion: the fourth commandment is not applicable in heaven. The seventh-day Sabbath can be applied only to the inhabitants of our planet. God is Spirit; therefore, heavenly beings honour the Creator as He really is, in spirit and in truth, always. God is to be honoured indiscriminately every day.

"¹⁷ But Jesus answered them, <u>My Father worketh even until now</u>, and I work" (Jn. 5:17).

John 5:17 provides a clear picture of Sabbath observance in heaven – this verse confirms the fact that God the Father is always at work. Seventh-day Sabbath has a very particular role in God's plan of salvation of mankind – it points at eternal rest in Christ and through Christ.

B. Is the Seventh Commandment applicable in heaven?

"²⁷ God created man in his own image. In God's image he created him; male and female he created them. ²⁸ God blessed them. God said to them, "Be fruitful, multiply, fill the earth, and subdue it. Have dominion over the fish of the sea, over the birds of the sky, and over every living thing that moves on the earth" (Gen. 1:27-28).

"¹⁸ Yahweh God said, "It is not good for the man to

107

*be alone. I will make him a helper comparable to[c]
him""* (Gen. 2:18).

*"21 Yahweh God caused the man to fall into a deep
sleep. As the man slept, he took one of his ribs, and
closed up the flesh in its place. 22 Yahweh God made
a woman from the rib which had taken from the
man, and brought her to the man"* (Gen. 2:21-22).

"14 "You shall not commit adultery"" (Ex. 20:14).

According to the Book of Genesis, God created human beings
as male and female. He created them for a purpose: to marry,
procreate, and to bring the earth and everything on it under their
control – to live in harmony with the Creator and His creation.

God is Spirit! Therefore, the verse *"God created man in his
own image. In God's image he created him; male and female he
created them"* is to be analyzed spiritually. Human beings were
created in the image of God's Spirit, in the image of God's divine
attributes. One of these attributes is physically manifested in
the capacity of mankind to procreate – a clear physical expression (an image) of God's creative nature. This, however, should
not be misunderstood: the act of procreation applies only to
humankind.

God's divine nature is an awesome mystery; there are many
speculations in this regard. Sincere believers yearn for divine
glory – the glory that Adam and Eve had before their fall into
sin. However, there are people who, in their human weakness,
try to level God to their human standards. There are many
puzzling issues in the Bible; therefore, believers are tempted to
ask themselves certain question. One of those questions is: Do
angels in heaven procreate? Is it possible for a bodiless heavenly
being to perform such an act in heaven? No! Angels in heaven do
not marry and do not procreate! If angels do not procreate, then
neither are they capable of committing adultery – the act prohibited by the sixth commandment (Ex. 20:14) of the Decalogue.
This is confirmed by the following Bible verses:

"[30] For in the resurrection *they neither marry, nor are given in marriage*, but are as angels [l]in heaven" (Mt. 22:30).

"[25] For when they shall rise from the dead, *they neither marry, nor are given in marriage*; but are as angels in heaven" (Mk. 12:25).

"[35] but they that are accounted worthy to attain to that [k]world, and the resurrection from the dead, *neither marry, nor are given in marriage*: [36] for neither can they die any more: for they are equal unto the angels; and are sons of God, being sons of the resurrection" (Lk. 20:35-36).

On the basis of biblical evidence presented above, a definitive conclusion follows: the seventh commandment is not applicable in heaven. The commandment regarding adultery, which refers to a physical act, can be applied only to human beings here on earth!

C. Is the Sinaitic Covenant faultless?

A Pharisee, Saul from Tarsus (Apostle Paul), provides the answer to this question. Paul's Epistle to the Hebrews affirms that the covenant made on Mount Sinai is faulty (Heb. 8:7-13; Heb. 10:1). It is very obvious the fact that, if there were no inconsistencies regarding the old covenant, there would be no need of a new one (Jer. 31:31-33). The very sacrifices, the law, and the prophets point to the cross of Golgotha, that is, to the new covenant.

According to the Bible, the Ten Commandments are the basis of the covenant established on Mount Sinai (Ex. 34:27-28; Deut. 4:13; Deut. 9:9, 11, 15; 1Kg. 8:21). Therefore, it is necessary to conduct a thorough analysis of the law, more precisely, an analysis of what is tolerated, overlooked in the Ten Commandments and Torah. Ultimately, astonishing facts come out – the Ten Commandments and the entire Torah tolerate, that is, do not prohibit the following:

- Slavery, a common practice in Israel (Ex. 21:2; 2Kgs. 4:1; Neh. 5:5);

- Polygamy, just another common practice in Israel. The Old Testament patriarchs have the reputation of having many wives and concubines: King David had eight wives (1Sam. 18:27; 1Cron. 3:1-9); King Solomon (1Kgs. 11:3) was famous for having 700 wives and 300 concubines (Ex. 21:10-11; Deut. 17:17; Deut. 21:15-17; 1Sam. 1:1-2);

- Divorce (Deut. 24:1; Ezra. 10:19), indecent treatment of female war prisoners (Deut. 21:10-14; Num. 31:17-18, 40-41, 47-48). Both cases, according to Jesus' teaching, point at adultery (Mt. 5:31-32; Mt. 19:9; Mk. 10:11-12; Lk. 16:18);

- Religiously motivated killing was permitted by the law: the Israelites, carrying the Ark of the Covenant that contained the tablets of the Law (including the sixth commandment – *"You shalt not kill")*, were commanded to kill men, women, and children living in Canaan (Num. 21:3,35; Num. 31:7-8,17; Deut. 20:13-18; Deut. 3:6; Deut. 25:19; Jos. 6:21; Jos. 8:25-26; Ex. 13:17); killing of Israelites for breaking the law (Ex. 31:14-15; Lev. 20:9; Deut. 21:18-21; Num. 25:5; Deut. 13:15); "... *eye for eye and life for life"* rule (Ex. 21:23-24; Lev. 24:17-20; Deut. 19:21). God, however, did not punish Cain for killing His brother Abel (Gen. 4:15).

After a careful analysis of these controversial biblical episodes in the light of New Testament truth, inevitable deduction follows:
- The sixth and seventh commandments have been transgressed;
- The eighth, ninth, and tenth commandments have also been transgressed, as they are not applicable anymore when a person is taken into slavery or killed;
- The fifth commandment is transgressed, as God-fearing parents would never want their sons to behave in such a vicious manner;
- The fourth commandment is transgressed, as priests were breaking the Sabbath law on every Sabbath by offering sacrifices (Mt. 12:5; Num. 28:9-10) and performing circumcision (Jn. 7:22; Gen. 17:10-12; Lev. 12:3);

- The third commandment is transgressed, as vows and swearing were practiced in the Old Testament (Mt. 5:33-37; Mt. 23:16-22; Jas. 5:12; Lev. 19:12; Num. 30:2; Deut. 23:21);

- The second commandment is transgressed as slavery, polygamy, adultery...are a capricious form of idolatry;

- The first commandment is transgressed, as nobody committing such transgression can truly honour God.

The old covenant has an incontestable role in God's plan of redemption. It was based on the law, which was meant to lead Israelites to Christ (Gal. 3:17, 24-25). Animal sacrifices (the type) were pointing to Jesus Christ (the antitype). The old covenant was a forerunner of the new covenant established on the cross of Golgotha – a covenant of the Spirit. The law is a reminder of what sin is; the Spirit, however, gives life. The faultiness of the old covenant is evident. It is confirmed by the following New Testament verses:

> "7 For _if that first covenant had been faultless_, then would no place have been sought for a second" (Heb. 8:7).

> "13 In that he saith, A new covenant, _he hath made the first old_. But that which is becoming old and waxeth aged is nigh unto vanishing away" (Heb. 8:13).

> "19 (for _the law made nothing perfect_), and a bringing in thereupon of a better hope, through which we draw nigh unto God" (Heb. 7:19).

> "1 For _the law_ having a shadow of the good things to come, not the very image of the things, [a]_can never_ with the same sacrifices year by year, which they offer continually, _make perfect them that draw nigh_" (Heb. 10:1).

> "56 The sting of death is sin; and _the power of sin is the law_" (1Cor. 15:56).

"[10] but when that which is perfect is come, that which is in part shall be done away" (1Cor. 13:10).

"[6] But now _we have been discharged from the law_, having died to that wherein we were held; _so that we serve in newness of the spirit, and not in oldness of the letter_" (Rom. 7:6).

"[10] For _this is the covenant that_ [i]_I will make with the house of Israel_ After those days, saith the Lord; _I will put my laws into their mind, And on their heart also will I write them_: And I will be to them a God, And they shall be to me a people" (Heb. 8:10; Jer. 31:33).

"[6] who also _made us sufficient as ministers of a new covenant; not of the letter, but of the spirit_: for the letter killeth, but the spirit giveth life" (2Cor. 3:6).

"[14] but their [i]minds were hardened: for until this very day at the reading of the old covenant the same veil [j]remaineth, it not being revealed to them that it is done away in Christ. [15] _But unto this day, whensoever Moses is read, a veil lieth upon their heart_. [16] But whensoever [k]it shall turn to the Lord, the veil is taken away. [17] Now the Lord is the Spirit: and where the Spirit of the Lord is, there is liberty" (2Cor. 3:14-17).

"[36] Teacher, which is the great commandment in the law? [37] And he said unto him, [n]_Thou shalt love the Lord thy God_ with all thy heart, and with all thy soul, and with all thy mind. [38] This is the great and first commandment. [39] [o]And a second like unto it is this, [p]_Thou shalt love thy neighbor_ as thyself. [40] _On these two commandments the whole law hangeth, and the prophets_" (Mt. 22:36-40; also Mk. 12:28-31; Lk. 10:25-27).

Consequently, some may assert that there are two Gods: 1) God of the Old Testament – a God of war and punishment; 2) God of the New Testament – a God of peace and (agape) love. Thus, it may seem that we are dealing with divine dualism. On the other hand, some scholars question the authenticity and divine origin of certain aspects of the old covenant law:

- Was it God's divine command to imply bloodshed, to exterminate people, to plunder, to enslave or keep female war prisoners for Israelite male satisfaction? Or was it a human decision in the name of Yahweh?

- Wouldn't it have been better if Canaanites were converted into accepting God's commandments of the Sinaitic covenant; wouldn't it have been better a peace treaty with the descendants of Salem (Melchizedek's kingdom) than war?

- Are 613 laws of the Torah a set of divine laws or rather a religion-based constitution?

- Does the law that tolerates slavery and polygamy, and upholds patriarchal system where woman's identity and fundamental rights are at the discretion of man just because she is a woman, and where the first-born is privileged just because he happened to be born first reflect God's glory?

- Should 613 laws of the Torah be regarded as the absolute will of God or rather as a human concept of "God's will"? Does the old covenant law reflect divine perfection?

Some believers may argue that such an approach of the law casts doubt on the Holy Scripture. The response to this remark is this: such analysis of the law is questioning certain human ways of perception and interpretation of the word of God. Probably, the accusers should present their arguments to the One who inspired the writing of the manuscripts, which compose the New Testament (Paul's epistles in particular), as the New Testament questions certain aspects of the law.

In the Old Testament predominates the calling to obey the law, the Ten Commandments. This law was extended to 613 laws and rules. This "extension" interpreted the law and dealt with human behaviour in relation to the covenant (the law); it dealt with slavery, polygamy, divorce, manslaughter, and other social aspects in relation to the law.

On the other hand, the law, which is the basis of the Sinaitic (Mosaic) Covenant, was tolerant towards certain aspects of this "extension of the law." This tolerance on the side of the law caused (and is still causing) believers to ask themselves questions regarding practical applicability of the old covenant law. Does this mean that the law, which says: *"You shall not kill; You shall not commit adultery; You shall not steal..."* is not good? The (moral) law is holy, right, and good (Rom. 7:12)! Was there something wrong with the covenant that omitted, tolerated certain practices. Quite eidently, there must be something wrong with certain aspects of the "extension of the law." At that time, the law and its requirements was essential in people's daily life; however, it could not save them. Animal sacrifics required by the law could not make the person perfect – it takes faith to purify the heart and mind of a believer. This is confirmed by the following verses:

> *"[1] For <u>the law</u> having a shadow of the good things to come, not the very image of the things, [a]<u>can never with the same sacrifices year by year, which they offer continually, make perfect them that draw nigh</u>" (Heb. 10:1).*

> *"[6] For <u>I desire mercy, and not sacrifice</u>; and the knowledge of God more than burnt offerings" (Hos. 6:6; also Mt. 9:13; 12:7).*

> *"[19] Now we know that what things soever the law saith, it speaketh to them that are under the law; that every mouth may be stopped, and all the world may be brought under the judgment of God: [20] because [k]<u>by [l]the works of the law shall no flesh be [m]justified in his sight</u>; for [n]through the law cometh the knowledge of sin" (Rom. 3:19-20).*

In this case, individuals with radical convictions may argue that, if the Sinaitic covenant is not perfect, then the divine authority of Yahweh seems to be compromised. Such allegation is an evident non-sense! The so-called "faultiness" of the old covenant is to be understood from the perspective of its original purpose: the Sinaitic covenant was a precursor of God's new covenant established on Golgotha – the old covenant and its law was a shadow of the things to come, a shadow of Christ (Heb. 10:1-4; Col 2:16-17). In the same manner the Tabernacle, a physical representation of God's divine plan of salvation of mankind, was a copy of the Heavenly Tabernacle. Therefore, when that which is perfect comes, that which is in part shall be done away (1Cor 13:10). There is no doubt that certain particularities of the covenant established on Mount Sinai (Horeb) had to correspond to the people's mentality of those days.

For their enlightenment in this regard, they should give proper credit to Jeremiah 31:31-33 and Hebrews chapter 8.

God reveals Himself in a progressive way – the establishment of several covenants with mankind at different periods of human history is a confirmation of it. Believers under the new covenant have a new concept of God's law. God is Spirit; therefore, they worship God as He really is – *"in spirit and in truth."* They listen to the voice of the *"Word"*, and they follow Him – *"who was, who is, and who is to come"* – for it is written in the Scripture:

> *"⁶ Jesus saith unto him, I am the way, and the truth, and the life: no one cometh unto the Father, but* [d]
> *by me"* (Jn. 14:6).

The prophet Jeremiah (Jer. 31:31-34) announced to the people of Israel that the time is coming when Yahweh will make a *"new covenant"* with His people. This is the covenant: *"I will put my laws in their minds and written in their hearts"* – a covenant of the Spirit. Can a law based on (daily) sacrifices, which cannot take away sins (Heb. 10:1-4; Heb. 9:9-10), make people perfect? According to the New Testament, the law is not a full and faithful model of the real things (Heb. 10:1-2). In this respect, it is pertinent to mention that God's Providence in relation to His people is manifested through love (agape), not through law. However, due to the unpredictable nature of mankind and its limited comprehension of the will of God, the law is indispensable.

Is the Sinaitic covenant faultless? If it is, then why would God later speak of another covenant? Does the old covenant law reflect perfection? Well, Jesus Christ clearly state that the entire law and the prophets depend on the "two commandments of love." Therefore, Christ's commandment of love (agape) is a perfect law. This is a sensitive topic of discussion. The answer to these questions is left to the discretion of the reader!

Note: This brief exegetical analysis of the old covenant law is by no means intended to offend Jewish religion or obscure the image of the old covenant as such – it has nothing to do with the historical conflict between Palestinians and Jews. The purpose of this reasoning is to emphasize the incontestable authority of God's new covenant and propose an approach of the Holy Scripture in the light of the New Testament truth. It is meant to combat religious incoherence, fanaticism, and spiritually abusive indoctrination of people that has been persisting for a very long time.

D. Are Jesus' Commandments the Ten Commandments?

The topic concerning God's commandments is disputable nowadays. Many believers still stumble over the question regarding what one should keep: the Ten Commandments of the old covenant or Christ's Two Commandments of love (agape) of the new covenant. Some believers assert that Jesus' commandments are the Ten Commandments; others, however, uphold a different position. The answer to this question is found in the following New Testament verses:

> "[35] And one of them, a lawyer, asked him a question, trying him: [36] Teacher, which is the great commandment in the law? [37] And he said unto him, [n]_Thou shalt love the Lord thy God_ with all thy heart, and with all thy soul, and with all thy mind. [38] This is the great and first commandment. [39] [o]And a second like unto it is this, [p]_Thou shalt love thy neighbor_ as

thyself. ⁴⁰ <u>On these two commandments the whole law hangeth, and the prophets</u>" (Mt. 22:36-40).

"²⁸ *And one of the scribes came, and heard them questioning together, and knowing that he had answered them well, asked him, What commandment is the first of all? ²⁹ Jesus answered, <u>The first is, </u> ⁽ᵍ⁾<u>Hear, O Israel; </u> ⁽ʰ⁾<u>The Lord our God, the Lord is one: ³⁰ and thou shalt love the Lord thy God</u> ⁽ⁱ⁾with all thy heart, and ⁽ʲ⁾with all thy soul, and ⁽ᵏ⁾with all thy mind, and ⁽ˡ⁾with all thy strength. ³¹ <u>The second is this, </u> ⁽ᵐ⁾<u>Thou shalt love thy neighbor</u> as thyself. There is none other commandment greater than these*" (Mk. 12:28-31).

"²⁵ *And behold, a certain lawyer stood up and made trial of him, saying, Teacher, what shall I do to inherit eternal life? ²⁶ And he said unto him, What is written in the law? how readest thou? ²⁷ And he answering said, ⁽ʰ⁾<u>Thou shalt love the Lord thy God</u> ⁽ⁱ⁾with all thy heart, and with all thy soul, and with all thy strength, and with all thy mind; ⁽ʲ⁾<u>and thy neighbor</u> as thyself. ²⁸ And he said unto him, Thou hast answered right: this do, and thou shalt live*" (Lk. 10:25-28).

"⁹ *For this, ⁽ᵉ⁾Thou shalt not commit adultery, Thou shalt not kill, Thou shalt not steal, Thou shalt not covet, <u>and if there be any other commandment, it is summed up in this word, namely, Thou shalt love thy neighbor</u> as thyself. ¹⁰ Love worketh no ill to his neighbor: <u>love therefore is the fulfilment of the law</u>*" (Rom. 13:9-10).

"³⁴ <u>A new commandment I give unto you, that ye love one another; </u> ⁽ᵒ⁾*even as I have loved you, that ye also love one another*" (Jn. 13:34; also Jn. 15:12, 17; 1Jn. 3:23).

The verses quoted above unveil a new commandment: the "*commandment of love.*" Should this be regarded as the eleventh commandment?

It is very evident the fact that Jesus' commandments are much more than the Ten Commandments (and the Torah). Otherwise, one would have to assume that God's divine glory, His eternal attributes are limited to the Ten Commandments, to the 613 laws of Torah. Such assumption is irrational, and is not in harmony with the teaching of the New Testament! God's divine glory is much more than that – it is beyond our human comprehension!

How can one explain the following fact: keeping God's commandments, which do not prohibit slavery, polygamy... and many other things?

Jesus' teaching is very clear: "*love the Lord thy God and love thy neighbour*", not the law that allows or prohibits something!

Which commandments reflect God's divine and loving nature throughout the entire universe?

1) The Ten Commandments marked by the following particularities:
   - Do not prohibit slavery, polygamy, and so on;
   - The fourth and the seventh commandment do not apply in heaven.

2) Christ's Commandments of love (agape) marked by the following particularities:

   - The entire law (Ten Commandments, Torah) and the prophets depend on these two commandments;
   - God is love (agape).

The answer to this question is left to the discretion of the reader!

Note: Agape is one of several Greek words for love. In Christian theology, "*agape*"[24] refers to the love of God for humankind, as well as the human reciprocal love for God; the term necessarily extends to the love of one's fellow man. Agape love is divine, unconditional, self-sacrificing. God's agape love is clearly manifested in Jesus Christ – in His sacrificial death on the cross of Golgotha for the salvation of many. Agape is in contrast to "*eros*"[23], an affection of sexual nature. In this regard, it is pertinent to mention that certain people, whether deliberately or out of ignorance, tend to reduce God to the level of His creation and agape to eros; these individuals ascribe a moral status to immorality and teach others to regard perverted behaviour as a moral norm.

The Sanctuary

The Bible is a canonical collection of texts. These texts are considered sacred in Judaism and Christianity. The Bible, besides divinely inspired teachings and guidance, also contains allegorical language mostly incorporated in visions and prophetic messages. Some of these figures of speech are easier to understand, for instance: "*God's temple*" represents the believers, that is, the Spirit of God lives in them (1Cor. 3:16-17; 1Cor. 6:19; 2Cor. 6:16); "*incense*" are the prayers of the saints (Rev. 5:8); "*fine linen*" represent the righteousness (righteous deeds) of the saints (Rev. 19:8). However, biblical significance of certain allegories is beyond common understanding – it requires dedication through study and prayer. Biblically, God's will is revealed to mankind in different ways; therefore, the correct interpretation of divine revelation assumes a huge responsibility.

The questions regarding Divine Providence and the relationship between God and man have always been central in the thoughts of reasonable believers. Therefore, altars, places of worship, and temples were built to honour the divinity. Yahweh, the God of Israel, was central in the life of the people He brought out of Egypt. Israelites were commanded to build a sanctuary, a sacred place where the Ark of the Covenant was central, a place where divine presence of God was manifested.

"The Sanctuary was 'a copy and a shadow of heavenly things', a 'shadow of the good things to come' (Heb. 8:5; Heb. 10:1). Every shadow is cast by some body. What body was it which casts shadow of the Sanctuary? The Apostle Paul supplies the answer in Col. 2:17, 'Which are a shadow of the things to come; but the body is Christ's. Notice that it is Christ's body which casts that shadow. The Sanctuary was not a representation of Christ in His original glory, but in His incarnation.

Through sin, God and man were separated. In Jesus Christ they are brought back together again. In the Sanctuary of old,

God and man were brought together. There was also a place within which man might come, under certain conditions. Both places were within the sanctuary; God's presence in the inner apartment, and man's presence in the outer [...].

The veil of the sanctuary was the place at which God and man met. The veil was the only medium interposing between God and man, in that service. That temple veil <u>represented</u> Jesus Christ the God-man. More distinctively the veil represented the <u>flesh</u> or incarnation of Christ: 'enter into the holiest by the blood of Jesus…through the veil, that is to say, through <u>His flesh</u>' (Heb. 10:19-20).

The incarnate Christ is now the sole medium of approach between God and man, the antitype of the veil in the earthly sanctuary.

The veil of our Saviour's flesh was, at the Crucifixion, suspended between heaven and earth, on Calvary's cross, just as the veil hung between God and man in the temple. [...]

The earthly sanctuary represents the heavenly things; but the heavenly things are spiritual things. The heavenly sanctuary is not of the same creation as the earthly (Heb. 9:1; Heb. 9:11). If we are to understand the Old Testament teachings correctly, we must read them in the light of explanations given in the New Testament. Type must be interpreted by antitype.

How far remote is this conception from that of those who see in heaven an exact replica of two roomed building containing furniture (an ark, a table of shewbread, a golden candle stick, a golden altar of incense, a veil, a golden mercy seat etc.) in heaven."[10]

Is it reasonable to admit the presence of metal (gold), acacia wood, linen – materials which are subject to corrosion, decomposition – in the Heavenly Sanctuary? God is Spirit, and such physical earthly things are not compatible in the heavenly realm.

Let's be more specific. Is it spiritually correct to admit that the Heavenly Sanctuary contains two stone tablets with Ten Commandments carved on it, a gold jar containing manna, and Aaron's budded rod?

It is irresistibly logical to conclude that the three objects inside the Most Holy Place (within the Ark of the Covenant according to Hebrews 9:4) are a symbolic representation of God's divine plan of redemption of humankind.

Jesus said: *"I am the way, the truth, and the life"* (Jn. 14:6), that is:

- The way – Aaron's stick;
- The truth – Ten Commandments carved on two stone tablets;
- The life – manna in the gold jar.

Human sinful nature cannot comprehend God's divine glory. To some extent, however, this can be achieved by allegorical representation of the spiritual things. Therefore, allegorical language used in the Bible is due to limited human understanding of spiritual things. On the other hand, some believers take biblical allegories literally. However, such approach of the word of God is discordant and spiritually offensive – it gives birth to false teachings and controversial doctrines.

It is written in the Bible:

> *"Yahweh says, "<u>Heaven is my throne, and the earth is my footstool</u>. What kind of house will you build to me? Where will I rest?" (Is. 66:1; also Acts 7:4; Mt. 5:34).*

If so, then what was the logic of building the tabernacle and temple? This may seem confusing as long as we do not analyze these things spiritually. The Tabernacle had two divisions separated by a veil (curtain). The first one – the Holy Place – was accessible to man, thus representing the earth; in the second one – the Most Holy Place – was manifested the presence of Yahweh, thus representing the heaven. The veil, which separated the two rooms, and which was the only way into the Most Holy Place, represented the Word – Jesus Christ – who came into the world with a mission. Thus, physical things of the tabernacle are a representation of the spiritual things. This reasoning is confirmed by the following New Testament verses:

"[50] And Jesus cried again with a loud voice, and yielded up his spirit. [51] And behold, <u>the veil of the [u] temple was rent in two from the top to the bottom</u>; and the earth did quake; and the rocks were rent" (Mat. 27:50-51; also Mark. 15:38).

"[19] Having therefore, brethren, <u>boldness to enter into the holy place by the blood of Jesus</u>, [20] by the way which he dedicated for us, a new and living way, <u>through the veil, that is to say, his flesh</u>; [21] and having a great priest over the house of God" (Heb. 10:19-21).

"[24] For Christ entered not into a holy place made with hands, like in pattern to the true; <u>but into heaven itself</u>, now to appear before the face of God for us" (Heb. 9:24).

"[17] <u>which are a shadow of the things to come</u>; but the body is Christ's" (Col. 2:17).

"[22] And <u>I saw no [r] temple therein</u>: for the Lord God the Almighty, and the Lamb, are the [s] temple thereof" (Rev. 21:22).

The issue regarding the veil is a reality within Orthodox Churches where there still is a distinctive separating wall called the iconostasis, which reminds of the veil separating the two compartments of the biblical Tabernacle (or the Temple in Jerusalem). However, the veil symbolized Jesus Christ's flesh (Heb. 10:19-21). Jesus, on the cross of Golgotha, put an end to the veil. Jesus Christ is the only mediator between God and man (Jn. 14:6; 1Tim. 2:5).

Old covenant and the cross of Golgotha

Around two thousand years ago, the universe witnessed a unique event which has astonished both angels in heaven and inhabitants on earth. The "*Word*", by His own free will, left His heavenly glory and came into the world with a unique mission: to pay the ransom for the sins of mankind. On the Cross of Golgotha, Jesus Christ became the perfect sacrifice required as atonement for the salvation of many – a divine manifestation of God's eternal love.

Christ's Calvary on the Cross of Golgotha became the landmark between past and future, death and life, earth and heaven. On the Cross of Golgotha, Christ put an end to the old covenant and its sign, the Sabbath. The Word – Christ Jesus – put an end to sacrifices and all other practices required by the law. The cross of Golgotha marks the end of the Sinaitic covenant (the end of Mosaic Law) and the beginning of God's new covenant as follows:

- The law (including the Sabbath) was introduced 430 years after the covenant with Abraham (Gal. 3:17-18); it was in charge to lead the people to Christ (Gal. 3:19, 24-25; Rom. 10:1-4);

- Jesus Christ put an end to the law (2Cor. 3:6; Rom. 7:6; Rom. 8:1-3; Rom. 10:4; Eph. 2:15; 1Cor. 9:20-21; Gal. 5:18; 1Tim. 1:9-10);

- Christ put an end to Sabbath (Is. 1:13; Hos. 2:11; Col. 2:14-16; Gal. 4:9-11; Eph. 2:15; Mk. 2:27-28; Mt. 11:28;

- Jesus had been accused by Pharisees of transgressing the Sabbath of the fourth commandment (Mt. 12:9-14; Mk. 3:1-6; Lk. 6:1-2; Lk. 13:10-17; Jn. 5:17-18; Jn. 9:16);

- Through Christ, God made a new covenant with His people. It is a covenant of hearts and minds – a covenant of the Spirit (Jer. 31:31-33; Heb. 8:7-12; 2Cor. 3:6; Heb. 9:14-15);

- Believers of the new covenant are put right with God through faith, not through law (Rom. 3:19-24; Rom. 4:3; Rom. 5:1-2; Rom. 10:1-4; Gal. 2:15-16; Gal. 3:10-11);

- The 613 laws of the old covenant, the handwriting of ordinances had been replaced by the law of the Spirit (2Cor. 3:6; Rom. 7:6; Rom. 8:1-3; Eph. 2:15);

- The Ten Commandments of the old covenant had been replaced by the Two Commandments of (agape) love, "*love the Lord thy God and love thy neighbour*" (Mt. 22:36-40; Mk. 12:28-31; Lk. 10:25-27; Jn. 14:15; Rom. 13:9-10; Jn. 13:34; 15:12, 17, 1Jn. 3:23; 2Jn 6);

- The type (the veil separating two rooms of the Tabernacle, the law written or carved on stone tablets, animal sacrifices, and physical circumcision) had been replaced by the antitype (Jesus Christ, law of the Spirit, Lamb of God, spiritual circumcision). Thus, God has made known to us the mystery of His will: to bring all things in heaven and on earth together under one head, even Christ (Eph. 1:9-10).

God's chosen servants, the prophets, foretold that time is coming when God will make a new covenant with His people. To doubt the "*word of God*" or partially accept prophetic messages of the Bible means to put the Lord our God to the test.

Cotroversial questions

Religious controversy over sensitive topics has been going on for many centuries. Ideological discordances often incited religious conflicts and division within Christianity. In search for the truth, sincere believers often came up with exploratory questions; the actions of others, however, stirred up confusion among believers. Some of these questions are: Is the seventh-day Sabbath binding on Christians? Is the old covenant law binding on Christians? Are Christians under the law or under grace?

The law is holy and the commandment is holy, just, and good (Rom. 7:12). But it was the law that made us aware of what sin is. For, we would not have known what lust is, if the law did not say: do not covet (Rom. 7:7). Does this mean that what is good causes our death? Certainly not! It was sin that did it; by using what is good, sin brought death to us, in order that its true nature as sin might be revealed.

Sin came into the world as a result of Adam and Eve's disobedience to God. The original sin brought death into the world. Biblical expression *"for in the day that you eat of it, you will surely die"* (Gen. 2:17), which refers to the tree of the knowledge of good and evil that was in the middle of the Garden of Eden, should be perceived in a spiritual sense. Adam died 930 years after the expulsion from Eden – a physical consequence of the spiritual death that took place on the day Adam sinned by eating the forbidden fruit. The first human couple fell from God's grace. Later, God gave to mankind the law to set a standard of holiness; however, mankind could not meet that standard on its own.

What the law could not do, because human nature is weak, God did. He condemned sin in human nature by sending His own Son, who came with a nature like sinful human nature, to do away with sin. Therefore, there is no condemnation now for those who live in unity with Christ Jesus. For the law of the

Spirit, which brings us life in union with Christ, has set us free from the law of sin and death (Rom. 8:1-3).

According to the New Testament, Jesus Christ put an end to the law (Rom. 10:4; Rom. 7:6; 2Cor. 3:6; Eph. 2:15; Rom. 3:19-24). Christians are not anymore under the law written with ink or carved on stone tablets, because they are under the Spirit (2Cor. 3:6; Rom. 7:6; Gal. 5:18); they are not under law but under God's grace (Rom. 6:14). If we are under God's grace, does this mean that we shall sin, that is, shall we steal, kill, and commit adultery...? Certainly not! We have died to sin when we were baptized into union with Christ; we were also baptized into union with his death. Since we died with Christ, we believe that we will also rise and live as He did (Rom. 6:1-8). If we sin, we are no longer under God's grace; we fall under law and dishonour Christ, our actions demand Christ's crucifixion again – we find ourselves in a deplorable state. But if we live by the Spirit, we are under God's Grace and the law does not apply to us because the law is for law-breakers (1Tim. 1:9-10). Believers under the new covenant are put right with God through their faith in Jesus Christ, not by doing what the law requires (Rom. 3:19-23; Rom. 4:3; Rom. 5:1; Gal. 2:15-16; Gal. 3:10-11; Rom. 10:4). This is the secret of God's grace, which is not a secret to His people. For many, however, this is still a mystery: Christ put an end to the law; yet, those who break the law are charged with transgressing the law. The law is a reminder of what sin is; therefore, its significance in God's plan of salvation of mankind must not be neglected.

A. Is the seventh-day Sabbath binding on Christians?

The topic regarding Sabbath is quite complex. Any attempt to resolve this religious polemic based only on the fourth commandment is partial, thus incorrect. The seventh-day Sabbath goes hand in hand with the covenant made on Mount Sinai (Mount Horeb). The Ten Commandments are the basis of the Sinaitic covenant and Sabbath is the sign of that covenant, the sign of agreement between Yahweh and Israel. Both covenant and its sign occurred at the same time, same place – these are inter-connected, inseparable. Therefore, to solve the Sabbath contro-versy, it is necessary to take into account all aspects related to this matter. Partial approach of the Bible leads to fanaticism and extra biblical teachings – a nourishing ground for controversial doctrines.

The question regarding Sabbath comprises:

1. The fourth commandment.

2. The old covenant made on Mount Sinai and its sign, the Sabbath.

3. The Old Testament prophecies.

4. The New Testament teachings on the following topics:

- The old covenant law and Sabbath;

- The new covenant and its particularities;

- Christ's mission on earth.

Is the old covenant Sabbath applicable to believers under the new covenant? No, it isn't! This statement is confirmed by the following incontestable biblical evidence:

1) According to apostle Paul's letter to the Galatians, the law (including the Sabbath) was given 430 years after God's cove-nant with Abraham (Gal. 3:17-18), and was in charge to lead people to Christ (Gal. 3:19; Gal. 3:24-25).

Certain believers might object to Paul's statement in Galatians 3:17 regarding 430 years. However, the main issue in this verse is that the law was given after Abraham, after the deliverance of Israelites from Egyptian slavery, not before.

2) The prophets foretold the coming of the Messiah and establishment of God's new covenant with His people; they also predicted that Yahweh would put an end to Sabbath and Israel's religious festivities (Deut. 18:15,18; Ps. 2:6-9; Ps. 110:4; Is. 6:9-10; Is. 7:14; Is. 9:6; Is. 49:6; Is. 61:1; Jer. 23:5-6; Dan. 9:25-26; Hos. 11:1; Mic. 5:2; Zech. 9:9; Zech. 11:12-13; Zech. 12:10; Is. 42:6-7; Jer. 31:31-34; Heb. 8:7-13; Is. 1:13; Hos. 2:11).

Some believers consider Isaiah 1:13 and Hosea 2:11 irrele-vant because in the Old Testament predominates the calling for

Sabbath observance. Nevertheless, in the Old Testament is stated only once that the time is coming when Yahweh will make a new covenant with His people (Jer. 31:31-33). Yet, the entire New Testament is based on those verses mentioned only once: God's new covenant (established on the cross of Golgotha through Jesus Christ).

3) The new covenant sealed with the blood of Christ is a covenant of the Spirit, not of written law (2Cor. 3:6; Rom. 7:6).

4) Christ put an end to the law (2Cor. 3:6; Rom. 7:6; Rom. 8:1-3; Rom. 10:4; Eph. 2:15; 1Cor. 9:20-21; Gal. 5:18; 1Tim. 1:9-11) and also to Sabbath (Is. 1:13; Hos. 2:11; Col. 2:14-17; Gal. 4:9-11; Mk. 2:27-28; Mt. 11:28; Mt. 12:9-14; Mk. 3:1-6; Lk. 6:1-2; 13:10-17; Jn. 9:16). How did Jesus Christ put an end to the law? By fulfilling it (Mt. 5:17-18)! Christ put an end to the covenant based on that law and established a new covenant of the Spirit; by putting an end to the type, the shadow (Col. 2:16-17), Christ revealed Himself to the world as the antitype.

5) Jesus Christ came with two commandments of (agape) love – the whole law and the prophets depend on these two commandments (Mt. 22:36-40; Mk. 12:28-31; Lk. 10:25-27).

6) There's no commandment regarding the seventh-day Sabbath keeping in the New Testament; the observance of other nine commandments is mentioned many times.

7) If a Christian is bound to keep the old covenant Sabbath, then he should observe all other requirements of that covenant.

8) If believers of the new covenant are bound to keep Sabbath, the sign of the covenant between Yahweh and Israel established on Mount Sinai, a memorial of deliverance from Egyptian slavery, then such approach of the issue implies contradiction, compromise. The Holy Spirit is not a spirit of compromise!

9) Among the main causes which culminated in Jesus' arrested and ultimately to His crucifixion was the accusation of breaking the fourth commandment.

10) If Jesus, according to the Jewish law, physically broke the Sabbath law, yet spiritually He did not, does this imply the possibility that God makes exception regarding the implementation

of the law? No! That would contradict God's divine nature! Jesus is pure because He observed the Sabbath "*in truth and in spirit.*" If He is the "*Word (Logos)*", that is, the source of (eternal) life, then He is also the source of (eternal) rest! The seventh-day Sabbath was a shadow of the things to come (Col. 2:16-17), a physical representation of the spiritual rest! Christ is our true Sabbath!

Are Christians bound to the seventh-day Sabbath? No! Why? Because, as it was mentioned previously, the Holy Scripture teaches us so:

1) The prophets foretold that God would put an end to the old covenant, Sabbath, and religious festivities.

2) The New Testament provides clear evidence, which confirms that Christ is the end of the law (including Sabbath law); the apostles and other first century Christians were gathering for worship, prayer, and the Lord's Supper (Holy Communion) on the first day of the week.

3) Breaking the Sabbath law was one of the three main accusations that led to Jesus' arrest and finally to His crucifixion – the accusers were Sabbath-keepers.

4) For a Christian, the old covenant Sabbath observance implies absurdity as follows:

- The seventh day is holier than other days, therefore God is honoured less on other days of the week;

- It suggests the concept of dualism, which leads to honouring Yahweh on the seventh day of the week and dishonouring God, the Creator, on other days of the week – every day is holy in regard to sin.

Some may say that, the One who said: "*You shall not murder; You shall not commit adultery; You shall not steal...*"; also said: "*keep the Sabbath holy.*" At first impression, this statement seems quite appealing. However, the Bible always provides answers to provocative and speculative arguments. Therefore, the One who said: do not kill, do not commit adultery, do not steal..., also stated the following:

"*13 Bring no more vain offerings. Incense is an*

130

abomination to me; new moons, <u>Sabbaths, and convocations: I can't bear with evil assemblies</u>" (Is. 1:13).

"[11] <u>I will also cause all her celebrations to cease</u>: her feasts, her new moons, <u>her Sabbaths, and all her solemn assemblies</u>" (Hos. 2:11).

"[27] And he said unto them, <u>The sabbath was made for man, and not man for the sabbath</u>: [28] so that the Son of man is lord even of the sabbath" (Mk. 2:27-28).

"[28] <u>Come unto me</u>, all ye that labor and are heavy laden, <u>and I will give you rest</u>" (Mt. 11:28).

"[23] But the hour cometh, and now is, when the <u>true worshippers shall worship the Father in spirit and truth</u>: [g]for such doth the Father seek to be his worshippers. [24] [h]<u>God is a Spirit: and they that worship him must worship in spirit and truth</u>" (Jn. 4:23-24).

Jesus, according to Mark 2:28 and Luke 6:5, is "*Lord of the Sabbath*." If Jesus is Lord of the Sabbath, then true believers should honour Him, not the seventh day of the week; the Son of man is Lord every day, not just of the seventh day. This means that we should honour Him as He really is, in spirit and in truth every day. Did Christ die on the cross for Sabbath-keepers or for those who honour God seven days a week? The following verses shine a new light on the understanding of this topic:

"[16] <u>Let no man therefore judge you in</u> meat, or in drink, or in respect of a feast day or a new moon or <u>a sabbath day</u>: [17] which are a shadow of the things to come; but the body is Christ's" (Col. 2:16-17).

"[9] but now that ye have come to know God, or rather to be known by God, how turn ye back again to the weak and beggarly [b]rudiments, whereunto ye desire to be in bondage over again? [10] <u>Ye observe</u>

days, and months, and seasons, and years. [11] I am afraid of you, lest by any means I have bestowed labor upon you in vain" (Gal. 4:9-11).

"[1] Brothers, my heart's desire and my prayer to God is for Israel, that they may be saved. [2] For I testify about them that they have a zeal for God, but not according to knowledge. [3] For being ignorant of God's righteousness, and seeking to establish their own righteousness, they didn't subject themselves to the righteousness of God. [4] For Christ is the fulfillment[a] of the law for righteousness to everyone who believes" (Rom. 10:1-4 WEB).

"[14] For he is our peace, who made both one, and brake down the middle wall of partition, [15] having abolished in his flesh the enmity, even the law of commandments contained in ordinances; that he might create in himself of the two one new man, so making peace" (Eph. 2:14-15).

"[6] who also made us sufficient as ministers of a new covenant; not of the letter, but of the spirit: for the letter killeth, but the spirit giveth life" (2Cor. 3:6).

"[28] Come unto me, all ye that labor and are heavy laden, and I will give you rest" (Mt. 11:28).

Is the fourth commandment binding on Christians? Did Jesus keep the Sabbath according to the Jewish law? If He did, then why Pharisees and teachers of the law were plotting to kill Him for allegedly breaking the Sabbath law (Mt. 12:9-14; Mk. 3:1-6; Lk. 6:2; Lk. 13:10-17; Jn. 5:17-18; Jn. 9:16)? In reality, Jesus did not break the Sabbath because He is the fulfillment of the law and the prophets (Mt. 5:17-18). The new covenant established on the cross of Golgotha put an end of the old covenant and its sign, the Sabbath!

Certain believers might argue that, according to the New Testament, Jesus never stated directly that He has come to put an end to the "*sign*" of the Sinaitic covenant. Well, according to the New Testament, Jesus never stated directly that He has come to put an end to old covenant, sacrifices, circumcision, and so on. Yet, on the cross of Golgotha, Jesus Christ put an end to all these; yet, through daily practice of their faith, Christians have been confirming this biblical reality for almost two millenniums. Would it be pertinent to assert that Christ put an end to the old covenant, but did not put an end to the sign of that covenant? No!

The central issue in Paul's letter to the Hebrews chapter 4 is the promise of "*rest*." This promised rest is based on people's faith, not on obeying the law or keeping seventh day of the week. So, the people who believe in this promise will rest from their work. God is Spirit and His rest is in spirit; therefore, those who believe will also receive that rest in spirit. The Scripture teaches that everyone must die once, and after that be judged by God (Heb. 9:27), thus some will receive eternal rest and some will receive condemnation.

It is very obvious the fact that Sabbath-keeping believers will affirm that God never changes, thus His laws are unchangeable – a very reasonable observation. God is holy, eternal, and unchangeable. Halleluiah! However, God's approach towards His creation is different every time. Each covenant between God and humankind has a specific promise; each covenant, in comparison to the previous one, contained certain particularities. Circumcision was the sign of the Abrahamic covenant; seventh-day Sabbath was the sign of the Sinaitic (Mosaic) covenant; the Holy Spirit is God's seal on believers under the new covenant established on the cross of Golgotha, as this is a covenant of the spirit. God never changes! However, God's revelation of His will to mankind each time is distinctive.

Again, Sabbath-keepers will argue that Sinaitic covenant is eternal and Sabbath is an everlasting sign. Their statement makes sense from the Old Testament perspective! However, the following biblical verses bring to light a different reality:

"*31 Behold, the days come, says Yahweh, that I will*

make a new covenant with the house of Israel, and
with the house of Judah: [32] not according to the
covenant that I made with their fathers in the day
that I took them by the hand to bring them out of
the land of Egypt; which my covenant they broke,
although I was a husband to them, says Yahweh.
[33] But this is the covenant that I will make with the
house of Israel after those days, says Yahweh: I will
put my law in their inward parts, and in their heart
will I write it; and I will be their God, and they shall
be my people" (Jer. 31:31-33).

"[13] Bring no more vain offerings. Incense is an abom-
ination to me; new moons, Sabbaths, and convoca-
tions: I can't bear with evil assemblies" (Is. 1:13).

"[11] I will also cause all her celebrations to cease: her
feasts, her new moons, her Sabbaths, and all her
solemn assemblies" (Hos. 2:11).

These verses confirm the fact that Yahweh, the God of Israel,
was going to make a new covenant with His people, and put
an end to Sabbath and religious festivities. Thus, the "*(eternal)*
Sinaitic covenant" and the "*(eternal) Sabbath sign*" become
terminable, limited to the new covenant that was to be established. In this case, it is appropriate to affirm that the expression
"*eternal*", which is biblically attributed to the Sinaitic covenant
and Sabbath, was in effect for generations until the old covenant
was replaced by the new one. The cross of Golgotha marks the
end of the covenant established on Mount Sinai (Horeb) – it
also marks the beginning of the new covenant established on the
cross of Golgotha.

Certain believers, however, consider that "*new covenant*" in
Christ did not put an end to Sabbath-keeping; therefore, they
regard themselves as believers of the new covenant and at the
same time keep the old covenant Sabbath. To be a Christian,
that is to say, to be a believer under God's new covenant and
at the same time keep Sabbath, the sign of the old covenant,
reflects partiality and ignorance of Scripture. Christians of Jewish

descent who, to conform with religious tradition of their ances-
tors chose to observe the Sabbath, demonstrate a very honourable act. This, however, reflects compromise – the Holy Spirit
does not condone compromise.

Other believers assert that the prophecy concerning God's
new covenant has not come true yet, therefore, they dishonour
Christ's Calvary on the Cross – for them the destruction of the
Temple in 70 AD, which put an end to sacrifices and offerings,
and the emergence of Christianity seem to be just random historical incidents. Such believers are in dilemma. It seems that their
alternative is to observe the requirements of the Sinaitic covenant
sealed with the blood of animals – a disputable topic nowadays
– and hope for a new covenant.

The Sinaitic covenant and seventh-day Sabbath are interre-
lated, interconnected. The law, Sabbath being part of it, was in
charge of the people for many generations – it was meant to
lead them to Christ, that they might be justified by faith. When
justification by faith came, the old covenant law and its sign, the
Sabbath, are no longer needed. This reasoning is confirmed by
the following Bible verses:

> "*19 What then is the law? It was added because of
> transgressions, till the seed should come to whom
> the promise hath been made; and it was ordained
> through angels by the hand of a mediator*" (Gal.
> 3:19).

> "*24 So that the law is become our tutor to bring us
> unto Christ, that we might be justified by faith.
> 25 But now that faith is come, we are no longer under
> a tutor*" (Gal. 3:24-25).

The argument based on Genesis 2:2-3 and Exodus 20:8-11,
according to which the seventh-day Sabbath was sanctified at
creation, thus was observed ever since, is inconsistent. The fact
that the words "*Sabbath*" and "*Sabbath-keeping*" are not found
in the Book of Genesis, and that there is no biblical evidence to
confirm that patriarchs before Moses were keeping the Sabbath is

a confirmation of it. Therefore, it is quite evident that seventh-day Sabbath keeping was ordained on Mount Horeb (Sinai).

B. Is the old covenant law binding on Christians?

The old covenant law is still a debatable topic within Christianity nowadays. Many believers assert that the Ten Commandments are binding on Christians; others, however, strongly believe that Christians are bound to Christ's Two Commandments of (agape) love. An explorative analysis of this issue leads to the following reasoning:

1) The law is for lawbreakers, not for the righteous (1Tim. 1:9-11). There is no condemnation to them which are in Christ Jesus, who live not after the flesh, but after the Spirit. For the law of the Spirit of life in Christ Jesus has set him free from the law of sin and of death (Rom. 8:1-2). If a believer is led by the Spirit, he is not under the law (Gal. 5:18). According to the New Testament, Christ has brought the law to an end, so that everyone who believes is put right with God (Rom. 10:4).

2) If a believer sins, he falls from God's Grace and becomes bound to the Ten Commandments, as the law gives him knowledge of what sin is – transgression of the law (1Jn. 3:4; Rom. 7:7).

3) Jesus' two commandments of love (agape): "*love your God and love your neighbour*" are much greater than the Ten Commandments. There is no greater commandment than these two – the entire law and the prophets depend on these two commandments (Mt. 22:36-40; Mk. 12:28-31; Lk. 10:25-27; Rom. 13:9-10).

4) Are Christians bound to the covenant established on Mount Sinai, as the Ten Commandments are the "<u>basis</u>" of that covenant (Ex. 34:27-28; Deut. 4:13; Deut. 9:9,11,15; 1Kg. 8:21)? If one is bound to something, then he becomes the subject of that something. God is Spirit, and this Spirit is the source of eternal life. If one put his faith in the Spirit, the result will be eternal life. If one puts his faith in the law carved on stone tablets, the consequence will be the one similar to a

stone tablet, for humankind in its imperfection cannot obey the entire law.

5) Sabbath keeping is not mentioned in the New Testament; however, the calling to observe the other nine commandments is stated many times. Therefore, the New Testament mentions keeping of only <u>nine commandments of the Decalogue</u>. As Jesus Christ put an end to the Sinaitic covenant, He also put an end to the sign of that covenant – the seventh-day Sabbath. Jesus said: "*come to me ... and I shall give you rest*" (Mt. 11:28); thus, believers have rest (Sabbath) in Christ and through Christ. The old covenant Sabbath was a shadow of things to come (Col. 2:16-17), a shadow of the true Sabbath, Christ Jesus.

The law was introduced because of human wickedness and stands as a constant reminder of sin: do not do this or that. However, the law has a relative effectiveness, as it cannot fully comprise human potential to sin. That is why Christ's two commandments of (agape) love, on which depend the entire law carved on stone tablets or written in the Torah (Pentateuch) and the prophets, are superior. God is love (1Jn. 4:8, 16); God's Providence throughout the universe is manifested through agape love. Therefore, the commandment of love is a perfect law.

Obeying the law is a consequence of faith. No one obeys anything unless he believes in it. No law can be observed without faith, without believing in the purpose of that law. So, the central thing in the law is faith. The voice of God speaks to us through our faith saying: "*be holy because I am holy!*" Therefore, anything that does not come from faith is a sin (Rom. 14:23). The law is inactive as long as there's no transgression of the law. When transgression occurs, the law becomes active; being activated by sin, it pinpoints towards the part that has been transgressed. Therefore, the law is for lawbreakers. If a commandment is transgressed, the lawbreaker is condemned by it. Apart from law, sin is dead (Rom. 7:8).

Abraham believed God and it was accounted to him for righteousness (Gal. 3:6-7; Rom. 4:13-16); Moses believed Yahweh, the God of Israel, and was found worthy of receiving the Ten

Commandments. The Old Testament patriarchs were accepted as righteous by God because of their faith. Their actions were the result of their faith; therefore, faith is central in the life of believers.

According to the Old Testament, it was believed that blessing and salvation come by keeping the law, the Ten Commandments. If this is so, then why did God later speak through his faithful servant, the prophet Jeremiah, of another covenant?

It is very evident the fact that the law regarding killing, committing adultery, stealing, and so on are still standing for those who are not led by the Spirit.

The central concern for Sabbath-keepers seems less the Decalogue but the fourth commandment. All their attention is directed towards safeguarding the seventh-day Sabbath. They apply as well the rule: if one commandment is broken, then the whole law is broken.

Christians keep the Ten Commandments. Christian fourth commandment sound like this: Worship the Lord your God in spirit and in truth every day. For He is the Sovereign Lord, holy and eternal, the Creator of heaven, earth, sea, and all that is in it; He is the source of life and the sustainer of the universe. Remember the dolorous passion of our Lord Jesus Christ on the cross of Golgotha; remember the day of His resurrection, a joyful day, a memorial of God's new creation.

Seventh-day Sabbath is a part of the Decalogue – the fourth commandment. Sabbath is also a part of the Sinaitic covenant – the sign of agreement between Yahweh and Israel. Seventh-day Sabbath is a memorial of deliverance from Egyptian slavery (Deut. 5:15). According to the New Testament, believers are free from the law, which once held them prisoners; no longer do they serve in the old way of a written law, but in the new way of the Spirit (Rom. 7:6). Therefore, Sabbath law is no longer applicable to believers under the new covenant.

The truth is that Christians are morally bound to Christ's commandments of the new covenant – a covenant of the spirit with its laws *put into people's minds and written on their hearts*"; they are no longer bound to the old covenant (sealed with the blood of animals) and to its sign, the seventh-day Sabbath. As prophesied, Jesus Christ put an end to the shadow – the old covenant and its ordinances (sacrifices, circumcision, Sabbath, and religious festivities). The curtain hanging in the Temple being torn in two, from top to bottom, when Jesus died on the cross (Mt. 27:51; Mk. 15:38; Lk. 23:45), and the destruction of Jerusalem and the Temple in 70 AD, which put an end to religious sacrifices and offerings – all these clearly confirm the fulfillment of Bible prophecy.

As mentioned before, the Decalogue represents only a relative reminder of what sin is. For a Christian, to be in harmony with the teachings of the New Testament, addition of at least several extra commandments to the Decalogue is absolutely necessary. These are: commandments to prohibit slavery and polygamy, as the Ten Commandments and Torah tolerate them, and a commandment to annul the useless physical circumcision, the sign of Abrahamic covenant, which later was incorporated into the Mosaic covenant. On the other hand, there are no specific laws regarding moral and judicial rights of women in the patriarchal society of the old covenant law; there are no specific laws regarding moral sexual conduct with concubines, widows, unmarried women, prostitutes, and women prisoners of war; the law regarding privilege and authority of the firstborn fails to demonstrate brotherly love and justice. Furthermore, a system governed by *"eye for eye and life for life"* rule does not reflect divine and loving nature of God as taught in the New Testament. The old covenant law and its practical applicability is a debatable issue for believers under the new covenant.

Some believers will assert that the Sinaitic Decalogue is compensated by Christ's two commandments of love. This is a very interesting remark. However, nobody uses a piece of new cloth to patch an old garment (Lk. 5:36-37) – reasonable believers hold onto the newness of God's new covenant established on Golgotha.

Christian believers are morally bound to Christ's

commandments of agape love. On these two commandments hang the entire law (Ten Commandments, Torah) and
the prophets. There is no law against such things as love, joy,
peace, patience, kindness, goodness, faithfulness, humility, and
self-control – the fruits of the Spirit (Gal. 5:22-23). The new
covenant believers are not subject to the Sinaitic covenant (Heb.
8:13). Those who maintain a different opinion on this biblical
issue have the freedom of choice; however, they should choose
wisely.

The Ten Commandments (the law) represent the basis of the
old covenant (Ex. 34:27-28; Deut. 4:13; Deut. 9:9, 11, 15; 1Kg.
8:21). Christ's two commandments of love represent the basis of
the new covenant. The Ten Commandments and the prophets
reflect Christ's two commandments of agape love (Mt. 22:36-
40). Christ's commandments reflect divine and loving nature of
God, as Christ is the image of the invisible God (Col. 1:15; Heb.
1:3), and as God is agape love (1Jn. 4:8,16). Christians are put
right with God through faith, not through law; for the "*letter
(law) killeth, but the Spirit giveth life*" (2Cor. 3:6). Observance of
the law is a consequence of faith. God's new covenant established
on Golgotha has clear authority over the covenant established on
Mount Sinai. This reasoning is confirmed by the following Bible
verses:

> "27 *Yahweh said to Moses, "Write you these words:
> for <u>in accordance with these words I have made a
> covenant with you and with Israel</u>." 28 He was there
> with Yahweh forty days and forty nights; he neither
> ate bread, nor drank water. <u>He wrote on the tablets
> the words of the covenant, the ten commandments</u>"
> (Ex. 34:27-28).*

> "13 *He declared to you <u>his covenant</u>, which he
> commanded you to perform, <u>even the ten command-
> ments</u>. He wrote them on two stone tablets" (Deut.
> 4:13).*

> "11 *It came to pass at the end of forty days and forty*

nights, that Yahweh gave me <u>the two stone tablets, even the tablets of the covenant</u>" (Deut. 9:11).

"⁸ Moses took the blood, and sprinkled it on the people, and said, "<u>Look, this is the blood of the covenant</u>, which Yahweh has made with you concerning all these words""" (Ex. 24:8).

"³¹ Behold, <u>the days come, says Yahweh, that I will make a new covenant</u> with the house of Israel, and with the house of Judah" (Jer. 31:31).

"²⁷ And <u>he took</u> [p]<u>a cup</u>, and gave thanks, and gave to them, saying, Drink ye all of it; ²⁸ <u>for this is my blood of the</u> [q]<u>covenant</u>, which is poured out for many unto remission of sins" (Mt. 26:27-28; also Mk. 14:23-24).

"²⁰ And the cup in like manner after supper, saying, <u>This cup is the new covenant in my blood</u>, even that which is poured out for you" (Lk. 22:20).

"²³ For I received of the Lord that which also I deliver unto you, that the Lord Jesus in the night in which he was [h]betrayed took bread; ²⁴ and when he had given thanks, he brake it, and said, This is my body, which [i]is for you: this do in remembrance of me. ²⁵ In like manner also the cup, after supper, saying, <u>This cup is the new covenant in my blood</u>: this do, as often as ye drink it, in remembrance of me" (1Cor. 11:23-25).

"³⁶ Teacher, which is the great commandment in the law? ³⁷ And he said unto him, [n]<u>Thou shalt love the Lord thy God</u> with all thy heart, and with all thy soul, and with all thy mind. ³⁸ This is the great and first commandment. ³⁹ [o]And a second like unto it is this, [p]<u>Thou shalt love thy neighbor</u> as thyself. ⁴⁰ On these two commandments the whole law hangeth, and the prophets" (Mt. 22:36-40).

"34 _A new commandment I give unto you, that ye love one another;_ [o]_even as I have loved you, that ye also love one another_" (Jn. 13:34; also Jn. 15:12,17; 1Jn. 3:23).

"6 who also _made us sufficient as ministers of a new covenant; not of the letter, but of the spirit_: for the letter killeth, but the spirit giveth life" (2Cor. 3:6).

"9 For this, [e]_Thou shalt not commit adultery, Thou shalt not kill, Thou shalt not steal, Thou shalt not covet, and if there be any other commandment, it is summed up in this word, namely, Thou shalt love thy neighbor as thyself._ 10 Love worketh no ill to his neighbor: _love therefore is the fulfilment of the law_" (Rom. 13:9-10).

"19 Now we know that what things soever the law saith, it speaketh to them that are under the law; that every mouth may be stopped, and all the world may be brought under the judgment of God: 20 because [k]_by_ [l]_the works of the law shall no flesh be_ [m]_justified in his sight; for_ [n]_through the law cometh the knowledge of sin_. 21 But now apart from the law a righteousness of God hath been manifested, being witnessed by the law and the prophets; 22 even _the righteousness of God through faith_ [o]_in Jesus Christ unto all_ [p]_them that believe_; for there is no distinction; 23 for all [q]_have sinned, and fall short of the glory of God;_ 24 _being justified freely by his grace through the redemption that is in Christ Jesus_" (Rom. 3:19-24).

"3 For what saith the scripture? [d]And _Abraham believed God, and it was reckoned unto him for righteousness_" (Rom. 4:3).

"1 Being therefore _justified_ [a]_by faith,_ [b]_we have peace with God through our Lord Jesus Christ;_ 2 through whom also we have had our access [c]_by_ *faith into this grace wherein we stand; and [d]we [e] rejoice in hope of the glory of"* (Rom. 5:1-2).

"¹ Brethren, my heart's [a]desire and my supplication to God is for them, that they may be saved. ² For I bear them witness that they have a zeal for God, but not according to knowledge. ³ For being ignorant of God's righteousness, and seeking to establish their own, they did not subject themselves to the righteousness of God. ⁴ For Christ is the end of the law unto righteousness to every one that believeth" (Rom. 10:1-4).

"⁵ We being Jews by nature, and not sinners of the Gentiles, ¹⁶ yet knowing that a man is not [l]justified by the works of the law but through faith in Jesus Christ, even we believed on Christ Jesus, that we might be justified by faith in Christ, and not by the works of the law: because by the works of the law shall no flesh be" (Gal. 2:15-16).

"¹⁰ For as many as are of the works of the law are under a curse: for it is written, [k]Cursed is every one who continueth not in all things that are written in the book of the law, to do them. ¹¹ Now that no man is justified [l]by the law before God, is evident: for, [m] The righteous shall live by faith" (Gal. 3:10-11).

Are Christians bound to the Ten Commandments of the Sinaitic covenant? This question is quite complex. Christ put an end to the law. However, did He not put an end to the moral law (do not kill, do not steal, do not commit adultery, and so on)? Christians are under God's grace, not under law. A believer under grace is not subject to the law; for the law is not for the righteous, but for the lawless and disobedient (1Tim. 1:9-10). Nevertheless, a believer living in concordance with the will of God, morally, ought to be able to make the distinction between good and evil. Therefore, for those who are led by the Spirit, the Ten Commandments are a reminder of what is good and what is evil; however, for those who are <u>under the law</u>, the Decalogue is binding.

The Ten Commandments, as mentioned previously, harbour contradiction: do not prohibit slavery and polygamy; tolerate social, judicial, and religious discrimination of women; uphold unjustified privilege and authority of the firstborn. A society governed by the law that tolerates slavery, polygamy, gender inequality, and many other things is compromised morally. In this case, Christ's Two Commandments of love entirely substitute the Ten Commandments (the law). God is love (1Jn. 1:8, 16). Agape love reflects God's caring and loving nature – the Divine Providence. Love is beyond law, beyond human comprehension. The following Bible verses confirm this reasoning:

"24 So that <u>the law is become our tutor to bring us unto Christ, that we might be justified by faith</u>. 25 But now that faith is come, <u>we are no longer under a tutor</u>" (Gal. 3:24-25).

"6 who also <u>made us sufficient as ministers of a new covenant; not of the letter, but of the spirit</u>: for the letter killeth, but the spirit giveth life" (2Cor. 3:6).

"18 But <u>if ye are led by the Spirit, ye are not under the law</u>" (Gal. 5:18).

"36 Teacher, which is the great commandment in the law? 37 And he said unto him, [n]<u>Thou shalt love the Lord thy God</u> with all thy heart, and with all thy soul, and with all thy mind. 38 This is the great and first commandment. 39 [o]And a second like unto it is this, [p]<u>Thou shalt love thy neighbor</u> as thyself. 40 On these two commandments the whole law hangeth, and the prophets" (Mt. 22:36-40).

"34 <u>A new commandment I give unto you, that ye love one another</u>; [o]even as I have loved you, that ye also love one another" (Jn. 13:34; also Jn. 15:12,17; 1Jn. 3:23).

God is Spirit (Jn. 4:24). God is also love (1Jn. 4:8, 16) and light (1Jn. 1:5). God's new covenant established on the cross of Golgotha is a covenant of the Spirit. It is based on Christ's two commandments of love. Therefore, Christians are servants of the new covenant – not of the law (written or carved on stone tablets) but of the Spirit; for the law kills, but the Spirit gives life (2Cor. 3:6).

Are Christians bound to Christ's Two Commandments of love, the basis of God's new covenant established on the cross of Golgotha, or to the Ten Commandments, the basis of the Sinai covenant? Are Christians to serve in newness of the spirit or in oldness of the letter? This is a good question to consider for those with a sincere heart.

C. How are people converted to Adventism?

Christianity has always been confronted with various challenges. Extra-biblical teachings and spiritually abusive doctrines have often inflicted division and confusion among believers. Therefore, such things cannot pass unnoticed. A devout Christian may be puzzled by the following question: How do Adventists, despite several incontestable biblically controversial doctrines, manage to convert believers of other religious denominations to Adventism? The answer to this question is simple: by promoting tendentious interpretation of the Bible.

Seventh-day Adventists are indoctrinated with the following teachings:

1) Adventists keep the Ten Commandments; other believers keep only nine (or eight) commandments.

2) Seventh-day Sabbath is God's perpetual sign of His eternal covenant with His people; it is a symbol of redemption in Christ [Belief 19 (Belief 20 following the insertion of a new belief in 2005)].

3) Sabbath is the seal of God; Sunday is the mark of the beast (Ellen G. White's writings).

4) On October 22, 1844 Christ entered into the Most Holy Place of the Heavenly Sanctuary; on this date, Christ entered the second and last phase of His atoning ministry, the investigative judgment of the professed believers [Belief 23 (Belief 24 following the insertion of a new belief in 2005), Ellen White's writings].

5) Ellen G. White is the Lord's messenger (a prophet) and her writings are a continuous and authoritative source of truth in Adventist Church [Belief 17 (Belief 18 following the insertion of a new belief in 2005), vow 8, and other Adventist publications].

6) Seventh-day Adventist Church is the remnant church of God of the last days [Belief 12 (Belief 13 following the insertion of a new belief in 2005)].

Christian response to these allegations is this:

1) Christians keep *"Christ's Two Commandments of love"* of God's new covenant. On these two commandments depends the whole law and the prophets (Mt. 22:36-40; Mk. 12:28-31; Lk. 10:25-27; Rom. 13:9-10).

Adventists endeavor to keep the Ten Commandments (the law). Nevertheless, just as the Israelites of the Old Testament, Adventists are facing similar problems concerning the relative comprehension of practical application of the law (including Sabbath). In reality Adventists break the Sabbath law on every Sabbath day.

2) Seventh-day Sabbath is a sign of the covenant between Yahweh and Israel (Ex. 31:13, 16-17; Ezek. 20:12, 20), a memorial of deliverance from Egyptian slavery (Deut. 5:15). Thus, Sabbath is not a sign of the covenant between Yahweh and Christians – Sabbath keeping makes no sense under the new covenant. The word *"Sabbath"* does not occur in the Books of Genesis and Revelation. There are no verses in the New Testament to confirm Sabbath keeping; however, the observance of nine remaining commandments is mentioned many times.

For a Christian, the Lord's Supper (Holy Communion) and the Baptism are the symbols of redemption in Christ (Lk. 22:19-20; 1Cor. 11:23-25; Mt. 26:26-28; Mk. 14:22-23; Mt. 28:19). Jesus Christ had been accused by the Pharisees of breaking the Sabbath law (Mt. 12:9-14; Mk. 3:1-6; Lk. 13:10-17; Jn. 5:17-18; Jn. 9:15-16; Mt. 12:1-2 also Mk. 2:23-34; Lk. 6:1-2). Therefore, Sabbath (the seventh-day of the week) cannot be a symbol of redemption in Christ for believers under the new covenant.

The law of the Sinaitic covenant (including Sabbath) was given 430 years after the covenant with Abraham, and was in charge of believers to lead them to Christ (Gal. 3:17-19, 24-25). On the cross of Golgotha, Jesus Christ put an end to the Sinaitic covenant and its law (Jer. 31:31-33; Heb. 8:7-13; 2Cor. 3:6; Rom. 7:6; Rom. 8:1-3; Rom. 10:1-4; Eph. 2:15; 1Cor. 9:20-21; Gal. 3:10-11; Gal. 5:18; 1Tim. 1:9-10; Jn. 13:34). If Christ put an end to the old covenant, it is very evident that He also put an end to the sign of that covenant – the seventh-day Sabbath (Is. 1:13; Hos. 2:11; Col. 2:14-17; Gal. 4:9-11; Eph. 2:15; Mk. 2:27-28; Mt. 11:28). Jesus Christ fulfilled the law and the prophets (Mt. 5:17-18; Jn. 17:4-6; Jn. 19:30; Mt. 11:28).

3) The Holy Spirit is God's seal on His people (Eph. 1:13; Eph. 4:30; 2Cor. 1:22). Sunday, the first day of the week, is a memorial of Jesus Christ's "resurrection", a memorial of a new creation, a day of joy; it is a day when the apostles and other first century Christians were meeting for prayer, worship, and the Lord's Supper (Holy Communion). Christians are believers of God's new covenant sealed with the blood of Jesus, the Lamb of God – it is a covenant of the Spirit, not of the written law (2Cor. 3:6; Rom. 7:6).

Seventh-day Sabbath is never presented in the Bible as the seal of God but as a sign of the covenant between Yahweh and the people He brought out of Egypt.

4) The sanctuary doctrine, which is partially described in Belief 23 (Belief 24 following the insertion of a new belief in 2005), contradicts the teachings of the New Testament. The

"October 22, 1844 Christ" of the Sanctuary doctrine is a blasphemous myth.

5) Any prophet is tested by his prophecy. If the prophecy comes true, then he is a true prophet of God. Ellen White failed this test – her so-called "prophecies" did not come true. Lately, several truth seekers have demonstrated Ellen G. White's plagiarism in her writings – there are many copies and borrowings in her so-called "inspired writings." Certain teachings and advice of Ellen White are contradictory.

6) The remnant church represents those believers who honour God in spirit and in truth, those who have the seal of God, the Holy Spirit, those who keep the commandments of God and the testimony of Jesus Christ. The true remnant church of God cannot accept the "October 22, 1844 Christ" of the blasphemous sanctuary doctrine. God's divine glory is much more than the Ten Commandments, much more than 613 laws of the Torah – it is beyond our comprehension!

Believers who manifest partiality regarding the "*word of God and the testimonies of Jesus*" are compromised. God is Spirit; therefore, true believers worship God "*in spirit and in truth*", not through man-made doctrines!

Those who accept Adventist teachings initially do not see doctrinal double standards of the Advent Church. Later, some of those believers discover the hidden side of the truth; however, they find themselves already deeply rooted in that religious system. For some of them, leaving that church seems rather a creaky decision – too much self-sacrifice at stake.

Seventh-day Advent Church seems to have some success these days in those countries where people have limited access to information, therefore limited choice.

The Lord's Day

The Holy Scripture provides many references regarding the day of the Lord. Nowadays, there is a tendency to speculate on this topic. Some believers assert that the seventh-day Sabbath is the Lord's Day. Such an assumption, however, is inconsistent because the entire Christianity identifies the Lord's Day with the day of resurrection of Jesus Christ, which took place on Sunday – the first day of the week. It is nonsense to assert that the Lord's Day is the seventh-day Sabbath – the day when Jesus Christ lay dead in a tomb. The Lord's Day is a day of the living Christ, not of a dead one.

According to the Old Testament, Sabbath is a "*sign*" of the covenant between Yahweh and the people He liberated from Egyptian slavery (Ex. 31:13, 16-17; Deut. 5:15; Ezek. 20:12). The fourth commandment Sabbath is part of the law. Due to its demands, what to do and what one is not allowed to do on the seventh day, the Sabbath has become rather a burden despite its significance – "*Sabbath*" meaning "*rest.*" In fact, Sabbath keeping was mandatory; transgressing the Sabbath law was punished with death penalty (Ex. 31:15; Ex. 35:2). God's new covenant is based on commandment of (agape) love; therefore, it cannot uphold a law that brings death. Believers of the new covenant are under grace, not under law. The assertion, "Sabbath is the Lord's Day", is unreasonable.

In the Old Testament, the day of the Lord is described as a day of God's anger and fury, a day of punishment (Is. 13:9; Amos. 5:20; Zeph. 1:14-15). Nevertheless, the Bible also declares that God's glorious day is coming, the day of our Lord Jesus Christ's return. For some people, this will be a day of judgment; for God's people, however, it will be a day of joy and reward.

In the New Testament, the Lord's Day is described as a day of joy and peace. On this day, Christians were assembling to commemorate Jesus Christ's resurrection, partake of the Lord's

Supper (Holy Communion), and pray together. Early Christians identified Sunday, the first day of the week, as:

1) The day when Jesus Christ was resurrected (Mt. 28:1-9; Mk. 16:1-7; Lk. 24:1-7; Jn. 20:1-9).

2) The day when Jesus appeared to the apostles and many other believers (Mt. 28:1, 9, 16-18; Mk. 16:9-14; Lk. 24:1, 13-35; Jn. 20:1, 14-20, 26-27).

3) The day when the Holy Spirit descended from heaven upon the followers of Jesus Christ (Acts 2:1-4). This refers to Pentecost, which always falls on the first day of the week (Lev. 23:15-16).

The word "*Lord*" in the New Testament is often associated with two particular words. These are: the "*Lord's Day*" and the "*Lord's Supper*." It makes sense to partake of the Lord's Supper on the Lord's Day! Partaking of the Lord's Supper on Saturday (Sabbath) does not sound good!

Controversy over the Lord's Day is stirred up by those who do not give proper credit to the New Testament. Some believers consider that a little bit of compromise is condoned by God, thus they consciously attribute certain characteristics of the Sinaitic covenant to the new covenant established on the cross of Golgotha. On the other hand, some consider that the verse "*I was in the Spirit on the Lord's day*" (Rev. 1:10) refers to the seventh-day Sabbath. In this regard, it is nonsense to assert that John, a Christian, identified the Lord's Day with the seventh-day Sabbath – the day when Jesus lay dead in a tomb; John received the Revelation on the first day of the week – on the Lord's Day, the day of resurrection of our Lord Jesus Christ!

A. Historical evidence of early Christian worship on the first day of the week[25]

The following extracts from historical documents confirm that early Christians were gathering for worship on Sunday, the first day of the week:

- BARNABAS (100 AD): "We keep the eighth day [Sunday] with joyfulness, the day also on which Jesus rose from the dead" (*The epistle of Barnabas, 15:6-8*).

- BARNABAS (100 AD): "Moreover God says to the Jews, 'Your new moons and Sabbaths I cannot endure.' You see how he says, 'The present Sabbaths are not acceptable to me, but the Sabbath which I have made in which, when I have rested [heaven: Heb 4] from all things, I will make the beginning of the eighth day which is the beginning of another world.' Wherefore we Christians keep the eighth day for joy, on which also Jesus arose from the dead and when he appeared ascended into heaven" (*15:8f, The Epistle of Barnabas, 100 AD, Ante-Nicene fathers, vol.1, p.147*).

- JUSTIN (150 AD): "But if we do not admit this, we shall be liable to fall into foolish opinion, as if it were not the same God who existed in the times of Enoch and all the rest, who neither were circumcised after the flesh, nor observed Sabbaths, nor any other rites, seeing that Moses enjoined such observances... For if there was no need of circumcision before Abraham, or of the observance of Sabbaths, of feasts and sacrifices, before Moses; no more need is there of them now, after that, according to the will of God, Jesus Christ the Son of God has been born without sin, of a virgin sprung from the stock of Abraham" (*Dialogue With Trypho the Jew, 150-165 AD, Ante-Nicene Fathers, vol. 1, p. 206*).

- JUSTIN (150 AD): "And on the day called Sunday, all who live in cities or in the country gather together to one place and the memoirs of the apostles or the writings of the prophets are read, as long as time permits; then, when the reader has ceased, the president verbally instructs, and exhorts to the imitation of these good things [...] But Sunday is the day on which we all hold our common assembly, because it is the first day on which God, having wrought a change in the darkness and matter, made the world; and Jesus Christ our Saviour on the same day rose from the dead. For He was crucified on the day before that of Saturn (Saturday); and on the day after that of Saturn, which is the day of the Sun, having appeared to His apostles and disciples, He taught them these things, which we have submitted to you also for your consideration" (*First apology of Justin, Weekly Worship of the Christians, Ch.68*).

- JUSTIN (150 AD): "We are always together with one another. And for all the things with which we are supplied we bless the Maker of all through his Son Jesus Christ and through his Holy Spirit. <u>And on the day called Sunday there is a gathering together in the same place of all who live in a city or a rural district</u>. (There follows an account of a Christian worship service, which is quoted in VII.2.) <u>We all make our assembly in common on the day of the Sun, since it is the first day</u>, on which God changed the darkness and matter and made the world, and Jesus Christ our Saviour arose from the dead on the same day. <u>For they crucified him on the day before Saturn's day</u>, and on the day after (which is the day of the Sun) he appeared to his apostles and taught his disciples these things" (*Apology, 1, 67:1-3, 7; First Apology, 145 AD, Ante-Nicene Fathers, Vol. 1, p. 186*).

- CLEMENT of ALEXANDRIA (190 AD): "he does the commandment according to the Gospel and <u>keeps the Lord's Day</u>, whenever he puts away an evil mind...glorifying the <u>Lord's resurrection</u> in himself" (*Vii.xii.76.4*).

- TERTULLIAN (200 AD): "<u>We solemnize the day after Saturday in contradiction to those who call this day their Sabbath</u>" (*Tertullian's Apology, Ch 16*).

- TERTULLIAN (200 AD): "Let him who <u>contends that the Sabbath is still to be observed a balm of salvation, and circumcision on the eighth day because of threat of death</u>, teach us that in earliest times righteous men kept Sabbath or practiced circumcision, and so were made friends of God. ...Therefore, since God originated <u>Adam</u> uncircumcised, and <u>inobservant of the Sabbath</u>, consequently his offspring also, <u>Abel</u>, offering Him sacrifices, uncircumcised and <u>inobservant of the Sabbath</u>, was by Him commended... <u>Noah</u> also, uncircumcised – yes, and <u>inobservant of the Sabbath</u> – God freed from the deluge. For <u>Enoch</u>, too, most righteous man, uncircumcised and inobservant of the Sabbath, He translated from this world... <u>Melchizedek</u> also, "the priest of most high God," uncircumcised and <u>inobservant of the Sabbath</u>, was chosen to the priesthood of God" (*An Answer to the Jews 2:10; 4:1, Ante-Nicene Fathers Vol. 3, p. 153*).

- TERTULIAN (200 AD): "Others... <u>suppose that the sun is the god of the Christians, because it is well-known that we regard Sunday as a day of joy</u>" (*To the Nations 1:133*).

- The DIDASCALIA (225 AD): "The apostles further appointed: <u>On the first day of the week let there be service</u>, and the reading of the Holy Scripture, and the oblation <u>because on the first day of the week our Lord rose from the place of the dead</u>, and on the first day arose upon the world, and <u>on the first day of the week he ascended up to heaven</u>, and on the first day of the week he will appear at last with the angels of heaven" (*Didascalia 2*).

- CYPRIAN (250 AD): "<u>The eighth day, that is the first day after the Sabbath, and the Lord's Day</u>" (*Epistle 58, Sec 4*).

- IGNATIUS (250 AD): "If, therefore, those who were brought up in the ancient order of things <u>have come to the possession of a new hope, no longer observing the Sabbath, but living in the observance of the Lord's Day, on which also our life has sprung up again by Him and by His death</u>-whom some deny, by which mystery we have obtained faith, and therefore endure, that we may be found the disciples of Jesus Christ, our only Master [...] <u>Let us therefore no longer keep the Sabbath after the Jewish manner</u>, and rejoice in days of idleness; for "he that does not work, let him not eat." For say the [holy] oracles, "In the sweat of thy face shalt thou eat thy bread." <u>But let every one of you keep the Sabbath after a spiritual manner</u>, rejoicing in meditation on the law, not in relaxation of the body, admiring the workmanship of God, and not eating things prepared the day before, nor using lukewarm drinks, and walking within a prescribed space, nor finding delight in dancing and plaudits which have no sense in them. <u>And after the observance of the Sabbath, let every friend of Christ keep the Lord's Day as a festival, the resurrection-day, the queen and chief of all the days [of the week]</u>. Looking forward to this, the prophet declared,

"To the end, for the eighth day", on which our life both sprang up again, and the victory over death was obtained in Christ, whom the children of perdition, the enemies of the Saviour, deny, "whose god is their belly, who mind earthly things," who are "lovers of pleasure, and not lovers of God, having a form of godliness, but denying the power thereof [...]" (*Epistle of Ignatius to the Magnesians, Chapter IX*).

- IGNATIUS (250 AD): "On the day of the preparation, then, at the third hour, He received the sentence from Pilate, the Father permitting that to happen; at the sixth hour He was crucified; at the ninth hour He gave up the ghost; and before sunset He was buried. <u>During the Sabbath He continued under the earth in the tomb in which Joseph of Arimathaea had laid Him. At the dawn of the Lord's day He arose from the dead</u>, according to what was spoken by Himself, "As Jonah was three days and three nights in the whale's belly, so shall the Son of man also be three days and three nights in the heart of the earth." <u>The day of preparation, then, comprises the passion; the Sabbath embraces the burial; the Lord's Day contains the resurrection</u>" (*Epistle of Ignatius to the Trallians, chap. 9*).

- EUSEBIUS (300 AD): "They did not, therefore, regard circumcision, <u>nor observe the Sabbath neither do we; ...because such things as these do not belong to Christians</u>" (*Ecc. Hist., Book 1, ch.4*).

- EUSEBIUS (300 AD): "[The Ebionites] <u>were accustomed to observe the Sabbath and other Jewish customs but on the Lord's Day to celebrate the same practice as we in remembrance of the resurrection of the Saviour</u>" (*Church History III.Xxvii.5*).

- EUSEBIUS (300 AD): "They [the pre-Mosaic saints of the Old Testament] did not care about circumcision of the body, neither do we [Christians]. <u>They did not care about observing Sabbath, nor do we</u>. They did not avoid certain food, neither did they regard the other distinctions <u>which Moses first delivered</u> to their posterity to be observed as symbols; <u>nor do Christians of the present day do such things</u>" (*Church History 1:4:8*).

- EUSEBIU of CAESAREA (300 AD): "The day of his

[Christ's] light... was the day of his resurrection from the dead, which they say, as being the one truly holy day and the Lord's day, is better than any number of days as we ordinarily understand them, and better than the days set apart by the Mosaic Law for feasts, new moons, and Sabbaths, which the Apostle [Paul] teaches are the shadow of days and not days in reality" (*Proof of the Gospel 4:16:186*).

- ATHANASIUS (345 AD): "The Sabbath was the end of the first creation, the Lord's Day was the beginning of the second, in which he renewed and restored the old in the same way as he prescribed that they should formerly observe the Sabbath as a memorial of the end of the first things, so we honor the Lord's day as being the memorial of the new creation" (*On Sabbath and Circumcision 3*).

- APOSTOLIC CONSTITUTIONS (350 AD): "[...] And on the day of our Lord's resurrection, which is the Lord's day, meet more diligently, sending praise to God that made the universe by Jesus, and sent Him to us, and condescended to let Him suffer, and raised Him from the dead. Otherwise what apology will he make to God who does not assemble on that day to hear the saving word concerning the resurrection, on which we pray thrice standing in memory of Him who arose in three days, in which is performed the reading of the prophets, the preaching of the Gospel, the oblation of the sacrifice, the gift of the holy food?" (*Constitutions of the Holy Apostles, book 2*)

- APOSTOLIC CONSTITUTIONS (350 AD): "[...] But keep the Sabbath, and the Lord's day festival; because the former is the memorial of the creation, and the latter of the resurrection. But there is one only Sabbath to be observed by you in the whole year, which is that of our Lord's burial, on which men ought to keep a fast, but not a festival. For inasmuch as the Creator was then under the earth, the sorrow for Him is more forcible than the joy for the creation; for the Creator is more honourable by nature and dignity than His own creatures" (*Constitutions of the Holy Apostles, book 7*).

- APOSTOLIC CONSTITUTIONS (350 AD): "How we

ought to assemble together, and to celebrate the Festival Day of Our Saviour's Resurrection. <u>On the day of resurrection of the Lord, that is, the Lord's day, assemble yourselves together, without fail</u>, giving thanks to God, and praise Him for those mercies God has bestowed upon you through Christ, and has delivered you from ignorance, error, and bondage, that your sacrifice may be unspotted, and acceptable to God, who has said concerning His universal Church: "In every place shall incense and a pure sacrifice be offered unto me; for I am a great King, saith the Lord Almighty, and my name is wonderful among the heathen" (*Constitution of the Holy Apostles, book 7*).

- CYRIL of JERUSALEM (350 AD): "<u>Fall not away</u> either into the sect of the Samaritans or into Judaism, for Jesus Christ has henceforth ransomed you. <u>Stand aloof from all observance of Sabbath</u> and from calling any indifferent meats common or unclean" (*Catechetical Lectures 4:37*).

- COUNCIL of LAODICEA (360): "<u>Christians should not Judaize and should not be idle on the Sabbath, but should work on that day</u>; they should, however, particularly reverence <u>the Lord's day and, if possible, not work on it, because they were Christians</u>" (*Canon 29*).

- AUGUSTINE (412 AD): "<u>Well, now, I should like to be told what there is in the Ten Commandments, except the observance of the Sabbath, which ought not be kept by a Christian</u>... Which of these commandments would anyone say that the Christian ought not to keep? It is possible to contend that it is not the Law which was written on those two tables that the apostle [Paul] describes as 'the letter that kills' [2Cor 3:6], but the law of circumcision and the other sacred rites which are now abolished" (*The Spirit and the Letter 24*).

B. Is the Lord's Day of pagan origin?

Certain Sabbatarian arguments concerning the *"Lord's Day"* are based on extra-biblical assertions of Arthur Weigall, which were published in his book, The Paganism of Our Christianity. According to A. Weigall, Christian Sunday worship has its origin in pagan Mithraism. However, the truth is that Arthur Weigall also states the following:

1) #28: The "Lord's Day" (Sunday) is of pagan origin: "The Hebrew Sabbath having been abolished by the Christians, the Church made a sacred clay of Sunday, partly because it was the day of resurrection, but largely because it was the weekly festival of the sun; for it was a definite Christian policy to take over the pagan festivals endeared to the people by tradition, and to give them a Christian significance. But, as a solar festival, Sunday was a sacred day of Mithra; and it is interesting to notice that since Mithra was addressed, as Dominus, 'Lord', Sunday must have been 'the Lord's Day' long before the Christian times" (The Paganism of Our Christianity, Arthur Weigall, 1928, p.136)[26][27].

2) #29: Jewish Sabbath and the Sunday Lord's Day both are of pagan origin: "In the early Christian Church there were no festivals, holy days, or Sabbaths"…"I have, already mentioned that Sunday, too, was a pagan holy-day; and in this chapter I propose to discuss the origin of this custom of keeping one day in the week as a Sabbath, or "day of rest", and to show that the practice was forcefully opposed by Jesus Christ. The origin of the seven-day week, which was used by the Jews and certain other peoples, but not till late by the Greeks and Romans, is to be sought in some primitive worship of the moon, for the custom of keeping the day of the new moon and that of the full moon as festivals, which is widely found in antiquity, implies the recognition of a cycle of about 14 days, of which a week of seven days is a half, the actual length of a week thus determined being 7 3/8 days. Now the Babylonians had an early adopted the seven-day week, and their calendars contain directions for the abstention from certain secular acts on stated days, which seemed to correspond to seventh days, and called "Sabbath"; and though the Jewish Sabbath cannot be directly traced to Babylonian usage, the institution is obviously derived from

moon-worship and from the concomitant recognition of number seven as calendaristically sacred. The Jews attribute the holiness of the 'seventh day' to the fact that God was supposed to have rested from His six-day creative labours on that day; but this was itself a legend derived from Babylonian mythology, and was not the original reason why the seventh day was a day of rest" (*The Paganism of Our Christianity*, Arthur Weigall, 1912, p. 209, 210-211)[26][27].

3) #30: Conclusion of entire book:

Almost all of Christianity is of pagan origin! "A fact which must be clear to those who have read the foregoing chapters is that Christianity developed into a religion in a lurid pagan environment, which could not fail to have its influence upon the new faith" (*The Paganism in Our Christianity*, Arthur Weigall, 1928, p. 242)[26][27].

According to A. Weigall, almost all of Christianity is of pagan origin – an open attack on Christianity. The following (selected) quotations from the same source[24][25] confirm it:

- The twelve disciples derive from Zodiac (*p. 25*);
- The 27 books of the New Testament Canon are not valid (*p. 37*);
- The name Mary is of pagan origin (*p. 41*);
- The virgin birth is of pagan origin (*p. 44, 47, 60*);
- Jesus born in a stable and wrapped in swaddling clothing is of pagan origin (*p. 52*);
- Miracles of Jesus are of pagan origin (*p. 58*);
- Jesus' Crucifixion was a Jewish human sacrifice of pagan origin (*p. 69, 76*);
- Ascension is of pagan origin (*p. 100*);
- Jesus descends into Hades is of pagan origin (*p. 113*);
- Jesus "the Rock of Salvation" is of pagan origin (*p. 129*);
- Jesus "the slain Lamb of God" is of pagan origin (*p. 131, 132*);
- Jesus "the Shepherd" is of pagan origin (*p. 136*);
- Baptism and the Lord's Supper both are of pagan origin (*p. 134, 146-147*);

- The idea of blood atonement for the sins is of pagan origin (*p. 152, 158*);

- Incarnate Logos of John 1:1 is of pagan origin. The "pre-existent angel" is a 4th century concept (*p. 172, 173-175*);

- The Trinity is of pagan origin (*p. 182*);

- The "Lord's Day" (Sunday) is of pagan origin (*p. 209, 210-211*);

- Jewish Sabbath and the Sunday Lord's Day are both of pagan origin (*p. 136, 209, 210-211*);

- Conclusion of entire book: Almost all of Christianity is of pagan origin! (*p. 242*).

The book asserts that Sunday has its origin in Mithraism and Sabbath has its origin in Babylonia pagan worshiping. If Arthur Weigall is such a valuable scholar, then why not taking into account all his statements.

Should these provocative allegations be viewed as a sincere attempt to solve a religious polemic or a stratagem orchestrated by the same deceptive spirit who some two thousand years ago instigated first century Christians into rejecting the "*Gospel of Salvation*" preached by the apostle Paul to believers of Gentile origin? It is very evident the fact that this is a direct attack on Christianity. Its aim is to provoke confusion among believers who are weak in faith and ultimately seduce them into rejecting Christ and God's new covenant. These provocateurs do not come with solutions to the problem — their weapon of choice of is an open denial of God's Word. Consequently, unaware people are led astray, thus the chain of deception continues.

C. Are Saturday and Sunday of pagan origin?

In ancient times, days of the week were named after the planets of our solar system and pagan deities. Saturday, "*Dies Saturni*", was the day of the planet Saturn and also the day of Saturn, the Roman god of agriculture; Sunday, "*Dies Solis*", was the day of the sun; Monday was the day of the moon... and so on – such naming of the days of the week is still in use nowadays. Pagan worship was practiced every day.

The rise of Christianity – the new religion of the first century

– definitively changed the course of history. On the cross of Golgotha, Jesus Christ – the prophesied Messiah – established God's new covenant. On Sunday, three days after His death and burial, Jesus was resurrected; on Sunday, Jesus revealed Himself to the apostles and other believers; on Pentecost, which always falls on Sunday, the Holy Spirit descended upon the apostles and other followers of Christ; on Sunday, the first day of the week, Christians were assembling for the worship and partaking the Lord's Supper. All these have one thing in common: Sunday. According to the logic of A. Weigall, Jesus Christ's resurrection, the descent of the Holy Spirit upon believers on the day of Pentecost, Christian habit of assembling for worship on Sunday, and so forth, all these imply Mithra worship. Such assertion is absurd! Does the verse "*I was in the Spirit on the <u>Lord's Day</u>*" (Rev. 1:10) imply that John (a Christian Jew), who received the Apocalypse, was a Mithra worshiper? Certainly not!

Are Saturday and Sunday of pagan origin? The real issue here is a provocation – its aim is to obscure and distort the image of Christianity. Consistent historical evidence confirms that conspiracy, deception, and distorted interpretation of the Bible are often the weapons of choice of the occult.

Christians do not regard Sunday as a day of worship of the sun. For them, Sunday, the first day of the week, represents the "*day of resurrection of our Lord Jesus Christ – the Lord's Day*."

The teaching according to which "Sunday worship is sun worship" is a conspiracy. Promoters of this deception often use as an arguments the Egyptian obelisk located in the center of St. Peter's Square (Vatican), which they associate with Egyptian worship of the sun. Nevertheless, they deliberately neglect two facts: 1) the <u>cross</u> on top of the obelisk; 2) the following <u>inscription</u> on base of the obelisk: "*Christus Vincit, Christus Regnat, Christus Imperat, Christus ab omni malo plebem suam defendat*", which means "Christ is the victor, Christ is the king, Christ is the ruler, may Christ defend His people from all evil."

A reasonable, unbiased believer cannot assume that, due to an obelisk, Christianity is a sun-worship religion, just as one cannot assume that ancient Israelite religion was a pagan-worship religion just because of the existence on its territory of some pagan altars and isolated pagan worship. A definitive conclusion cannot be based on a block of stone. Therefore, regardless of the motives [symbol of Christ's victory over the power of darkness, aesthetics, or non-Christian influence (infiltration) to obscure the Roman Catholic Church], which led to the erection of the obelisk, it should not be a burden for true Christians. In this regard, it is pertinent to mention that the real intention of the Renaissance architects was to incorporate Gregorian calendar – the new calendar of the western Christianity – into St. Peter's Square located in front of St. Peter's Basilica in Vatican City. However, for those who have doubts about this matter, the following verse may be useful.

> "21 They say unto him, Caesar's. Then saith he unto them, Render therefore unto Caesar the things that are Caesar's; and unto God the things that are God's" (Mt. 22:21; also Mk. 12:17; Lk. 20:25).

Associating Sunday, the day of Christ's resurrection, with pagan worship of the sun and consequently polluting people's faith with such deceptive teaching has a very specific purpose: 1) to create a bad image of the "Lord's Day"; 2) to discredit Christianity in general. The enemies of Christianity should not be underestimated – their hostility is manifested in various forms and has no limits.

Some believers assert that certain Christian holidays have a pagan background. They say that on December 25, the day when western society celebrates Christmas, was a pagan holiday before Christianity became official religion of the Roman Empire; they assert that on this date was celebrated the "Birthday of the Unconquered Sun (Dies Natalis Solis Invicti)"[28]. What about hundreds of millions of Orthodox believers celebrating Christmas on the 7th of January, as the Orthodox Church still use Julian calendar? If certain pagan holidays have been replaced by Christian holidays, then wise believers should perceive the work of the Holy Spirit in this because Christians honour God on these particular holydays, not some pagan deities. However, officiation and spiritual manifestation of these holidays, its impact on the people, is another topic of discussion.

Other believers assert that Christian holidays seem to be commercialized, thus giving the impression of celebrating things, of buying and selling, of idolatry, therefore, lacking spiritual discernment. The truth is that perception and interpretation of the Bible varies from one individual to another. For some believers, certain religious practices are very important; for others, however, such things seem to be irrelevant or even offensive spiritually. Secularism often makes use of religious discordances to the detriment of Christianity.

Vital role of both the Orthodox and Catholic Churches within Christianity is incontestable. These two churches carry the torch of Christian faith passed down by the apostles for almost two millennia. This mission came with a cost clearly described in the Bible (Jn. 12:24) – many "grains of wheat (saints)" had to fall into the ground and die to produce the fruit of Christianity the mankind enjoy nowadays. However, there are certain things of which both churches are not comfortable to talk about: controversial decisions and actions taken in the past that somewhat damaged the image of Christianity. In this regard, there is a tendency among some believers in Western society to speculate on these controversial episodes of Christianity. These believers, however, seem to omit certain historical facts:

- Both churches (Byzantine and Roman Catholic) had to face similar provocations, and both churches were involved in the use of military force to solve religious conflicts. Eastern caesaropapism and Western papocaesarism often imposed its authority on the people;

- Religious persecution of believers who propagated teachings considered as heretical by the Byzantine Church and Muslim military expansion in the East determined many people to seek refuge on the territory of the former Western Roman Empire. Consequence, Western Europe became a nourishing ground for pseudo-Christian ideologies and other biblically controversial teachings that constantly erode Christianity;

- Both churches had disputes over ecclesiastical and theological differences, which consequently led to schism in 1054. However, the permanent alienation between Orthodox and Catholics took place in 1204, when the fourth crusade sacked Constantinople. On this date, the Byzantine splendor much envied by Rome was crushed.

Regarding the controversy over the day of rest and worship, it is very obvious that promotors of "Sunday – day of the sun" deception, deliberately or out of ignorance, neglect an undisputable fact: "<u>Saturday – day of the Saturn</u>", a reality of historical and religious importance constantly overlooked by some scholars and preachers.

Which of the following days is of paramount importance for a Christian?

- "Dies Saturni" (day of the Saturn);
- "Dies Solis" (day of the sun);
- "*Dies Domini*" (the Lord's Day).

Definitely, it is the "*day of resurrection of Jesus Christ, our Lord and Saviour.*" Halleluiah!

The Sabbath controversy

The Holy Scripture is divinely inspired and represents a source of truth for believers. The Creator, in His Providence, has granted mankind the freedom to choose. It is our Christian duty to use this freedom in the light of truth revealed in the New Testament. Freedom of choice based on compromise is in contradiction with the word of God, thus can be used as a weapon of darkness.

Nowadays, the topic concerning Sabbath observance under the new covenant still is a stumbling stone for some believers. These believers regard seventh-day Sabbath, the sign of the old covenant, as an integral part of the new covenant established on the cross of Golgotha. In this sense, to resolve this ideological confusion and prevent the spread of biblically controversial teachings, a thorough analysis of the Scripture is absolutely indispensable.

A. What does the Holy Scripture teach about the seventh day of the week?

In the Holy Scripture it is written:

1) Sabbath, the seventh day of the week, is a day of rest, a holy day (Ex. 20:8-11).

2) Sabbath is an eternal sign of the eternal covenant between Yahweh and Israel, a sigh of sanctification (Ex. 31:13, 16-17; Ezek. 20:12, 20).

3) Sabbath is a memorial of deliverance from Egyptian slavery (Deut. 5:15).

The Holy Scripture also teaches the following:

1) The Law (including Sabbath) came 430 years after the covenant with Abraham (Gal. 3:17); it was introduced through Moses on Mount Sinai, and was in charge of people to bring them to Christ (Gal. 3:19, 24-25).

2) God has made a new covenant with his people; it is a covenant with God's law put in their minds and written in their hearts – a covenant of the Spirit, not of written law (Is. 42:6-7; Jer. 31:31-33; Heb. 8:7-12; 2Cor. 3:6).

3) According to this new covenant, the Holy Spirit is God's seal (sign) on His people (Eph. 1:13; Eph. 4:30; 2Cor. 1:22).

4) According to the Old Testament, the following days are also declared holy:

- Fifteenth day of the first month is holy (Ex. 12:2, 6, 14, 16; Lev. 23:6-7; Num. 28:17-18);

- Twenty-first day of the first month is holy (Ex. 12:16; Lev. 23:8; Num. 28:25);

- First day of the seventh month is holy (Lev. 23:23-25; Neh. 8:2, 9-11);

- Tenth day of the seventh month is holy (Lev. 23:26-32; Num. 29:7);

- Fifteenth day of the seventh month is holy (Lev. 23:33-35; Num. 29:12).

Do Sabbath keepers observe these holy days?

5) According to the Old Testament, the following religious holidays and practices are declared everlasting:

- Passover Festival (Ex. 12:12-14, 24);
- Festival of Unleavened Bread (Ex. 12:17; Lev. 23:6,14);
- Day of Atonement (Lev. 16:29-34);
- Festival of Tabernacle (Lev. 23:34, 41);
- Bread offerings (Lev. 24:5-8);
- Daily Burned Offerings (Ex. 29:38-42);
- Circumcision (Gen. 17:9-14; Ex. 12:44, 47-49);

Do Sabbatarians observe these everlasting requirements?

6) The first Apostolic Council of Jerusalem was decreed that Gentile converts to Christianity keep these necessary rules: eat no food that has been offered to idols, eat no blood, eat no animal that has been strangled, and to abstain from sexual immorality (Acts 15:28-29). Seventh-day Sabbath observance is not mentioned. Was that an incident?

7) According to Paul's letter to the Colossians, Sabbath is a

shadow of things to come (Col. 2:16-17);

8) Adventists may claim that, according to the Book of Acts, the apostle Paul kept the Sabbath. However, a careful analysis of the Book of Acts unveils the following biblical reality:

- Paul was preaching in the synagogues on Sabbath to Jews and to Greeks converted to Judaism – it is very obvious that Paul's preaching on Sabbath was purely evangelical;

- According to Acts 21:20-21, Paul had been accused of teaching Jews that were living among the Gentiles to forsake Moses (the Law);

- Riots against Paul instigated by the Jews in several cities confirm the fact that the apostle Paul was not living in accordance with the Law of Moses – Paul was not a Sabbath keeper;

- There is no biblical evidence of Christian worship on Sabbath.

Seventh-day Adventists assert that Jesus Himself kept the Sabbath – rather a rhetorical attempt to resuscitate a lost cause. Jesus had been circumcised on the eighth day; He also kept religious holy days required by the Jewish law. However, Jesus observed the Sabbath *"in spirit and in truth"*, not according to the law. Adventists deliberately omit an undeniable biblical reality: Pharisees plotted to kill Jesus for transgressing the Sabbath. Ultimately, Jesus had been arrested, condemned, and crucified for allegedly transgressing the <u>first</u> and of the <u>fourth commandments</u> as mentioned previously (see: Jn. 5:17-18; Mt. 12:9-14; Mk. 3:1-6; Lk. 6:2; Lk. 13:10-17; Jn. 9:16).

The sun does not set for about three months during the summer solstice of the polar circle zone. There's no sunrise-sunset and morning-evening cycle during this period of the year. How does the forth commandment Sabbath apply to people living there? What about Sabbath keeping during the polar nights of the winter solstice – the opposite phenomenon of polar days of the summer solstice?

B. What does the Holy Scripture teach about the first day of the week?

In the Holy Scripture it is written:

1) Jesus Christ was resurrected on Sunday, the first day of the week (Mt. 28:1-9; Mk. 16:1-7; Lk. 24:1-7; Jn. 20:1-9).

2) Jesus Christ revealed Himself to His followers on the first day of the week (Mt. 28:1, 9, 16-18; Mk. 16:9-14; Lk. 24:1, 13-35; Jn. 20:1, 14-20, 26-27).

3) The promised gift, the Holy Spirit, descended upon Christian believers on the day of Pentecost – the birthday of the Christian church (Acts 2:1-4). Jewish feast of Pentecost always fell on Sunday, the first day of the week (Lev. 23:15-16).

4) Early Christians assembled for prayer and partaking of the Holy Communion on the first day of the week (Acts 20:7; 1Cor. 11:17-22; 1Cor. 16:1-2).

Sunday, the first day of the week, is a miniature of the Easter – the Christian Pascha crowned with the resurrection of Jesus Christ. Nevertheless, some believers will argue that the death and resurrection of our Lord Jesus Christ should be commemorated every day. That is true! Christians honour the memory of Christ's death and resurrection daily through prayer and public profession of their Christian faith. However, they also assemble on Sunday for worship and partaking of the Holy Communion (also called the Eucharist or Lord's Supper).

Many Christians assert that, just as the Sinaitic covenant had a sign, the Sabbath, God's new covenant also has a sign. In this sense, there are differences of opinion as follows:

- The cross, on which God, through Christ, established a new covenant with His people;

- Sunday, the day of the resurrection of Jesus Christ, a day of rest and worship for Christians;

- Baptism, the rite of submersion or affusion in water, symbolizing the believer's death to sin, the burial of the old life, and the resurrection to walk in the newness of life in

Jesus Christ – the sacrament of initiation into Christ's holy church and admission into the Christian community;

- The Lord's Supper (Holy Communion), the rite or sacrament of partaking of the bread and wine symbolizing the body and blood of Jesus that sealed God's new covenant.

All the above mentioned symbol and rites are equally important. These values clearly define Christian identity and reflect the mystery, the beauty, and the glory of God's new covenant in Christ. However, this new covenant is a covenant of the spirit (2Cor. 3:6; Rom. 7:6); therefore, the sign of the new covenant should be a spiritual one: the Holy Spirit – the seal of God (Eph. 1:13; 4:30; 2Cor. 1:21-22). True believers worship God in spirit and in truth (Jn. 4:24) – they perceive and evaluate these Christian practices spiritually.

C. Saturday Sabbath or Sunday Sabbath?

Biblical significance of Sabbath, the seventh day of the week, can be summarized as follows:

- Sabbath is a sign of the Sinaitic covenant between Yahweh and Israel, a sign of sanctification;
- A memorial of delivery from Egyptian slavery;
- A memorial of the old creation under curse (Gen. 2:2; Gen. 3:17-19; Rom. 8:22-23);
- Sabbath is under the law;
- A shadow of things to come;
- Sabbath is a day of a dead Christ;
- For believers under the new covenant, Sabbath keeping involves contradiction (Is. 1:13; Hos. 2:11; Col. 2:14-17; Gal. 4:9-11; Marc 2:27-28; Mat. 11:28);
- Sabbath was never part of the message of the Gospel of Grace; it has nothing to do with salvation.

According to the New Testament, Sunday, the first day of the week, has the following biblical significance:

- Sunday is the day of the resurrection of our Lord Jesus Christ;
- On this day, Jesus revealed Himself to the apostles and other believers;

- On Pentecost, which always falls on Sunday, the Holy Spirit descended upon the apostles and other followers of Jesus Christ – the birthday of the Christian church;

- The day when early Christians assembled for worship and partaking of the Lord's Supper (Holy Communion);

- Weekly memorial of Christ's resurrection, a memorial of a new creation (2Cor. 5:17; Gal. 6:14-15);

- A day of joy;

- Sunday, the first day of the week, means the *"Lord's Day!"*

Is Saturday a Christian Sabbath? No! It was a Sabbath only for the believers under the old covenant!

Is Sunday a Christian Sabbath? In the New Testament, there is no commandment to confirm it! Christians, however, have a new day: the day of the resurrection of our Lord Jesus Christ, a memorial of a new creation. Sunday, the first day of the week, is a day of joy and rest, but is not the Sabbath of the fourth commandment.

What is the Christian Sabbath? The Lord Jesus Christ is the true Christian Sabbath! True believers honour God every day. God is Spirit; true rest (Sabbath) is a rest in spirit and in truth. The following Bible verses confirm the verity of this statement:

> *"24 [h]God is a Spirit: and they that worship him must worship in spirit and truth" (Jn. 4:24).*

> *"27 And he said unto them, The sabbath was made for man, and not man for the sabbath" (Mk. 2:27);*

> *"so that the Son of man is lord even of the sabbath" (Mk. 2:28; also Lk. 6:5; Mt. 12:8).*

> *"28 Come unto me, all ye that labor and are heavy laden, and I will give you rest" (Mt. 11:28).*

> *"4 In him was life; and the life was the light of men. 5 And the light shineth in the darkness; and the darkness [b]apprehended it not" (Jn. 1:4-5).*

> *"6 Jesus saith unto him, I am the way, and the truth,*

and the life: no one cometh unto the Father, but [d]
by me" (Jn. 14:6).

Biblical message in Mark 2:28, Luke 6:5 and Matthew 12:8 is very clear: if Jesus is Lord of the Sabbath, then true believers should honour Him, not seventh day of the week. The Son of man is Lord every day, not just on the seventh day. This means that we should honour Him as He really is, in spirit and in truth, every day. In John 14:6, Jesus Christ is revealed as the "*life*." If <u>Jesus is the "*life*"</u>, thus the source of eternal life, this means that <u>Jesus is also the "*rest*"</u>, that is, the source of eternal rest (eternal Sabbath)!

Jesus Christ is the "*way, the truth, and the life*" (Jn. 14:6); He is also the rest (Mt. 1:28) – our true Sabbath. However, if a

Christian wishes to have a day of rest and worship, than let this day be the day of the resurrection of our Lord Jesus Christ!

According to the Old Testament, Yahweh declared to the people He brought out of Egypt that "*they won't enter into my rest*" (Ps. 95:11; Heb. 3:11; Heb. 4:3). Later, God spoke of another day: "*Today, oh that you would hear his voice! Don't harden your hearts*" (Ps. 95:7-8; Heb. 3:15; Heb. 4:7). Paul's Letter to the Hebrews chapter 4 provides more details in this regard. According to the apostle Paul, Israelites did not enter God's rest because they did not believe. However, those who believe enter that rest. Therefore, to enter God's rest is a matter a faith – it is to believe in the "*word of God and the testimony of Jesus Christ*." The following Bible verses corroborate this reasoning:

> "*7 for he is our God. We are the people of his pasture, and the sheep in his care. <u>Today, oh that you would hear his voice! 8 Don't harden your heart</u>, as at Meribah, as in the day of Massah in the wilderness, 9 when your fathers tempted me, tested me, and saw my work" (Ps. 95: 7-9).*

> "*10 Forty long years I was grieved with that genera-tion, and said, "It is a people that errs in their heart.*

They have not known my ways." [11] Therefore I <u>swore in my wrath, "They won't enter into my rest"</u>" (Ps. 95:10-11).

"[3] [c]For <u>we who have believed do enter into that rest</u>; even as he hath said, [d][e]As I sware in my wrath, [f]They shall not enter into my rest: although the works were finished from the foundation of the world" (Heb. 4:3).

"[6] Seeing therefore it remaineth that some should enter thereinto, and they to whom [j]the good tidings were before preached failed to enter in because of disobedience, [7] <u>he again defineth a certain day, To-day</u>, saying in David so long a time afterward (even as hath been said before), [k]<u>To-day if ye shall hear his voice, Harden not your hearts</u>" (Heb. 4:6-7).

"[8] For <u>if [l]Joshua had given them rest, he would not have spoken afterward of another day</u>. [9] There remaineth therefore a sabbath rest for the people of God. [10] For he that is entered into his rest hath himself also rested from his works, as God did from his" (Heb. 4:8-10).

"[13] Bring no more vain offerings. Incense is an abomination to me; new moons, <u>Sabbaths</u>, and convocations: <u>I can't bear with evil assemblies</u>" (Is. 1:13).

"[11] <u>I will also cause all her celebrations to cease</u>: her feasts, her new moons, <u>her Sabbaths</u>, and all her solemn assemblies" (Hos. 2:11).

"[14] having blotted out [g]the bond written in ordinances that was against us, which was contrary to us: and he hath taken it out of the way, nailing it to the cross; [15] [h]having despoiled the principalities and the powers, he made a show of them openly, triumphing over them in it. [16] <u>Let no man therefore judge you</u> in meat, or in drink, or <u>in respect of a feast day or a new moon or a sabbath day</u>: [17] which *are a shadow of the things to come; but the body is Christ's" (Col. 2:14-17);*

"9 but now that ye have come to know God, or rather to be known by God, how turn ye back again to the weak and beggarly [b]rudiments, whereunto ye desire to be in bondage over again? 10 Ye observe days, and months, and seasons, and years. 11 I am afraid of you, lest by any means I have bestowed labor upon you in vain" (Gal. 4:9-11).

"14 For he is our peace, who made both one, and brake down the middle wall of partition, 15 having abolished in his flesh the enmity, even the law of commandments contained in ordinances; that he might create in himself of the two one new man, so making peace" (Eph. 2:14-15).

"11 Now that no man is justified [l]by the law before God, is evident: for, [m]The righteous shall live by faith" (Gal. 3:11).

Bible verse "...*I desire mercy, not animal sacrifice...*" (Hos. 6:6; Mt. 9:13; 12:7) seem to be in contrast with the old covenant law! Mercy is a manifestation of the work of the Holy Spirit on the mind and heart of believers; whereas animal sacrifices, offerings, and circumcision represent a physical manifestation of the requirements of the law. God desires our kindness and goodness, our daily conduct "*in spirit and in truth*" – these are not subject to the law. Jesus Christ is the end of the old covenant and its law (the Sabbath law); Christ is the beginning of a new covenant, a covenant governed by the two commandments of (agape) love!

According to the Old Testament, Sabbath – the seventh day of the week – is a memorial of creation (Ex. 20:8-11) and deliverance from Egyptian bondage (Deut. 5:15). According to the New Testament, Sunday – the first day of the week – is a memorial of Christ's resurrection, a memorial of a new creation and deliverance from bondage of sin.

"7 And upon the first day of the week, when we were

gathered together to break bread, Paul discoursed with them, intending to depart on the morrow; and prolonged his speech until" (Acts 20:7).

"17 Wherefore if any man is in Christ, [h]he is a new creature: the old things are passed away; behold, they are become new" (2Cor. 5:17).

"14 But far be it from me to boast, except in the cross of our Lord Jesus Christ, through which the world has been crucified to me, and I to the world. 15 For in Christ Jesus neither is circumcision anything, nor uncircumcision, but a new creation" (Gal. 6:14-15 WEB).

"6 who also made us sufficient as ministers of a new covenant; not of the letter, but of the spirit: for the letter killeth, but the spirit giveth life" (2Cor. 3:6).

"4 but when the fulness of the time came, God sent forth his Son, born of a woman, born under the law, 5 that he might redeem them that were under the law, that we might receive the adoption of sons. 6 And because ye are sons, God sent forth the Spirit of his Son into our hearts, crying, Abba, Father" (Gal. 4:4-6).

"4 even as he chose us in him before the foundation of the world, that we should be holy and without blemish before [c]him in love: 5 having foreordained us unto adoption as sons through Jesus Christ unto himself, according to the good pleasure of his will, 6 to the praise of the glory of his grace, [d]which he freely bestowed on us in the Beloved: 7 in whom we have our redemption through his blood, the forgiveness of our trespasses, according to the riches of his grace" (Eph. 1:7).

"28Come unto me all you that labour and are heavy laden, and I will give you rest" (Mt. 11:28).

Lord's rest or seventh day rest?

This question turns out to be a test of faith and knowledge of the word of God for many believers. The Epistle of Paul to the Hebrews chapter 4 provides a valuable clue in this regard.

Long ago God declared to the people of Israel: "*I swore in my wrath, "They won't enter into my rest"*" (Ps. 95:11; Heb. 4:3-5). They did not enter into God's rest because they did not believe (Heb. 3:18-19; Heb. 4:6), because they did not accept it with faith (Heb. 4:2). There are, then, others who are allowed to receive it. This is shown by the fact that God sets another day, which is called "*Today*" (Heb. 4:6-7). Many years later God spoke of it through David in the Scripture already quoted: "*Today, oh that you would hear his voice! Don't harden your heart*" (Ps. 95:7-9; Heb. 4:7). What is the significance of the word "*today*" in this context? It means today, tomorrow, the day after tomorrow; it means any day (Heb 3:13). It means that any time, when someone hears the voice of God speaking to him about the Gospel of Salvation, he should not be stubborn – he should believe.

According to the fourth commandment, the day of rest is associated with the creation. However, there's no biblical evidence to confirm that, after the completion of His work of creation, God continued creating, which would imply another cycle of mornings and evenings, days and nights, thus another seventh day rest. This biblical reasoning confirms the fact that God's rest is continuing even today. God the Creator is eternal and His rest is also eternal! On the other hand, Jesus clearly stated that His Father always works (Jn. 5:17).

The Bible states: "*They won't enter into my rest!*" The message of this verse is very clear: they won't enter into "*God's <u>rest</u>*", not God's <u>day of rest</u>.

One of God's divine attributes is omnipotence. God always works (Jn. 5:17); therefore, God never rests. On the other hand, it is common sense to affirm that God, in His omnipotence, is always at His works and always at rests. God is Eternal Spirit! His rest is eternal. Therefore, God offers his children every day rest, eternal rest. One day of rest per week does not reflect God's divine and loving character revealed in the New Testament through Jesus Christ. Physically, we rest whenever we are tired, exhausted. For a Christian, however, true rest is a rest in spirit through the Holy Spirit.

It is very evident the fact that the expression "*my rest*" mentioned in Psalm 95:11 and Hebrews 4:3-5 has a spiritual significance meaning "*God's peace*" – the blessing that comes from the Holy Spirit. And even though God is always at His work, this should be understood as God's work of providence.

Jesus said:

> "[28] <u>Come unto me</u>, all ye that labor and are heavy laden, <u>and I will give you rest</u>" (Mt. 11:28).

> "[6] *Jesus saith unto him, <u>I am the way, and the truth, and the life: no one cometh unto the Father, but</u>* [d] <u>by me</u>" (Jn. 14:6).

For a Christian, the Word – *Christ Jesus* – is the source of life and rest. Christian Sabbath, the true rest, is in Christ and through Christ!

Ellen G. White – Prophetic visions or prophetic blunders?

Most Seventh-day Adventists consider Ellen G. White a prophet. Outside Adventist Church, however, prophetic authority of Ellen G. White is very controversial. To solve this Adventist prophetic puzzle, a thorough analysis of Ellen White's writings is indispensable; therefore, quotations from her writings regarding prophetic visions, teachings, and advices are absolutely necessary.

A. Ellen G. White's failed prophecies

Ellen G. White wrote[29][30][31]:

- I have seen that the 1843 chart (Wm. Miller's) was directed by the hand of the Lord and that it should not be altered that the figures were as he wanted them" (*Early Writings, p. 64 edition 1882*).

- "As God has shown me in holy vision...we heard the voice of God like many waters, which gave us the day and hour of Jesus' coming" (*Early Writings, pp.15, 34,285*).

- (First Vision 12/1844) "It was just as impossible for them (those that gave up their faith in the 1844 movement) to get on the path again and go to the city, as all the wicked world which God had rejected. They fell all the way along the path one after another," (Foregoing now deleted) "until we heard the voice of God like many waters, which gave us the day and hour of Jesus' coming. The living saints, 144.000 in number, knew and understood the voice, while the wicked thought it was thunder and an earthquake" (*A Word to the Little Flock, p.14, edition 1847*).

- **Ellen G. White forgets the hour proclaimed**: - "I have not the slightest knowledge as to the time spoken by the voice of

God. I heard the hour proclaimed, but had no remembrance of that hour after I came out of vision" (*Selected Messages 1, p.298, edition 1889*).

- **Ellen G. White lost her visions**: "In our frequent change of location in the early history of the publishing work, I have crossed the plains no less than 17 times I lost all traces of the first publishing work"..."And here I pause to state that any of our people having in their possession a copy of any or all of mine first views, as published prior to 1851, will do me a great favour if they will send them to me without delay" (*Selected Messages 1, p.60*).

- **White blames her failed prophecy on the members of the Seventh-day Adventist Church!** "Thus the work was hindered, and the world was left in darkness. Had the whole Adventist body united upon the commandments of God and the faith of Jesus, how widely different would have been our history" (*Selected Messages, Book 1, p.299*).

- "For a time after the disappointment in 1844, I did hold, in common with the advent body, that the door of mercy was forever closed to the world...I was shown in vision, and still believe, that there was a shut door in 1844" (*Selected Messages, Book 1, p.63*).

- "I was shown that... the door was opened in the most holy place in the heavenly sanctuary, where the ark is, in which are contained the Ten Commandments. This door was not opened until the mediation of Jesus was finished in the holy place of the sanctuary in 1844. Then Jesus rose up shut the door of the holy place, and opened the door into the most holy place, and passed within the second veil, where he now is standing by the ark" (*Early Writings, p.42*).

- "We gathered about Jesus, and as He closed the gates of the city, the curse was pronounced upon the wicked. The gates were shut. Then the saints used their wings and mounted to the top of the wall of the city" (*Early Writings, p.53*).

- "It is well known that many were expecting the Lord to come at the 7th month, 1845. That Christ would then come we firmly believed. A few days before the time passed, I was at Fairhaven, and Dartmouth, Mass, with a message on this point of time. At this time, Ellen was with the band at Carver, Mass, where she saw in vision, that we should be disappointed" (*A Word to the Little Flock p. 22, by James White 1847*).

- Ellen G. White prophesied the end of the world in 1843, 1844, 1845, and 1851: "Now time is almost finished (1851) and what we have been 6 years learning they will have to learn in months" (*Early Writings, p.57*).

- "[...] at the close of the 2300 days, in 1844, began the work of investigation and the blotting out of sins" (*Great Controversy, p.552*).

- "[...] Unto 2300 days, then the sanctuary be cleansed" was fulfilled in 1844 (*Great Controversy, pp.484, 475, 486*), that it was the heavenly sanctuary that was cleansed (*p.475*), and that it was the confessed sins of God's people that defiled the heavenly sanctuary" (*p.480*).

- "[...] The Proclamation, Behold the Bridegroom cometh in the summer of 1844, led thousands to expect the immediate advent of Christ. At the appointed time the Bridegroom came, not to the earth, as the people expected, but to the Ancient of Days in heaven to the marriage, the reception of His kingdom. They that were ready went in with Him to the marriage and the door was shut [...]" (*Great Controversy, p.487*).

- "[...] This work of examination of character, of determining who are prepared for the kingdom of God, is that of Investigative Judgment" (*Great Controversy, p.489*).

- "[...] in 1844...our High Priest entered the holy of holies... to perform the work of investigation judgment. The only cases considered are those of the professed people of God" (*Great Controversy, p.546*).

- "As the sins of the people were anciently transferred in figure to the earthly sanctuary by the blood of the sin-offering, so our sins are, in fact transferred to the heavenly sanctuary by the blood of Christ" (*Great Controversy, p.266, edition 1886*).

- "As anciently the sins of the people were by faith placed

upon the sin-offering and through its blood transferred in figure to the earthly sanctuary so in the new covenant the sins of the repentantly are by faith placed upon Christ" and transferred, in fact, to heavenly sanctuary" (*Great Controversy, p.421, edition 1911*).

- "When Christ by virtue of His blood removes the sins of His people from the heavenly sanctuary at the close of His ministration, He will place them upon Satan, who in execution of the judgment, must bear the final penalty" (*Great Controversy, p.481, edition 1927*).

B. Ellen G. White's visions and remarks

Ellen G. White wrote[32][33][34]:

- "In ancient times God spoke to men by the mouth of the prophets and apostles. In these days He speaks to them by the Testimonies of His Spirit" (*Testimonies for the Church, vol.4, pp.147, 148. Testimony 27; 1876*).

- "If you lessen the confidence of God's people in the Testimonies He has sent them, you are rebelling against God as certainly as were Korah, Dathan, and Abiram" (*Testimonies for the Church, vol.5, p. 66. Testimony 31; 1882*).

- "Yet, now when I send you a testimony of warning and reproof, many of you declare it to be merely the opinion of Sister White. You thereby insult the Spirit of God" (*Testimonies 5, p.64*).

- "The Lord gave me a view of the heavenly sanctuary... Jesus raised the cover of the ark, and I beheld the tablets of stone on which the Ten Commandments were written. I was amazed as I saw the forth commandment in the very centre of the ten precepts with a soft halo of light encircling it. Said the angel, it is the only one which defines the living God who created the heaven and the earth and all things that are therein" (*Life Sketches of Ellen G. White, pp.95 and 96*).

- "The four on the first (tablet) shone brighter than the other six. But the fourth, the Sabbath commandment, shone above them all...The holy Sabbath looked glorious a halo glory was all around it. I saw that the Sabbath commandment was not nailed to the cross" (*Early Writings of Ellen G. White, p.33*).

- "I saw that God had not changed the Sabbath, for he never changes. But the pope had changed it from the seventh day to the first day of the week; for he was to change times and laws" (*Early Writings of Ellen G. White, p.33*).

- "The pope has changed the day of rest from the seventh to the first day" (*Early Writings of Ellen G White, p.65*).

[**Note:** The Emperor Constantine issued a decree in 325 AD that the people should rest on Sunday, first day of the week – a reality historically confirmed. This decree has in fact ratified something that was being practiced by Christians for almost three hundred years. Papacy came to power much later].

- "The seal of God is revealed in the observance of the Seventh-day Sabbath" (*Testimonies, vol.8, p.117*).

- "The enemies of God's law, from the ministers down to the least among them, have a new conception of truth and duty. Too late they see that the Sabbath of the fourth commandment is the seal of the living God" (*Great Controversy, p.640*).

- "Here we find the mark of the beast. The very act of changing the Sabbath into Sunday, on part of the Catholic Church, without any authority from the Bible" (*The Mark of the Beast, by Ellen G. White, page 23*).

- "The Sunday Sabbath is purely a child of Papacy. It is the mark of the beast" (*Adventist Review, vol.1, No.2, August, 1850*).

- "To obey the commandments is the only way to obtain His favour" (*Testimonies, vol.2, p.84*).

- "From what was shown to me, there is a great work to be accomplished for you before you can be accepted in the sight of God" (*Testimonies, vol. 2, p.84*).

- "You have a great work to do...It is impossible for you to be saved as you are" (*Testimonies, vol.2, p.316*).

- "When the Saviour's hands were bathing those soiled feet, and wiping with the towel, the heart of Judas thrilled through and through with the impulse then and there to confess his sin" (*Desire of the Ages, p.645*).

- "He was weak and feeble through pain and suffering, caused by the scourging and blows which he had received, yet they laid on him the heavy cross upon which they were soon to nail him. But Jesus fainted beneath the burden. Three times they laid on him the heavy cross, and three times he fainted" (*Spiritual Gifts, vol.1, p.57*).

- "The Lord has given me a view of other worlds. Wings were given me, and an angel attended me from the city to a place that was bright and glorious" (*Early Writings, p.39*).

- "All angels that are commissioned to visit the earth hold a golden card, which they present to the angel at the gates of the city" (*Early Writings, p.39*).

- "Pray for the sick – We should first find out if the sick one has been withholding tithing or has made trouble in the church" (*Healthful Living, p.37*).

- "It is a sin to be sick; for all the sickness is the result of transgression" (*Councils on Health, p.37*).

- "His (Judas's) weight had broken the cord by which he had hanged himself to the tree. In falling, his body had been horribly mangled, and dogs were now devouring it. His remains were immediately buried out of site" (*Desire of the Ages, p.722*).

- "Satan appeared to be by the throne, trying to carry on the work of God. I saw them (Christians) look up to the throne, and prayed, 'Father, give us thy Spirit'. Satan would then breathe upon them an unholy influence" (*Early Writings, p.56*).

- "After Satan was shut out of heaven, with those who fell with him, he realized that he lost all the purity and glory of heaven forever. Then he repented and wished to be reinstated in heaven. He was willing to take his proper place or any place that might be assigned to him...He and his followers repented, wept and implored to be taken back into the favour of God. But no, their sin their hate, their envy and jealousy, had been so great that God could not blot it out. It must remain to receive its final punishment" (*Spiritual Gifts, vol.1, p.18, 19*).

C. Ellen G. White's teachings on diet

Ellen G. White wrote[33][30]:

- "The health reform, I was shown, is a part of the 'third angel's message' and is just as closely connected with it as are arm and hand with the body" (*Testimonies vol.1, p.486*).

- "God gave light on health reform, and those that reject it reject God!" (*Series B, No.6, p.31. EGW address to the General Conference in Orkland, published in the General Conference Bulletin, 1903, pp.84-88*).

- Ellen G. White was a health reformer but not a follower of health reform principles: "It has been reported that I have not followed the principles of health reform as I have advocated them with my pen; but I can say that I have been a faithful health reformer. Those who have been members of my family know that this is true" (*Councils on Diet and Foods, p.494*).

- "But since the Lord presented before me, in June, 1863, the subject of meat eating in relation to health, I have left the use of meat" (*Counsels on Diet and Food, p.482*).

- Ellen G. White has been eating meat and oysters for 67 years, and for 31 years after her first vision on health reform (in 1863): "I have a large family which often numbers sixteen. In it there are men who work at plow and who fell trees...Meat has not been used by us since the Brighton camp-meeting (held in 1894)..." (*Testimony Studies on Diet and Foods, p.67*).

- "Since the camping of Brighton I have banished meat from my table" (*1894: Spalding & Morgan Collection, p.81, paragraph 1*).

- "...If you can get few cans of good oysters, get them" (*Letter 16, 1882 – Manuscript Release No.852: The Development of Adventist Thinking, page 2, paragraph 3*).

- "I do not preach one thing and practice another. I do not present to my hearers rules of life for them to follow while I make an exception in my case" (*Selected Messages, Book 2, p.302, Letter 12, 1888*);

- "Those who digress occasionally to gratify the taste in eating a fattened turkey or other meats, pervert their appetites, and are not the ones to judge the benefits of the system of health reform. They are controlled by taste, not by principles" (*Counsels on Diet and Foods, p.399*).

- "Cheese should never be introduced into the stomach (*Testimonies to the Church, vol.2, p.68*).

- "Eggs should not be placed upon your table. They are an injury to your children" (*Testimonies to the Church, vol.2, p.70*).

- "Children are not allowed to eat flesh meat, spices, butter, cheese, pork, rich pastry...These things do their work of deranging the stomach" (*Testimonies, vol.3, p.136*).

- "You place on your table butter, eggs, and meat, and your children partake of them. They are fed with the very things that will excite their animal passions, and then you come to meeting and ask God to bless and save your children. How high do your prayers go?" (*Testimonies, vol.2, p.362*).

- "The use of swine's flesh is contrary to his express commandments" (*Testimonies to the Church, Vol.2, p. 96*).

- "It is just as much sin to violate the laws of our being as to break one of the Ten Commandments" (Eating a slice of bacon is as sinful as committing adultery) [*Testimonies to the Church, vol.2, p.70*].

- In the following verses, Mrs. White says, "pork is nourishing and strengthening food" and rebukes a brother for teaching that it was forbidden food: "...I saw that your views concerning swine flesh would prove no injury to you if you have them to yourself; but in your judgment and opinion you have made this question a test. If God requires his people to abstain from swine's flesh, He will convince them on the matter. If it is the duty of the church to abstain from swine flesh God will discover to more than two or three" (*Testimonies, vol.1, pp.206-207*).

- "We have positive testimony against tobacco, rich cakes, spirituous liquors, snuff, tea, coffee, flesh meat, butter, spices, mince pies" (*Testimonies vol.3, p.21*).

- "Tea and coffee drinking is a sin, an injurious indulgence, which like other evils, injures the sole" (*Counsels on Diet and Foods, p.425, edition 1896*).

- "The salads are prepared with oil and vinegar, fermentation takes place in the stomach, and the food does not digest, but decays or putrefies; as a consequence, the blood is not nourished, but becomes filled with impurity, and liver and kidney difficulties appear" (*Counsels on Diet and Foods, p.345*).

- "It is not well to eat fruits and vegetables at the same meal. If the digestion is feeble, the use of both will cause often distress and inability to put forth mental efforts" (*Counsels on Diet and Foods, p.112*).

D. Ellen G. White's diverse observations

Ellen G. White said[34][35][36]:

- "Some women have naturally small waists. But rather than regard such forms as beauty, they should be viewed as defective" (*The Health Reformer, November 1, 1871, paragraph 23*).

- "Many have lost their reason and become hopelessly insane by following this deforming fashion (hairpiece). Yet the slaves to fashion will continue to thus dress their heads, and suffer horrible disease and premature death, rather than be out of fashion" (*The Health Reformer, October 1, 1871, paragraph 11*).

- "Eating of pork has produced scrofula, leprosy, and cancerous tumours. Pork eating is still causing the most intense suffering to the human race" (*Counsels on Diet and Foods, p.393, paragraph 2*).

- "More die as the result of following the fashion than from other causes" (*Healthful Living, p.64, paragraph 275*).

- "If any among us are sick, let us not dishonour God by applying to earthly physicians, but apply to the God of Israel..." (*To those who have the seal of the Living God, January 31, 1849, paragraph 13*).

- "More deaths have been caused by drugs-taking than from all other causes combined. If there was in the land one physician in the place of thousands, a vast amount of premature mortality would be prevented" (*Selected Messages, Book 2, p.450, paragraph 2*).

- "I have been shown that the true followers of Jesus will

discard picnics, donations, shows, and other gathering for pleasure" (*1Testimony for the Church, p.288*).

- "A view of things was presented before me in which students were playing games of tennis and cricket...They were presented to me as a species of idolatry" (*Counsel to Parents, Teachers, and Students, p.350*).

- Taking pictures is idolatry: "This making and exchanging of photographs is a species of idolatry. Satan is doing all he can to eclipse heaven from our view. Let us not help him by making picture-idols" (*Message to Young People, p.316, paragraph 3, chapter title: Self Gratification. A Species of Idolatry*).

E. Ellen G. White – Prophetess or plagiarist?

Increasing disputes over the writings of Ellen G. White have become a stimulus for a thorough analysis of the history of Adventism. Several truth seekers have been determined to subject Ellen White's writings to a meticulous comparative analysis. They have concluded that her writings contain many borrowings and copies from other books published by other authors at different periods of time. Therefore, many of Ellen White's so-called inspired writings are rather inspired copies and borrowings. Dr. Walter Rea, former Adventist pastor, is one of those truth seekers who through his intensive research has demonstrated Ellen White's plagiarism[25] and published it in his book, The White Lie. Many pastors began to question the authority of Ellen White's "inspired writings." Consequently, some of them resigned, others were compelled to resign, and yet others were fired for rejecting the inspiration of Ellen White[37]. After all, it seems that certain people knew that there were some borrowings in Ellen White's writings; however, they chose to keep it from uninformed Adventists masses.

The books below represent the main sources of Ellen White's plagiarism[29][38][39]:

- The Great Teacher, by John Harris, 1836, 1870;
- The Life of our Lord and Saviour Jesus Christ, by John Fleetwood, 1844;

- Walks and Homes of Jesus Christ, by Daniel March, 1856;
- The Life of Christ, by William Hanna, 1863;
- Life Incidents, by James White, 1868;
- Night Scenes in the Bible, by Daniel March, 1868-1870;
- History of Protestantism, by J. A. Wylie, LL.D.1876;
- The Bible History, by Alfred Edersheim, 1876;
- The Life of Christ, by Frederic W. Farrar, 1877;
- The Life and Times of Jesus Christ the Messiah, by Alfred Edersheim, 1883;
- The Life and Work of Christ, by Cunningham Geikie, 1883.

Do Adventists know that before Ellen White published her book, The Great Controversy, there was already another book in circulation, The Great Controversy between God and Man[40], by Horace L. Hasting, 1858, Boston?

There were many publications on health reform in the 18th and 19th centuries promoting moderation on food and drinks, abstinence from alcohol, coffee, tea, tobacco, meat, etc. What an abundant source of inspiration for Ellen White! Could one of these sources be: Philosophy of Health[41], by L. B. Coles, 1853?

There are certain good things about Ellen White's writings, no doubt about that. The problem, however, is the source of those good things. Are her writings a direct inspiration from above, that is, from God? As mentioned before, thorough analysis of this issue reveals a different picture: her writings contain many borrowings and copies from other books! Whether or not, at that time, there was a law concerning plagiarism is less relevant now; what matters is the fact that the source of her writings are predominantly other books written by other authors. In this regard, some Adventists could argue that a person cannot write so many valuable books without divine guidance. That is an interesting observation! However, it is also a known fact that Mr. White made a very good income on royalties from the books she published.

F. Ellen G. White – Visions or seizures?

At the age of nine, Ellen G. White (born Ellen Gould Harmon) had a severe accident inflicted by a classmate who threw a stone at her, hitting her in the face (nose) – the fact stated in her biography. However, what is not mentioned but can be deduced these days is the fact that, most probably, she suffered a double head injury, as she fell on the ground unconscious. This incident had devastating physical and mental consequence on Ellen G. Harmon, as she had to drop school and never come back due to her health status, which for several years would not allow her to do that. Was Ellen G. Harmon aware of her health status? Of course, since her childhood! Her parents took her to several doctors, who, at that time, could not be of much help. Growing up in a family of believers, it is very obvious the fact that the young Ellen often found her refuge and comfort in reading the Bible.

Before going any further, it is appropriate to mention that Ellen G. Harmon had good results at school before the accident, and that such mishap can occur to anyone.

Going through Ellen White's writings, one can find description of her status during the visions. In medical terminology, her status may be described as altered state of consciousness and cardiorespiratory hypofunction. Nowadays, a person manifesting such symptoms may be suspected, among others, of a certain form of epilepsy. From medical point of view, people who had a severe head injury may later develop a certain form of epilepsy – the fact clinically confirmed.

Ellen White's writings provide a clear description of her mental status: visual, auditory, and olfactory hallucinations, which, most probably, are the consequence of head injury. In this regard, there is considerable evidence that Ellen White suffered of post-traumatic epilepsy. Therefore, her visions should be rather regarded as the product of constant reading of religious material combined with her mental condition. Hypergraphia, quite probably, is one of the symptoms of her mental status – it is a well-known fact that Ellen White wrote many books.

1) Visual, auditory, and olfactory hallucinations symptoms from Ellen G. White's own words[42]:

Hearing voices and smelling flowers:
EGW MS 29, 1901 – 'That Wednesday evening, still dreading the next day's carousal, she found a little anteroom and lay down. She fell asleep, but soon was awaken by a voice speaking to her. As she gained her senses, she knew what it meant. "<u>The room was filled with sweet fragrance, as beautiful flowers</u>". Then she fell asleep again once more and was awaken in the same way' (*The Early Elmshaven Years, vol.5, 1900-1905, by Arthur L. White (1981), p.23, paragraph 6*).

Seeing light and smelling flowers a hundred or more times:
MS 43a, 1901, – EGW mentions "a hundred times or more". In reporting the experience, she says, "I was asking the Lord where I should go and what I should do. I was for backing out.... Well, while I was praying and was sending up my petition, there was, <u>as has been a hundred times or more, a soft light circling around in the room, and fragrance like the fragrance of flowers, of a beautiful scent of flowers</u>" [*MS 43a, 1901. Ellen G. White (1981), p.53*].

Light filled the room, odor of violets, and heard a voice telling her to go to Dr. Kellogg's house:
Kellogg interview, 1907, p.66, – *Interview between J. H. Kellogg MD and Elders G. W. Amadon, and A. C. Bordeau. Notarized October 7, 1907, by J. T. Case, p.66*. "The third letter stated, 'Last Friday night when we were having family prayer, <u>a light filled the room and an odor of violets and a voice spoke to me and said, Go to Dr. Kellogg's house</u>' and so I am coming". (*EGW Estate letter, K-33 dated February 23, 1901, and is reproduced in "The Blue Book" called "A Response to An Urgent Testimony", p.53 by Charles Steward MD in 1907*).

None of the family saw the light or smelled a fragrance or heard voices:
General Conference Bulletin, 1901, p.204 – Did the others kneeling in worship that Friday evening <u>see the light and noticed the fragrance</u>? This is very natural question, which she

answered as she recounted the incident on April 11 at the general Conference session: "Though none of the family saw what I saw, or heard what I heard, yet they felt the influence of the Spirit, and were weeping and praising God" *(--GCB 1901, p.204)*.

After smelling the roses, seeing a silvery light her pain disappeared:

Salamaca, New York November 3, 1890 – After this, weary, weak, and perplexed, she thought to retire to her room and pray. Climbing the stairs, she knelt by the bed, and before the first word of petition had been offered she felt that the room was filled with the fragrance of roses. Looking up to see whence the fragrance came, she saw the room flooded with a soft, silvery light. Instantly her pain and weariness disappeared. The perplexity and discouragement of mind vanished, and hope and comfort and peace filled her heart. [*Life Sketches of Ellen G. White (1915), p. 310; Life Sketches pp. 310-320*].

A room filled with light, a white cloud with pink edges, hearing angels singing as well as the voice of Jesus:

Elmshaven, California March 2, 1907 – 9 Testimonies, pp. 66-67. The room was filled with light, a most beautiful, soft, azure light, and I seemed to be in the arms of the heavenly beings. This peculiar light I have experienced in the past in times of special blessings, but this time was more distinct, more expressive, and I felt such peace, peace so full and abundant no words can express it. I raised myself into a sitting posture, and I saw that I was surrounded by a bright cloud, white as snow, the edges of which were tinted with deep pink. The softest, sweetest music was filling the air, and I recognized the music as the singing of the angels. Then a voice spoke to me, saying: Fear not; I am your Saviour. Holy angels are all about you... Again I felt asleep, and when I awoke I heard music, and I wanted to sing. Then someone passed my door, and I wondered if that person saw the light. After a time the light passed away, but the peace remained. [*Life Sketches of Ellen G. White (1909), page 66-67*].

2) Doctors' letters and conclusion[42]:

Letter to John H. Kellogg MD from his brother Merritt G. Kellogg MD, August 1, 1906:

Healdsburg, Calif. Aug 1, 1906

J.H. Kellogg MD

Battle Creek, Mich.

Dear Brother John,

page 6

Now about my position as to the testimonies of Mrs. E. G. White. I think that in much of her writings we have clear evidence that the Spirit of God guided her thoughts as she wrote, but her inspiration came to her through the Holy Scripture contained in the Bible. The Bible has been her constant study and has been a source of her inspiration

Her early vision was the result of an abnormal nervous condition and the subject of the visions were the results of her conceptions of things when in a normal condition. Of this I am full convinced.

Your Brother,

Signed: M. G. Kellogg

Dr. Merritt G. Kellogg wrote the following letter regarding Ellen White's condition while in a vision to his brother J. H. Kellogg:

June 3, 1906,

In 1868, after talking with Dr. Trall, I began to suspect that Mrs. White's visions might not be what we had there unto supposed them to be, and from that time onward I have been studying both Mrs. White and her visions, dreams and testimonies...

I have seen Mrs. White in vision quite a number of times between 1852 and 1859, in every instance she was simply in a state of catalepsy. In each instance she was suddenly seized, fell unconscious, and remained unconscious during the full time the fit lasted; every vital function was reduced to the lowest point compatible with life; pulse almost stopped and infrequent breathing so slight as to be imperceptible except when she uttered short sentences; pupils dilated to great width, sense of hearing blunted; in fact was wholly unconscious, yet her mind was accurately active, the action being automatic and wholly involuntary, the whole vision being a conglomerated mental rehearsal of previous conceptions, senses, meditations, and suggestions so vividly reproduced on her mind as to be to her a living reality. <u>Catalepsy assumes many forms on its various victims, but in her case some phase of all forms was produced. I have seen many cases</u>. Mrs. L. Hall's description of Mrs. White's condition in vision agrees with mine.

<table>
<tr><td>**Physicians**</td><td>**Consultants**</td></tr>
<tr><td>Dr. John Harvey Kellogg</td><td>Dr. Thor W. Hudson</td></tr>
<tr><td>Dr. R.C. Norton</td><td>Dr. J.W. Snyder</td></tr>
<tr><td>Dr. Norman Estella</td><td>Dr. B.H. Palmer</td></tr>
</table>

Battle Creek, Inc
Miami Springs, (Miami) Florida
March 3, 1933

Mr. R. B. Tower,
246 Zerr Court,
Glandale, California

Dear Sir,
I have your letter of February 18 in which you speak of some tests being applied by me to Mrs. White while in vision. There is no truth whatsoever in this statement to which you refer. I never saw Mrs. White while she was in a state of vision. It is my belief that her condition while in vision was that of <u>catalepsy</u>. This is a nervous state allied to hysteria in which sublime visions are usually experienced. The muscles are set in such a way that ordinary tests fail to show any evidence of respiration, but the application of more delicate tests show that there are slight

breathing movements sufficient to maintain life. Patients sometimes remain in this condition for several hours.

Yours truly,

John Harvey Kellogg

Dr. William S. Sadler
533 Diversey Parkway
Chicago
September 19, 1966

Charles D. Willis, M.D.
1427 – 12th Ave.
San Francisco, California

Dear Dr. Willis,

Replying to your letter about Mrs. White's visions let me say that I have talked over these things many times with Elder Loughborough many years ago.

I never saw Mrs. White in a vision. From my talk with her, and with those who did observe her visions, I came to the conclusion that they were <u>distinctly cataleptic seizures</u>. There is nothing reported in connection with her visions that I have not seen in my own patients.

Furthermore, as Dr. M. G. Kellogg predicted, she would have no visions subsequently to the menopause, and this is true, with the change of life this phenomenon entirely disappears.

No, I do not do any more travelling. I am 91 years old now, and my last trip to the Pacific Coast was about thirty years ago. But if you ever are in Chicago I trust you will come to see me.

Sincerely,
William S. Sadler, M.D.

Dr. William S. Sadler
533 Diversey Parkway
Chicago
December 17, 1962

Charles D. Willis, M.D.
521 S. Woods Ave.
Fullerton, California

Dear Dr. Willis,

Replying to your of December 13 let me say that you were accurately informed about a group of questions which I once submitted to Mrs. White.

When up with my wife about 5:00 o'clock one morning in June, 1906 studying for our final examination in Neurology, I happened to glance down at the end of the bench we were sitting in on in McKinley Park and noticed a folded onion skin carbon copy of some sort. This proved to be a carbon addressed to the General Conference Committee by Mrs. White in which my name was mentioned among others with a statement something as follows:

> "Whatever problems you have concerning my work which bother you if you would write me frankly it would afford me an opportunity to help."

I wrote Mrs. White a full and lengthy letter frankly stating all my problems. I never received an answer to these questions. A short time later Sarah McIntyre, her companion, telephoned me of Mrs. White's disturbance upon receipt of my letter and suggested that she did not know how to reply to it. I assured Mrs. McIntyre that it was not necessary to reply, that, as far as I was concerned the whole matter could be forgotten, and evidently it was, for I never heard any more about it.

I have been asked for a copy of these questions by at least a half-dozen people in subsequent years, but I have never felt that I would be justified in making public that which was personal correspondence. I have never participated in any of the attacks which have been made upon Mrs. White as my wife and I regarded her as a personal friend. I so enjoyed the hospitality of her home and the many, many personal conversations we had I always felt under obligation to hold in the strict confidence.

Quite regardless of any question of her special gift which always impressed me as the "discernment of spirits" and from my conference with Dr. M. G. Kellogg, J. Loughborough and others, I was satisfied that her psychoneurologic status connected with her visions was very similar to that of our well-known catalepsy.

That this diagnosis was correct, was born out by the fulfillment of the predictions of Dr. M.G. Kellogg who evidently arrived at this same diagnosis because he predicted quite accurately that Mrs. White would never have any of these visions subsequently to her menopause, and this I understood was just what happened. None of my cataleptic female patients have ever had any seizures 90 days following their last menstruation.

With Mrs. White and her family I carefully inquired into her early accident of head injury during adolescence, and I became thoroughly satisfied that none of her phenomena had substantiated the diagnosis of Jacksonian epilepsy.

I assume that you know of my background and my early association with Dr. Kellogg and his work and of my close association with the Whites for two or three years, in which I was a member of the Board of Trustees of St. Helena Sanitarium, going up to Board meetings regularly every two weeks and usually having Sunday morning breakfast with Mrs. White.

My first introduction to the study of Mrs. White and her "visions" dated from the contact with my father-in-law, Smith Moses Kellogg, with whom Elder and Mrs. White made their home for about six months when they first went to establish the work at Battle Creek. You should recall that my wife, Dr. Lena Kellogg Sadler, was the eldest daughter of Smith Moses Kellogg.

Please tell me more about yourself and how you came to be interested in these matters as I am much intrigued by your letter of inquiry.

Sincerely,
William S. Sadler, M.D.

Note: The letters quoted above are by no means intended to undermine the image of Ellen G. White. These are meant to bring to light a medical reality, which was less familiar to the people about a hundred and fifty years ago. n

G. Who was Ellen G. White?

The fact that sensitive topics contrary to Adventist doctrinal teachings are being avoided in the Seventh-day Adventist Church is not something unusual. Doubts concerning Ellen White's prophetic authority among Adventists are usually tacit. Certain things are known to them; however, there still are many realities of which most Adventists are not aware of. Therefore, it would be unjust to overlook the following facts regarding Ellen White:

1. To teach that children must not consume eggs, cheese, butter, meat – food of indisputable nutritional value essential for the growth during childhood and adolescence – is a malicious act or a sign of mental instability. On the other hand, could it be that Mrs. White's children were eating only vegetables because their mother, the Lord's messenger, would not allow them to eat any food of animal origin? The reality reveals a different picture!

2. Mrs. White had a good eye for business. Her main income was the royalties from the books she published. She was receiving from $8000 to $12000 a year on the books she wrote while in the employ of the General Conference[43].

She forced the publishing house to continue to pay her 10 per cent on the retail price of her books. This is confirmed by Mrs. White's own words[43]:

- "[...] Then, if my brethren did not awake to the situation, I was to make no delay in taking the book into my own hands, the Lord would prepare the way before me" (*Special Instruction Regarding Royalties, p.7*).

- "No one can have been hurt financially more than I was hurt. [...] This was a dishonest transaction towards me, and it was unfaithful stewardship towards God" (*Special Instruction Regarding Royalties, page 9*). This refers to the period when "The Great Controversy" lay for nearly two years dead in the office, as another book "Bible Reading" was crowded in before The Great Controversy for which she did not get 10 per cent, whereas she got 10 per cent on "The Great Controversy."

3. Some people might wonder whether Mrs. White, under certain circumstances, took advantage of her position of authority. This is less relevant now! However, having the reputation as the Lord's messenger (the prophet), Ellen White became a person of authority within the Seventh-day Adventist Church. Analyzing her writings, it can be inferred that one of Mrs. White's influential phrases that had considerable effect on certain people would be: "I was told in a vision...!" Ordinary people dared not challenge the authority of the person who received "prophetic messages and visions from God", whereas the educated people were usually avoiding public futile confrontations. Some believers, however, challenged the so-called "visions and messages of the prophetess" and ended up leaving the Seventh-day Adventist Church.

Adventist doctrinal recipes

Seventh-day Adventism has a very complex doctrinal structure. Its fundamental ideology, the outcome of Millerite movement, has been conceived after the "Great Disappointment of October 22, 1844."

The following doctrinal teachings imposed on Adventist believers identify the Seventh-day Adventist Church and at the same time separate it from other religious denominations:

1. The sanctuary doctrine

The concept "sanctuary doctrine" as such is little known to most Adventists nowadays. However, the message of this doctrine is thoroughly described in Ellen G. White's writings and partially expressed in Belief 23 (Belief 24 following the insertion of a new belief in 2005) – it stands at the core of Adventism.

The sanctuary doctrine asserts the following:

- On October 22, 1844 AD, Christ, instead of returning to earth as some were expecting, entered into the Most Holy Place of the Heavenly Sanctuary;

- On October 22, 1844 AD, Christ entered the second and last phase of His atoning ministry – it is a work of investigative judgment.

Analyzing these doctrinal claims in the light of the New Testament truth, the inevitable conclusion follows:

- Jesus Christ was not ascended to the throne (right-hand side) of the Father on the day of Ascension;

- Christ's ministry of atonement was not finished on the cross of Golgotha – it was only the first phase of His atoning ministry.

Such allegation is not in harmony with the Bible – it is rather a blasphemy. Who is this Christ, who on October 22, 1844 allegedly entered into the Most Holy Place (to the Father), entered the second and last phase of His atoning ministry?

2. Ellen G. White

Seventh-day Adventists have been indoctrinated with the teaching that Ellen G. White is the Lord's messenger – a prophet. To become an Adventist, a believer is to accept the doctrine according to which the gift of prophecy was manifested in the ministry of Ellen White, and that her writings are a "continuous and authoritative source of truth which provides for the church comfort, guidance, instruction, and correction" [Belief 17 (Belief 18 following the insertion of a new belief in 2005) and other Adventist publications].

Ellen G. White – her prophetic visions, inspired writings and teachings – represents one of the three pillars of Adventism. The other two pillars are: the Sanctuary doctrine and the Sabbath.

Ellen White's alleged "inspired writings and teachings" represent an authority in the Seventh-day Adventist Church. Adventist homes are loaded with these writings and books attributed to their prophet. It often seems easier to consult Ellen White's writings than personally study the Bible. Her books on diet – what to eat and drink – are followed meticulously. The famous phrase "Ellen White said..." is quite commonly used among Adventists. If someone is more daring and asks a rather unconventional question, such person may be refuted with the remark: "Don't you agree with Adventist principles?" Many Adventists do not realize that, to a certain extent, Ellen White (her writings) has become a form of idolatry for them. This ellenwhitolatry may be found in sermons, Sabbath school, religious literature, and in many aspects of Adventist everyday life. The arrogant feeling "we feel sorry for the ignorance of those Sunday keepers!" is shared by many; however, spiritual awakening among many sincere Adventists urges them to adopt a different approach in this regard. The real issue, however, is that Adventists are the ones who need to be pitied.

Some Adventists assert that, in comparison to other Christian denominations, they have a prophet. However, if a non-Adventist manifests an investigative, critical attitude towards Ellen White's prophetic authority, he will be told that, according to Adventist doctrine, Ellen White is the Lord's messenger, not a prophet. This, however, is a weird remark! How is the person receiving prophetic visions and messages from God called in the Bible? Aren't these messengers of God biblically called the prophets? The very title of Belief 17(18) – The Gift of Prophesy – contradicts them. The central issue in Belief 17(18) and baptismal vow 8 is the "gift of prophecy"; therefore, doctrinally, Ellen White is a prophet. Ultimately, it appears that Adventists have a prophet whose writings contain many borrowings and copies from other sources – Ellen G. White is being accused nowadays of plagiarism[29].

It is very obvious that doctrinal teaching regarding the "gift of prophecy" is a sensitive topic within the Adventist Church. In this regard, the following biblical verses may be helpful:

> *"9 But in vain do they worship me, Teaching as their doctrines the precepts of men" (Mt. 15:9; also Mk. 7:7-8);*

> *"18 Let no man rob you of your prize [i]by a voluntary humility and [j]worshipping of the angels, [k]dwelling in the things which he hath [l]seen, vainly puffed up by his fleshly mind" (Col. 2:18).*

3. The Sabbath

According to the fourth commandment of the Sinaitic covenant, Sabbath, the seventh day of the week, is a day of rest and worship, a holy day. Ideologically, however, Adventist Church goes much further. Its subjects are indoctrinated with the following teachings:

a) Sabbath is God's perpetual sign of His eternal covenant between Him and His people [Belief 19 (Belief 20 following the insertion of a new belief in 2005)]; seventh-day Sabbath is binding on Christians (Vow 6).

However, the Holy Scripture teaches us that Sabbath is a

sign of the covenant made on Mount Sinai between Yahweh and Israel (Ex. 31:13, 16-17; Ezek. 20:12, 20), a memorial of deliverance from Egyptian slavery (Deut. 5:15). The word "*Sabbath*" is not found in the Books of Genesis and Revelation. On the other hand, it was prophesied that God would put an end the Sinaitic covenant and to the Sabbath (Jer. 31:31-33; Hos. 2:11; Is. 1:13). This prophecy was fulfilled by Jesus Christ. The cross of Golgotha marks the end of the old covenant and its sign – the Sabbath; therefore, the seventh-day Sabbath is not binding on Christians.

b) Sabbath is a symbol of our redemption in Christ [Belief 19 (Belief 20 following the insertion of a new belief in 2005)].

However, a believer, accordance to the New Testament, is redeemed by the sacrificial death of Jesus Christ; therefore, the symbol of our redemption is the Holy Communion. The assertion "Sabbath is a symbol of our redemption in Christ" is not in harmony with the teaching of the Gospel – it is rather a blasphemy.

c) Sabbath is the seal of God (Ellen White's writings and other Adventist publications).

The logic of this teaching is that the final test of believers is keeping the law (Sabbath law); therefore, Christian believers are saves by keeping the law, not by grace.

However, the Sabbath is never presented in the Bible as the seal of God. On the other hand, in the New Testament is stated very clearly that the Holy Spirit is the seal of God on His people (see Eph. 1:13; Eph. 4:30; 2Cor. 1:22).

d) Sunday-keeping is the mark of the beast (Ellen White's writings and other Adventist publications).

However, according to the logic of this allegation, all Christian believers who have been observing Sunday, the first day of the week, for almost 2000 years have the mark of the beast. Such allegation is an insult to the entire Christianity.

e) Adventists anticipate the enactment of a National Sunday law. According to this law, Sunday will become a national day of rest and worship. Implementation of this law will jeopardize religious freedom; therefore, Sabbath keepers (Adventists) will be persecuted, even killed.

This peculiar teaching can still be found in Ellen White's famous book, The Great Controversy. Its principal target seems to be the Roman Catholic Church, as its teaching is based on distorted interpretation of Bible prophecy according to which the Papacy is identified as the beast of Revelation (that is, the Pope is the Antichrist) and Sunday worship is the mark of the beast. Would followers of Christ's commandments "love your God and love your neighbour" agree to such an aberrant law? No! Would Jews worldwide allow such a thing to happen? No!

What Adventists scholars deliberately overlook is the fact that Pharisees were accusing and plotting to kill Jesus for transgressing the Sabbath law (Mt. 12:9-14; Mk. 3:1-6; Lk. 6:2; 13:10-17; Jn. 5:17-18; 9:16). How many sermons have been preached by Adventist pastors on these verses?

Do Adventists really observe the fourth commandment? If their answer is yes, then, to be in concordance with the Sabbath law regarding the distance permitted to walk on the Sabbath day, they should count their steps on Saturday. Practical applicability of the Sabbath law is a debatable issue among reasonable Adventists, as they drive cars or use other means of transportation on Sabbath day. Adventists abstain from working on Saturday; however, many goods of daily use are being produced on the day biblically called Sabbath. It seems alright for Sabbath keepers that others work for them on the Sabbath day – questions of conscience do not seem to apply in this situation.

Carefully selected tranquil instrumental hymns that may be heard at the end of the service provide a feeling of spiritual elevation especially after a boring sermon, or after the Sabbath school when Adventist, being divided into study groups, are discussing and interfering with one another thus often creating the impression of a church being rather transformed into a market place.

Sermons overemphasizing the Sabbath and Ellen White are quite common. Such selective doctrinal approach, however, often gives the impression that Jesus is neglected, abandoned, humbly riding on a donkey, or simply crucified again by those arrogant doctrinal allegations.

For many Adventists, it is a habit to wear nice and fashionable clothes on Sabbath: a set of clothes for morning service, another set for afternoon service. Not to wear nice clothes for worship on Sabbath is regarded as disrespectful in some churches. Therefore, it is honorable to come to church on Sabbath wearing nice suits, ties. Jesus Christ, apostles, and prophets were also wearing nice and spiritually clean clothes.

There are other Sabbatarian denominations that emerged from the Protestant Reformation as a result of the so-called freedom of religion and freedom of expression. However, Sabbath keeping in the Adventist Church is somewhat marked by its doctrinal particularities, which are not found in other denominations.

4. Kosher food

It is a well-known fact that Adventists observe the Old Testament dietary law. This involves the notion of "clean and unclean food." Consequently, Adventist religious freedom is marked by prohibition: do not eat this, do not touch that, and so on. Such dependency on the law, however, does not identify with the new covenant of the spirit (2Cor. 3:6) and Christ's two commandments of love – it rather reflects a compromise!

The New Testament has a firm position regarding dietary laws as follows:

> "*10 And he called to him the multitude, and said unto them, Hear, and understand: 11 Not that which entereth into the mouth defileth the man; but that which proceedeth out of the mouth, this defileth the man*" (Mt. 15:10-11).

> "*16 And he said, Are ye also even yet without understanding? 17 Perceive ye not, that whatsoever goeth into the mouth passeth into the belly, and is cast out into the draught? 18 But the things which proceed out of the mouth come forth out of the heart; and they*

defile the man. [19] _For out of the heart come forth evil thoughts, murders, adulteries, fornications, thefts, false witness, railings:_ [20] _these are the things which defile the man; but to eat with unwashen hands defileth not the man"_ (Mt. 15:16-20).

"[14] _He called all the multitude to himself, and said to them, "Hear me, all of you, and understand._ [15] _There is nothing from outside of the man, that going into him can defile him; but the things which proceed out of the man are those that defile the man._ [16] _If anyone has ears to hear, let him hear!""_ (Mk. 7:14-16 WEB).

"[18] _And he saith unto them, Are ye so without under-standing also? Perceive ye not, that whatsoever from without goeth into the man, it cannot defile him;_ [19] _because it goeth not into his heart, but into his belly, and goeth out into the draught? This he said, making all meats clean._ [20] _And he said, That which proceedeth out of the man, that defileth the man._ [21] _For from within, out of the heart of men,_ [k] _evil thoughts proceed, fornications, thefts, murders, adulteries,_ [22] _covetings, wickednesses, deceit, lasciviousness, an evil eye, railing, pride, foolishness:_ [23] _all these evil things proceed from within, and defile the man"_ (Mk. 7:18-23).

"[2] _One man hath faith to eat all things: but he that is weak eateth herbs"_ (Rom. 14:2).

"[14] _I know, and am persuaded in the Lord Jesus, that nothing is unclean of itself: save that to him who accounteth anything to be unclean, to him it is unclean"_ (Rom. 14:14).

"[17] _for the kingdom of God is not eating and drinking, but righteousness and peace and joy in the Holy Spirit"_ (Rom. 14:17).

The message of Bible verses quoted above is very clear: what goes into the mouth defiles not a man, but what comes out of the mouth defiles a man. From within, out of the heart of men preceed evil thoughts and plans, which lead to murder, adultery, fornication, theft, false witness, blasphemy, and so on – these are the things that defile a man. Jesus, in His teachings, is more concerned about our bodies and the food we eat than hand washing.

Should this be regarded as an act of encouragement to consume food prohibited by the Old Testament dietary law? Not at all! The message is very clear: God's kingdom is not a matter of food or drink, but of righteousness, peace, and joy in the Holy Spirit (Rom. 14:7). If someone, for reasons of health or any other reason, decides to abstain from consuming certain food, there is no need to follow some religious laws or invent doctrines. God created man "*in His image*", not in the image of certain laws or doctrines!

Seventh-day Adventist Church has tendency to propagate vegetarianism. In support of this teaching, besides their own research, Adventists selectively adopt scientific discoveries achieved by non-Adventist highly specialized laboratories and medical research centers. In this sense, Adventists tend to identify themselves as vegetarians – a new image. The term "kosher" applies to average Adventists; however, more devoted Adventists become vegetarians and use among others the famous "soy products." Contemporary Jews are probably surprised by these Adventist teachings because "kosher dietary laws" in Jewish religion have nothing to do with vegetarianism.

Adventist dietary logic goes back to Daniel and his friends, four young Jewish exiles in Babylonia, who chose not to sit at the king's table, and who chose a vegetarian diet (Dan. 1:6-16). Their decision has a logical explanation: to sit at the king's table would mean to partake in everything thus eat unclean food and ultimately fall into idolatry and worship Babylonian pagan gods. Analyzing this sensitive issue, several logical questions cannot escape our attention: Were the four young men vegetarians before the exile, before they had been selected to serve at the royal court? Were they part of a religious group who were vegetarians? If they were, how did they eat the Passover lamb at Passover festival? Was it a real lamb or was it a "soy-lamb"? It was most probably a real lamb!

Adventists should not forget that they are not living in the Garden of Eden, but rather on the ground under a curse (Gen. 3:17-19). Abel, one of Adam's sons, was a shepherd. This means that he consumed pastoral products like milk, cheese, butter, and meat. Abel also brought a lamb, killed it, and gave the best parts of it as an offering to God (Gen. 4:4). Was sheepherding for Abel a hobby or a way to earning his living?

Was Jesus a vegetarian? No! Were apostles and prophets vegetarians? No! Could a Jew be a vegetarian and at the same time offer animal sacrifices and eat the Paschal lamb? Was the prophet Elijah fed with real meat or "soy meat", when ravens were commanded by God to bring him food (1Kg. 17:3-6)? What about the patriarchs before Moses – were they observing a dietary law? There's no biblical record to confirm it!

Vegetarianism has advantages and disadvantages. The right thing to do, in this case, is to avoid extremes. However, the combination "vegetarianism and (religious) fanaticism" has proved to have a bad reputation. A balanced diet that contains a reasonable quantity of proteins, cereals, vegetables, and fruits is the right choice. Fanatical abstinence from certain food is not in harmony with the teachings of the New Testament.

Vegans may argue that the killing animals to consume its flesh is unjust. This statement is very honourable! According to the Bible, however, God's instruction to Noah and his sons is not what the vegans constantly advocate (Gen. 9:1-4). On the other hand, if our Bible is a reliable translation of the original manuscript, God clothed the first human couple with clothes made of animal skins:

> "²¹ Yahweh God made coats of animal skins for Adam and for his wife, and clothed them" (Gen. 3:21).

This, however, proves to be a delicate topic. Where does the skin come from? To have clothes made of animal skin, one must first kill the animal. Well, the Book of Genesis does not provide any information on how God made clothes from animal skin for Adam and Eve. Some believers may argue that the Providence of God must have provided a solution for those animals whose skin served as clothing for the first human couple. The logical response to such an argument is this: God could as well have provided clothes made of wool, cotton, linen…, thus leaving those animals unharmed. Others may suggest that the animal skin used for clothing Adam and Eve was probably from animals that died of natural death. Well, there was no death in the Garden of Eden. **Note**: This reasoning is by no means intended to provoke religious discordance. On the contrary, it should serve as a stimulus for a more thorough analysis of the Bible.

5. The tithing

The concept of "tithing" has its origin in the Old Testament and was widely practiced under the Mosaic Law. The Israelites were to give 10 percent of the crops they grew and the livestock they raised to the priests (tabernacle/temple). Seventh-day Adventist Church has incorporated this practice into its fundamental doctrinal beliefs. The system teaches that the tithe (ten percent of the income) belongs to the Lord. A hundred percent of the tithing goes directly to the Conference treasury and no tithe funds can be used for local needs. Other offerings are in the form of collections performed two-three times on the (holy) Sabbath; collecting money (objects with "Caesar's image" on it) on Sabbath is not a sin. Tithing is regarded as an imperative duty – it belongs to the Lord! Somehow, other collections give the impression of not belonging to the Lord, as these are regarded as "other offerings." Adventists may argue that tithing is not mandatory in their church; however, baptismal vows 9, 11, and Belief 20(21) confirm that one cannot be baptized unless he accepts Adventist fundamental beliefs (including tithing). One who refuses to tithe will soon find himself in a dilemma.

There is another interesting fact about the Adventist Church:

boring and spiritually unconstructive sermons are tolerated by the church. Tithing, however, is a more delicate issue; specific sermons promoting tithing are being preached, as the entire Adventist system financially relies on it.

The Bible provides the following clues regarding tithing:

- In the Book of Genesis (the pre-Mosaic period) there are two biblical records of tithing: Genesis 14:18-20 and Genesis 28:20-22; however, practical applicability of tithing was manifest under the Mosaic Law;

- "*Abram gave him a tenth of all*" (Gen. 14:20). Abraham tithed to Melchizedek only once; he tithed from the spoils of war. In fact, Abraham returned all the spoils to the original owners and took nothing for himself; he accepted only what his men have used (Gen. 14:22-24). There is no record of Abraham tithing again;

- Jacob made a vow: "*and of all that thou shalt give me I will surely give the tenth unto thee*" (Gen. 28:22). The Scripture, however, does not provide a description on how Jacob gave a tithing to the Lord, as no Melchizedek or any other priest is mentioned at that time. On the other hand, it is a rather <u>peculiar bargain</u> on the part of Jacob in the following verses:

> "²⁰ *Jacob vowed a vow, saying, "<u>If</u> God will be with me, and will keep me in this way that I go, and will give me bread to eat, and clothing to put on, ²¹ so that I come again to my father's house in peace, and <u>Yahweh will be my God</u>*" (Gen. 28:20-21);

- In ancient Israel, two professions were required by the law to tithe: crop farmers and animal herders. That is, tithing was required from land produce and domestic animals herding (Deut. 14:22-23; Lev. 27:30-32);

- Jesus Christ was a carpenter by profession; carpenters were not required by the Law of Moses to tithe. Does the verse regarding the coin found in the mouth of a fish (Mt. 17:27) prove that He did? No, it was a Temple tax;

- Peter was a fisherman, Paul was a tent maker; fishermen and tent makers were not required to tithe. None of the twelve disciples were required. However, people of other professions, who were not crop farmers or animal herders, gave offering required by the law;

- Tithing had been practiced by Israelites under the Law of Moses;

- If tithing law is applicable to believers living under the new covenant, then all other old covenant religious practices (sacrifices, circumcision) and ordinances should be applicable as well – this would be nonsense. Partiality does not reflect the will of God;

- What about those believers who lived before Abraham? There are no biblical records of tithing before Abraham;

- In Deuteronomy 14:22-26 is described a more logical significance of tithing:

> "²³ You shall eat before Yahweh your God, in the place which he chooses, to cause his name to dwell there, the tithe of your grain, of your new wine, and of your oil, and the firstborn of your herd and of your flock; that you may learn to fear Yahweh your God always" (Deut. 14:23);

- The Lord Jesus Christ paid our debts on the cross of Golgotha;

- Thanks giving and praise are God's people debts to their Father and God;

- Christians did not practice tithing in the first century, the incipient period of Christianity – they were under the law of the Spirit of Grace, not under the Mosaic Law. However, Christians were giving free-will offerings to support Christian churches and assist needy believers;

- Donations and free-will offerings to support the church, mission of evangelization, needy brothers and sisters, and charity activities are the work of the Holy Spirit, not of the tithing law. Christians have another tithing law: give as much as the Holy Spirit inspires you to give;

- Tithing in the New Testament is called freewill offering (1Cor. 16:2; 2Cor. 9:7);

- God's kingdom is not a matter of food, drink, or tithing, but of righteousness, peace, and joy in the Holy Spirit – it is worship "*in spirit and in truth*";

- Giving is a sign of grace. The apostle Paul quotes Jesus' words: "*it is more blessed to give, than to receive*" (Acts 20:35). However, God's kingdom is not a matter of wealth and health propaganda, a prosperity gospel, that is, if you give you will be prosperous. And, if that is not effective, then the sermon regarding the poor widow putting her last two coins into the offering box (Lk. 21:1-4) is preached to induce guilt feelings among listeners;

- Mark 7:11-13 provides a very clear description of the significance of tithing. According to Jesus's teaching, offering (that is, tithing) is meant to assist the needy people:

> "*¹¹ but ye say, If a man shall say to his father or his mother, That wherewith thou mightest have been profited by me is Corban, that is to say, Given to God; ¹² ye no longer suffer him to do aught for his father or his mother; ¹³ making void the word of God by your tradition, which ye have delivered: and many such like things ye do*" (Mk.7:11-13).

- Tithing is very unfair for poor people and those with low income. On the contrary, such people should be helped;

- A person's income is a private matter. However, if a person's tithing is multiplied by ten, then those in charge of tithing can figure out the person's income; therefore, people's privacy is infringed;

- Tithing is prevalent in many Protestant denominations; however, tithing practice within the Adventist church is done with a particular emphasis: it belongs to the Lord!

In this sense, it is pertinent to ask the following question: how accurately is the tithing handled? Adventist leaders are silent about the financial misuse and corruption of the famous

Davenport Scandal[44] in which Adventist Church and church leaders (in the USA), who invested with Dr. Davenport, lost something like 77 million dollars in the late 1970's and early 1980's in that Ponzi scandal. It seems that nobody was found guilty for the fraud – a miracle. USA is not the only country with such incidents.

Note: The purpose of this comment is to combat controversial doctrinal teachings concerning tithing practice (an unnecessary burden for many believers), and to encourages freewill offering and a religious service free from the habit of collecting money on the day which is supposed to be totally consecrated to God.

6. Adventist Church is the remnant church.

This doctrinal teaching seems to have its origin in the Book of Revelation (Rev.12:17; 14:12; 18:4). Seventh-day Adventist Church indoctrinates its subjects with the teaching that their church is the remnant church of God because they keep God's commandments. In other words, the logic of this doctrine is that the final test of a Christian believer regarding salvation will be keeping the law.

The central issue in Revelation 12:17 and 14:12 is "*keeping God's commandments and the testimony of Jesus Christ.*" However, the question is which commandments: the Ten Commandments of the Sinaitic covenant or Christ's command-ments of God's new covenant established on the cross of Golgotha? The truth is that Christ's commandments are much more than the Ten Commandments, much more than 613 laws of the Torah, as the entire law of Torah and the prophets depend on these two commandments (Mt. 22:36-40). The truth is that this alleged "remnant church", besides the Ten Commandments, also keeps 27 Adventist fundamental beliefs (28 beliefs following the insertion of a new belief in 2005) and 13 baptismal vows. In other words, Adventists ought to accept: 1) Ellen G. White as the Lord's messenger (the prophet) and her writings as a continuing and authoritative source of truth in the church; 2) the "October 22, 1844 Christ" of the sanctuary doctrine.

Do Adventists really keep the Ten Commandments? If they do, then they have no need of Christ because they keep the law that can save them.

The Book of Revelation (the Bible in general) does not specify which religious denomination is going to be saved in the last days. Saved believers are those who listen to the voice of the Holy Spirit, who live their lives in harmony with God's will. This biblical reality is confirmed by the following verses:

> "[16] *And other sheep I have, which are not of this fold: them also I must [e]bring, and* <u>*they shall hear my voice*</u>*; and [f]they shall become one flock, one shepherd" (Jn. 10:16).*

> "[27] <u>*My sheep hear my voice, and I know them, and they follow me*</u>*: [28] and I give unto them eternal life; and they shall never perish, and no one shall snatch them out of my hand" (Jn. 10:27-28).*

Religious indoctrination of people is not something new – it has always existed. However, to indoctrinate believers, without providing a solid biblical evidence, that they are the "chosen people, the remnant church" is very dangerous and has unpredictable consequences. Many wars have been waged in the name of such arrogant religious claims and resulted in the loss of millions of lives – a reality historically confirmed. The so-called human wisdom and its standards is worthless in God's sight. God alone knows people's hearts and thoughts; God alone is the judge of our deeds.

7. The Clear Word Bible

This is an Adventist paraphrase of the Bible edited in 1994, by Jack J. Blanco[45] . This paraphrase, criticized by both Adventists and non-Adventists, is a selective modification of the Holy Scripture where alterations, additions, elimination had been made to uphold Adventist doctrinal teachings.

However, the Clear Word Bible is not produced or endorsed

by the Seventh-day Adventist Church – it is the private enter-
prise of an individual – and is not used for worship services.

8. Seventh-day Adventists Church and the Sola Sriptura

The schism within Western Christianity has a colouful and
controversial history. Protestant believers assert that the
Protestant Reformation started with five solas (solae)[46]:
- *Sola Scriptura* (by "Scripture alone");
- *Sola Fide* (by "Faith alone");
- *Sola Gratia* (by "Grace alone");
- *Solus Christus* (by "Christ alone");
- *Soli Deo Gloria* ("Glory to God alone").

The Seventh-day Adventist Church is a branch of
Protestantism. However, how much does it identify with the
"five solas"? The Gospel to which is added extra biblical teaching
(The sanctuary doctrine), extra biblical prophet (Ellen G. White,
her prophetic visions, writings, advices), and controversial interpretation of the Book of Revelation is no longer the Gospel of
our Lord Jesus Christ, no longer the "*Sola Scriptura*.

Baptism – Adventist doctrines exposed!

In Christianity, baptism [from the Greek noun baptisma (βάπτισμα)][47] is a religious ritual act with the use of water (immersion, affusion) by which a person is admitted into membership of the Church. Baptism represents a symbol of partaking in Christ's death and resurrection by the new-born Christian. Baptism in Seventh-day Adventist Church has a certain particularity: baptismal candidates are to accept "27 Adventist fundamental beliefs and 13 baptismal vows"[48][49][50].

Note: In 2005 was inserted another belief, fundamental belief number 11 "Growing in Christ"[49][50]. Since then, the Seventh-day Adventist Church has 28 fundamental beliefs. This, however, brought about some changes in the numerical order of those fundamental beliefs such as: belief number 12 became number 13, belief 17 became 18, belief 19 became 20, belief 23 became 24, and so forth.

Certain Adventist doctrinal teachings prove to be controversial and spiritually abusive. To solve this Adventist doctrinal equation, a thorough analysis of several Adventist fundamental beliefs and baptismal vows is absolutely indispensable.

Baptismal candidates, prior to baptismal immersion, publicly accept the thirteen baptismal vows. The acceptance of baptismal vows confirms the fact that baptismal candidates accept the 27(28) Adventist fundamental beliefs with which they have already been acquainted with during the indoctrination course. The following baptismal vows draw particular attention:

Baptismal Vow 6: Do you accept the Ten Commandments as still binding upon the Christians; and is it your purpose, by the power of the indwelling Christ, to keep this law, including the forth commandment, which requires the observance of the seventh day of the week as the Sabbath of the Lord?

Baptismal Vow 8: Do you accept the Biblical teaching of the spiritual gifts, and do you believe that the gift of prophecy in the remnant church is one of the identifying marks of that church?

Baptismal vow 9: Do you believe in God's Remnant Church, and is it your purpose to support the church by your tithes and offerings, your personal effort, and influence?

Baptismal Vow 11: Knowing and understanding the fundamental Bible principles as taught by the Seventh-day Adventist Church, it is your purpose, by the grace of God, to order your life in harmony with these principles?

Baptismal Vow 13: Do you believe that the Seventh-day Adventist Church is the remnant church of Bible prophecy, and that people of every nation, race, and language are invited and accepted into its fellowship? Do you desire membership in this local congregation of this world church?

Alternative baptismal vow introduced in 2005 consists of three affirmations. Affirmation 2 corresponds to the traditional vow 11.

Affirmation 2: Do you accept the teachings of the Bible as expressed in the Statement of Fundamental Beliefs of the Seventh-day Adventist Church and do you pledge by God's grace to live your life in harmony with these teachings?

1. Belief 17(18) – The gifts of prophecy

One of the gifts of the Holy Spirit is prophecy. This gift is an identifying mark of the remnant church and was manifested in the ministry of Ellen G. White. As the Lord's messenger, her writings are a continuous and authoritative source of truth which provides for the church comfort, guidance, instruction, and correction. They also make clear that the Bible is the standard by which, all teachings and experiences must be tested. Support is found in these bible passages. (Joel 2:28-29; Acts 2:14-21; Heb. 1:1-3; Rev. 12:17; 19:10.)

Ellen G. White wrote:
- "As God has shown me in holy vision...we heard the voice of

God like many waters, which gave us the day and hour of Jesus' coming" (*Early Writings, pp.15, 34, 285*).

- **Ellen G. White forgets the hour proclaimed**: "I have not the slightest knowledge as to the time spoken by the voice of God. I heard the hour proclaimed, but had no remembrance of that hour after I came out of vision" (*Selected Messages 1, p.298, edition 1889*).

- **Ellen G. White blames her failed prophesy on the members of the Seventh-day Adventist Church!** "Thus the work was hindered, and the world was left in darkness. Had the whole Adventist body united upon the commandments of God and the faith of Jesus, how widely different would have been our history" (*Selected Messages, Book 1, p.299*).

- "In ancient times God spoke to men by the mouth of the prophets and apostles. In these days He speaks to them by the Testimonies of His Spirit" (*Testimonies for the Church, vol.4, pp.147, 148. Testimony 27; 1876*).

- "If you lessen the confidence of God's people in the Testimonies He has sent them, you are rebelling against God as certainly as were Korah, Dathan, and Abiram" (*Testimonies for the Church, vol.5, p.66. Testimony 31*).

- "Yet, now when I send you a testimony of warning and reproof, many of you declare it to be merely the opinion of Sister White. You thereby insult the Spirit of God" (*Testimonies 5, p.64*).

Doctrinal teaching that Ellen G. White is the Lord's messenger, a prophet, represents one of the characteristics that identify the Seventh-day Adventist Church; however, it is a very sensitive topic.

Baptism is always very carefully planned. During the indoctrination course, baptismal candidates have been indoctrinated with the teaching that the gift (spirit) of prophecy was manifested in the ministry of Ellen G. White, that is to say, she is a prophet. The name, Ellen White, is not mentioned during the baptism ceremony. However, baptismal vows 8 and 11 confirm the opposite, that is, baptismal candidates accepts and vows to order their lives in harmony with the 27(28) Adventist fundamental beliefs, including belief number 17(18) "The Gift of prophecy", with which they became acquainted with during the indoctrination course. "And when the church hears the thirteen vows, to which baptismal candidate says "yes", it is assumed by all that the person has accepted Ellen G. White. If there are non-Adventist visitors present, they will not suspect anything cultic or unbiblical, so that they would ask the question: Who is this Ellen G. White that baptismal candidates are to accept before they are baptized into Christ?"[51] In other words, this ceremonial strategy gives the false impression that one does not need to accept Ellen White to be baptized.

It is saddening for a reasonable Christian to imagine the fact that, to be baptized, one has to accept the doctrine according to which Ellen G. White is the "Lord's messenger (a prophet)" and her writings are "a continuous and authoritative source of truth in the church." The following ironical remark seems pertinent: go and baptise in the name of the Father, and of the Son, and of the Holy Spirit, (and of Ellen White).

"...This gift (of prophecy) is an identifying mark of the remnant church and was manifested in the ministry of Elle G. White" [Belief 17(18), vow 8].

According to the New Testament, Christian believers are sealed by the "*Holy Spirit*" (Eph. 1:13; Eph. 4:30; 2Cor. 1:22); therefore, the Holy Spirit is the identifying mark (seal) on those who believe. Daily observance of Christ's two commandments of love: "*love your God and love your neighbor*" is a visible manifestation of this mark – the Holy Spirit. The following verses confirm it:

> "*13 in whom ye also, having heard the word of the truth, the [i]gospel of your salvation,—in whom, having also believed, ye were sealed with the Holy Spirit of promise*" (Eph. 1:13).

> "*30 And grieve not the Holy Spirit of God, in whom ye*

were sealed unto the day of redemption" (Eph. 4:30).

"²¹ Now he that establisheth us with you [i]in Christ, and anointed us, is God; ²² [j]who also *sealed us, and gave us the earnest of the Spirit in our hearts*" (2Cor. 1:21-22).

"¹ If I speak with the tongues of men and of angels, but have not love, I am become sounding brass, or a clanging cymbal. ² And *if I have the gift of prophecy, and know all mysteries and all knowledge*; and if I have all faith, so as to remove mountains, *but have not love, I am nothing*. ³ And if I bestow all my goods to feed the poor, and if I give my body [a]to be burned, but have not love, it profiteth me nothing" (1Cor. 13:1-3).

"⁸ Love never faileth: but *whether there be prophecies, they shall be done away*; whether there be tongues, they shall cease; whether there be knowledge, it shall be done away. ⁹ *For we know in part, and we prophesy in part*; ¹⁰ but when that which is perfect is come, that which is in part shall be done away" (1Cor. 13:8-10).

"²² But *the fruit of the Spirit is* love, joy, peace, longsuffering, kindness, goodness, faithfulness, ²³ meekness, self-control; *against such there is no law*" (Gal. 5:22-23).

"...As the Lord's messenger, her writings are a continuous and authoritative source of truth which provides for the church comfort, guidance, instruction, and correction..." [Belief 17(18)].

The assertion "Ellen White, the Lord's messenger" is an arrogant claim. A prophet is tested by his own words. If his prophecy comes true, then he is a true prophet of God. Ellen White failed this test. Her so-called prophecies and predictions didn't come true, her visions are questionable, and there is plagiarism in her writings – all these affect her image as a prophet. Such doctrinal teaching makes sense only to an utterly indoctrinated Adventist. Just imagine a church where the writings of a certain person have become an authoritative source of truth which provides comfort, guidance, instruction, and protection. Does Jesus Christ really condone such a doctrinal allegation?

"They also make clear that the Bible is the standard by which all teachings and experience must be tested" [Belief 17(18)].

This statement condemns the entire teaching of this doctrine: Ellen G. White, the Lord's messenger (a prophet), her failed prophecies, her questionable visions and teaching failed the test – such doctrinal claims are extra biblical, thus not in harmony with the Holy Scripture.

Ellen G. White played an undisputable role in the history of Adventism. Therefore, the purpose of Belief 17(18) is to defend the image of Ellen White as prophet. Many Adventists do not question doctrinal teachings of their church. By doing so, they fail to see the hidden side of the truth. Consequently, they submit to compromised teachings and even mislead others into accepting it.

2. Belief 23(24) – Christ's ministry in the heavenly sanctuary

There is a sanctuary in heaven, the true tabernacle which the Lord set up and not man. In it Christ ministers on our behalf, making available to believers the benefits of His atoning sacrifice offered once for all on the cross. He was inaugurated as our great High Priest and began His intercessory ministry at the time of His ascension. In 1844, at the end of the prophetic period of 2,300 days, He entered the second and last phase of His atoning ministry. It is a work of investigative judgment which is part of the ultimate disposition of all sin, typified by the cleansing of the ancient Hebrew sanctuary on the Day of Atonement. In that typical service the sanctuary was cleansed with the blood of animal sacrifice, but the heavenly things are purified with the perfect sacrifice of the blood of Jesus. The investigative judgment reveals to heavenly intelligences who among the dead are asleep in Christ and therefore, in Him, are deemed worthy to have part in the first resurrection. It also makes manifest who among the living are abiding in Christ, keeping the commandments of God and the faith of Jesus, and in Him, therefore, are ready for translation into His everlasting kingdom. This judgment vindicates the justice of God in saving those who believe in Jesus. It declares that those who have remained loyal to God shall receive the kingdom. The completion of this ministry of Christ will mark the close of human probation before the Second Advent. (Heb. 8:1-5; 4:14-16; 9:11-28; 10:19-22; 1:3; 2:16-17; Dan. 7:9-27; 8:13-14; 9:24-27; Num. 14:34; Ezek. 4:6; Lev. 16; Rev. 14:6; 20:12; 14:12; 22:12).

Ellen G. White wrote:
- "The Lord showed me in vision more than a year ago, that brother Crozier had the true light on the cleansing of the Sanctuary, & c; and that it was his will that Brother C. should write out the view which he gave us in the Day-Star Extra, February 7, 1846. I feel fully authorized to recommend that Extra to every saint" (*A Word to the Little Flock, p.12, April 21, 1847*).
- "in 1844...our High Priest entered the holy of holies...to perform the work of investigation judgment. The only cases considered are those of the professed people of God" (*The Great Controversy, p.546*).
- "...at the close of the 2300 days, in 1844, began the work of investigation and the blotting out of sins" (*The Great Controversy, p.552*).
- "This work of examination of character, of determining who are prepared for the kingdom of God, is that of Investigative Judgment" (*The Great Controversy, p.489*).
- "The Proclamation, Behold the Bridegroom cometh in the summer of 1844, led thousands to expect the immediate advent

of Christ. At the appointed time the Bridegroom came, not to the earth, as the people expected, but to the Ancient of Days in heaven to the marriage, the reception of His kingdom. They that were ready went in with Him to the marriage and the door was shut" (*The Great Controversy, p.487*).

- "I was shown that...the door was opened in the most holy place in the heavenly sanctuary, where the ark is, in which are contained the Ten Commandments. This door was not opened until the mediation of Jesus was finished in the holy place of the sanctuary in 1844. Then Jesus rose up shut the door of the holy place, and opened the door into the most holy place, and passed within the second veil, where he now is standing by the ark" (*Early Writings, p.42*).

- "For a time after the disappointment in 1844, I did hold, in common with the advent body, that the door of mercy was forever closed to the world...I was shown in vision, and still believe, that there was a shut door in 1844" (*Selected Messages, Book 1, p.63*).

Fundamental belief 23 (24) has its origin in blasphemous teaching called the "Sanctuary doctrine." In fact, this belief is a modified version of that doctrine to which certain facts have been deliberately omitted. In her writings, Ellen G. White provides a very clear description of Christ's ministry in the Heavenly Sanctuary, as she is the promoter of this peculiar teaching. This belief takes Adventists into the past, back to the year 1844. On this date, allegedly marking the fulfillment of prophecy of Daniel 8:14, Millerites were expecting Christ's return to earth. However, Christ did not come to earth as they were expecting, but entered into the Most Holy Place of the Heavenly Sanctuary; on this date, Christ entered the second and last phase of His atoning ministry – a work of investigative judgment. Analyzing these doctrinal allegations and Ellen White's writings one can easily infered the following remarks:

- On Ascension Day, Jesus Christ was ascended into the Holy Place of the Heavenly Sanctuary – on this day, Jesus was not ascended to the right-hand side of the Father (into the Most Holy Place);

- On October 22, 1844, Jesus Christ entered into the Most Holy Place of the Heavenly Sanctuary;

- Christ's ministry of atonement was not finished on the cross of Golgotha – it was only the first phase of His atoning ministry.

In other words, 14 verses of the New Testament, which clearly confirm the fact that, on Ascension Day, Jesus Christ was taken up to heaven and sat at the right-hand side of God the Father, are irrelevant or false. In this regard, it seems that the logic of this doctrine is pointing out double standards: God says one thing, and later does something else. If Jesus Christ, the prophesied Messiah, did not finished His ministry of atonement on the cross of Golgotha, and was not ascended to the throne of the Father 40 days after the resurrection, then this doctrine is heralding a different Christ. <u>Who</u> is that Christ?

The New Testament states clearly that Christ's mission of atonement was finished on the Cross of Golgotha as follows:

> *"¹ These things spake Jesus; and lifting up his eyes to heaven, he said, <u>Father, the hour is come; glorify thy Son, that the Son may glorify thee</u>"* (Jn. 17:1).

> *"⁴ I glorified you on the earth. <u>I have accomplished the work which you have given me to do</u>"* (Jn. 17:4 WEB).

> *"³⁰ When Jesus therefore had received the vinegar, he said, <u>It is finished: and he bowed his head, and gave up his spirit</u>"* (Jn. 19:30).

> *"¹⁵ [h]having despoiled the principalities and the powers, he made a show of them openly, triumphing over them in it"* (Col. 2:15).

On Ascension Day, Jesus Christ was ascended to the right-hand side of the Father, into the Most Holy Place of the Heavenly Sanctuary – Jesus Christ didn't have to wait until October 22, 1844. The veracity of this statement is confirmed by the following verses: Mk. 16:19; Lk. 22:69; Acts 2:33; Acts 7:55-56;

Rom. 8:34; Eph. 1:20; Col. 3:1; Heb. 1:3; Heb. 8:1; Heb. 10:12; Heb. 12:2; 1Pet. 3:22; Rev. 3:21; Rev. 12:5.

"The investigative judgment reveals to heavenly intelligences who among the dead are asleep in Christ and therefore, in Him, are deemed worthy to have part in the first resurrection" [Belief 23(24)].

Who are these "heavenly intelligences" to whom the Word – Christ Jesus – ought to give an account regarding who is worthy or not to take part in the first resurrection? It is very evident that such doctrinal teaching is biblically controversial. Therefore, Adventists are suggested to order their life in harmony with the "word of God", not with teachings based on erroneous interpretation of the prophecy of Daniel 8:14.

The Bible states very clearly that any human attempt to interfere with God's divine plan brings about unpredictable consequences. Millerite interpretation of the prophecy of Daniel 8:14 is erroneous; therefore, attributing the "1844 Disappointment" a biblical prophetic image is spiritually offensive. The sanctuary doctrine, in spite of its alleged good intention, generates unbiblical teachings and interpretations.

3. Belief 19(20) – The Sabbath

The beneficial Creator, after the six days of Creation, rested on the seventh day and instituted the Sabbath for all people as a memorial of Creation. The fourth Commandment of God's unchangeable law requires the observance of this seventh-day Sabbath as the day of rest, worship, and ministry in harmony with the teaching and practice of Jesus, the Lord of the Sabbath. The Sabbath is a day of delightful communion with God and one another. It is a symbol of our redemption in Christ, a sign of our sanctification, a token of our allegiance, and a foretaste of our eternal future in God's kingdom. The Sabbath is God's perpetual sign of His eternal covenant between Him and His people. Joyful observance of this holy time from evening to evening, sunset to sunset, is a celebration of God's creative and redemptive acts. (Gen. 2:1-3; Ex. 20:8-11;

Lk. 4:16; Is. 56:5,6; 58:13-14; Mt. 12:1-12; Ex. 31:13-17; Ezek. 20:12,20; Deut. 5:12-15; Heb. 4:1-11; Lev. 23:32; Mk. 2:27-28).

Ellen G. White wrote:

- "I saw that God had not changed the Sabbath, for he never changes. But the pope had changed it from the seventh day to the first day of the week; for he was to change times and laws" (*Early Writings of Ellen G. White, p.33*).

- "The pope has changed the day of rest from the seventh to the first day" (*Early Writings of Ellen G. White, p.65*).

- "The seal of God is revealed in the observance of the Seventh-day Sabbath" (*Testimonies, vol.8, p.117*).

- "To obey the commandments is the only way to obtain His favour" (*Testimonies, vol.2, p.84*).

- "From what was shown to me, there is a great work to be accomplished for you before you can be accepted in the sight of God" (*Testimonies, vol. 2, p.84*).

According to the Book of Genesis, the fall of Adam and Eve into sin brought the entire creation under a curse (Gen. 3:17-19). Thus it is pertinent to assume that the seventh day Sabbath became a memorial of creation under a curse! On the other hand, the Gospel states very clearly that among the main allegations, which led to Jesus' arrested and ultimately to His death sentence by crucified, was breaking the Sabbath law.

God, through Christ, established a new covenant with His people, a covenant of a new creation. Jesus Christ revealed to mankind a new law – the law of the Spirit with its two command-ments of love. How do Adventists regard these two commandments in relation to doctrinal expression "God's unchangeable law"? Are these new commandments regarded as "the Son contradicts the Father"? Does this imply exception regarding the implementa-tion of the law? How do Adventists doctrinally justify Pharisees' constant plot to kill Jesus for breaking the Sabbath?

"The Sabbath is God's perpetual sign of eternal covenant between Him and His people" [Belief 19(20)].

This is not quite so. The Holy Scripture clearly states the following: "*...it (Sabbath) is a sign between me (Yahweh) and you (Israel)*" (Ex. 31:13, 16-17; Deut. 5:15; Ezek. 20:12). For reasons of convenience, the founders of Seventh-day Adventism replaced the word "*you (Israel)*" with "*His people.*" Why? If a non-Adventist is told that Sabbath is a sign between "*God and Israel*", he will reply: I want to be a Christian not an Israelite. Another major reason for omitting the word "*Israel*" was to convey a misleading message: Sabbath is a perpetual sign of the covenant between Yahweh and Christians. The expression "*His people*" leaves an open door to ambiguous interpretations; the word "*Israel*" stays firm, therefore, any speculation is futile.

Adventists will argue that, according to the Old Testament, Israel is called God's chosen people. That is true! However, what they overlook is the fact that God's people under the new covenant are not the people of the old covenant. God's people under the "*new covenant*" are those who accept the "*word of God and the testimony of Jesus Christ*", those who worship God "*in spirit and in truth.*" God's new covenant is sealed by the blood of Jesus Christ, the Lamb of God, not by the blood of animals.

From the New Testament perspective, the popular expression "Israel is God's people" turns out to be an unsubstantial argument, as the house of Israel and the house of Judah rejected Jesus Christ, the prophesied Messiah, and God's new covenant (see: Mt. 27:22-26; Jer. 31:31-34; Heb. 8:7-13; Mt. 26:27-28; Lk. 22:19-20; 1Cor. 11:23-25). It is saddening for a believer under the new covenant to accept the idea that God's people are those who died during the forty years spent in the desert as a result of Yahweh's punishment, all those who were twenty years and older, all except Caleb and Joshua (Num. 14:29-30). The Holy Scripture declares that true descendants of Abraham are those who have faith (Gal. 3:6-7; Rom. 4:13-17), and that only a remnant of the people of Israel will be saved (Is. 10:21-22; Rom. 9:27). The topic regarding "*God's people*" is disputable. Humankind, having the freedom to choose between obedience and rebellion, is unpredictable; however, God knows His people

– all those who worship Him "*in spirit and in truth.*"

The central issue is that seventh-day Sabbath is a "*sign*" between Yahweh and the people delivered from Egyptian slavery. The Sabbath, a sign of the covenant between Yahweh and Israel, a memorial of deliverance from Egyptian slavery cannot be a sign for believers under the new covenant. God's new covenant in Christ is a covenant of the Spirit (2Cor 3:6; Rom. 7:6) and does not incorporate seventh-day Sabbath, the physical sign of the Sinaitic covenant. God finds the first covenant faulty and old (Heb. 8:7-8, 13). By speaking of a new covenant, God makes the first one old. And anything that becomes obsolete and outdated will soon disappear (Heb 8:13). Once the old covenant is abolished, the sign of that covenant is also abolished! Once the new covenant replaces the old one, the so-called "*eternal*" sign and the "*eternal*" Sinaitic covenant become <u>terminable</u>.

God's people under the new covenant, through the sacrificial death of Jesus Christ on the cross of Golgotha, are liberated from the bondage of sin, not from Egyptian slavery.

Seventh-day Adventists are regarded by many people as followers of the old covenant law – a somewhat uncomfortable image. In response to this, Adventists argue that they are Christians and, by baptism, they confess Christ as their Lord and Saviour, they confess their faith in the death and resurrection of Jesus Christ. That is true! However, at baptism, they accept and promise to order their live in harmony with the 27(28) Adventist fundamental beliefs, which include belief 18(19) – The Law of God. This belief presents the law (Ten Commandments) as <u>the basis of God's covenant</u> with his people, which is a reference to the covenant established on Mount Sinai. On the other hand, they must also accept Ellen White as the Lord's messenger and the "October 22, 1844 Christ" of the sanctuary doctrine – such teachings do not concordance with the Gospel!

Jesus said to His disciples:

> "*19 Go ye therefore, and make disciples of all the nations, baptizing them into the name of the Father and of the Son and of the Holy Spirit*" (Mt. 28:19).

225

Jesus never said that the way to the Father is: 27 beliefs and 13 vows – a product of human speculation). Why 27+13? Why not more or less? Is God's divine glory limited to 27(28) beliefs and 13 baptismal vows?

How does the Sabbath law apply in the polar circle zone[52] during the white nights of the polar summer, when the sun does not set for about two-three months? How does the Sabbath law apply during the winter polar night, the opposite phenomenon of the summer polar day, when the sun does not rise, that is, there is 24 hour night for several months? Some Sabbatarians may argue that there are other less prominent signs that differentiate day from night – in this case, astronomy courses required. As a suggestion, white polar nights may be regarded as a symbolic reminder of the "new heaven and new earth", which are to come, and where there is no need of the sun or the moon to shine on it, for the glory of God is its light; likewise, winter polar nights may be regarded as a symbolic reminder of what is contrary to God's glory. This reasoning is based on the following verse:

> "23 And the city hath no need of the sun, neither of the moon, to shine upon it: for the glory of God did lighten it, [t]and the lamp thereof is the Lamb" (Rev. 21:23).

"It (Sabbath) is a symbol of our redemption in Christ… a celebration of God's creative and redemptive acts" [Belief 19(20)].

What is this? The following Bible verses provide a very clear description of the symbols of Christian redemption in Christ:

> "19 And he took [d]bread, and when he had given thanks, he brake it, and gave to them, saying, This is my body [e]which is given for you: this do in remembrance of me. 20 And the cup in like manner after supper, saying, This cup is the new covenant in my blood, even that which is poured out for you" (Lk. 22:19-20; 1Cor. 11:23-25; Mt. 26:26-28; Mk. 14:22-23).

> "19 Go ye therefore, and make disciples of all the

nations, baptizing them into the name of the Father and of the Son and of the Holy Spirit" (Mt. 28:19).

"3 Or are ye ignorant that all we who were baptized into Christ Jesus were baptized into his death? 4 We were buried therefore with him through baptism into death: that like as Christ was raised from the dead through the glory of the Father, so we also might walk in newness of life" (Rom. 6:3-4).

"30 But of him are ye in Christ Jesus, who was made unto us wisdom from God, [q]and righteousness and sanctification, and redemption" (1Cor. 1:30).

According to the Old Testament, the Sabbath is related to the creation and Sinaitic covenant, but in nowise to redemption of mankind. If Sabbath observance is a symbol of our redemption in Christ, then what is the significance of the Holy Communion and baptism? Doctrinal allegation "Sabbath is a symbol of our redemption in Christ" is blasphemous!

How could the founders of Seventh-day Adventism assert that Sabbath is a symbol of their redemption in Christ, when, according to the Gospel, the accusation of transgression of the Sabbath law was one of the three main causes, which culminated in Jesus' arrest and ultimately to His death sentence by crucifixion? Adventist doctrinal expression "Sabbath (sign of the old covenant) is a symbol of our redemption in Christ" proves to be a myth. No myth can last forever! A practical example of such doctrinal claim concerning the Sabbath is this: a woman (biblical allegory of the church) remarries thus she becomes bound unto the new marriage (new covenant), but at the same time she wears the wedding ring (seventh-day Sabbath), a sign of the previous marriage (old covenant).

"It (Sabbath) is… a sign of our sanctification" [Belief 19 (20)].

This doctrinal allegation is based on the Old Testament teaching according to which people are sanctified by observing the seventh-day of the week as a holy day. However, it seems that the founders of Adventist, whether deliberately or out of ignorance, neglected the fact that sanctification is the work of the Holy Spirit, that is, believers are purified by the power of the Holy Spirit, not by the law (Sabbath law). Keeping the law is a consequence of the work of the Holy Spirit on believer's heart and mind. It seems that they overlooked the seal of God – the Holy Spirit – that sanctifies those who believe the word of God, the gospel of salvation (Eph. 1:13; Eph. 4:30; 2Cor. 1:21-22); they neglected the fact that Christians are ministers of the new covenant – a covenant of the spirit, not of the written law (2Cor. 3:6). How many Sabbath-keepers are truly sanctified therefore will be saved just because they observe the seventh-day Sabbath? Is God's kingdom a matter of keeping a certain day? In the spiritual world, physical things like seventh day Sabbath do not apply – God is always honoured! No one is justified by the works of the law, but by faith – the faith in Christ and through Christ (Rom. 4:9; Rom. 3:19-24; Rom. 5:1-2; Rom. 10:1-4; Gal. 2:15-16; Gal. 3:10-11).

Sanctification is the work of the Holy Spirit, that is, believers are sanctified by the presence of the Holy Spirit within them; therefore, the "*Holy Spirit*" is the sign (seal) of Christian sanctification, not the seventh-day of the week! The following Bible verses confirm this reasoning:

> "*13But we are bound to give thanks always to God for you, brethren beloved of the Lord, because God hath from the beginning chosen you to salvation <u>through sanctification of the Spirit</u> and belief of the truth*" (2Thess. 2:13).

> "*2 according to the foreknowledge of God the Father, in sanctification of the Spirit, unto obedience and sprinkling of the blood of Jesus Christ: Grace to you and peace be multiplied 2Elect according to the foreknowledge of God the Father, <u>through sanctification of the Spirit</u>, unto obedience and sprinkling of the blood of Jesus Christ: Grace unto you, and peace, be multiplied*" (1Pet. 1:2).

"*9 then hath he said, Lo, I am come to do thy will. He taketh away the first, that he may establish the second. 10 [c]By which will we have been sanctified through the offering of the body of Jesus Christ once for all*" (Heb. 10:9-10).

"*30 But of him are ye in Christ Jesus, who was made unto us wisdom from God, [q]and righteousness and sanctification, and redemption*" (1Cor. 1:30).

"*24 [h]God is a Spirit: and they that worship him must worship in spirit and truth*" (Jn. 4:24).

"*13 in whom ye also, having heard the word of the truth, the [i]gospel of your salvation,—in whom, having also believed, ye were sealed with the Holy Spirit of promise*" (Eph. 1:13).

"*30 And grieve not the Holy Spirit of God, in whom ye were sealed unto the day of redemption*" (Eph. 4:30).

"*21 Now he that establisheth us with you [i]in Christ, and anointed us, is God; 22 [j]who also sealed us, and gave us the earnest of the Spirit in our hearts*" (2Cor. 1:21-22).

"*47 Sanctify them in your truth. Your word is truth [a]*" (Jn. 17:17 WEB).

"It is a symbol of our redemption in Christ, a sign of our sanctification, a token of our allegiance, and a foretaste of our eternal future in God's kingdom" [Belief 19(20)].

The above quoted doctrinal allegation is arrogant and offensive. It undermines the fundamental values of Christianity such as: the symbols of redemption in Christ and God's seal (sign) of sanctification. On the other hand, such doctrinal allegation seems to be rather a pledge of allegiance to the Sinaitic covenant, as Sabbath is the sign of that covenant.

Adventists may argue that they have been baptized and

partake of the Lord's Supper, therefore, they pledge their allegiance to the new covenant. That is quite an interesting remark! However, at baptism they accept and promise to order their life in harmony with the doctrine according to which "Sabbath is a symbol of our redemption in Christ, a sign of our sanctification, and a token of our allegiance." Such a doctrinal allegation is in contradiction with the Gospel, with the New Testament teachings in general.

"...the observance of this seventh-day Sabbath as the day of rest, worship, and ministry in harmony with the teaching and practice of Jesus, the Lord of the Sabbath" [Belief 19(20)].

It is pertinent to affirm that these particular verses refer to Jesus of Nazareth who was circumcised on the eighth day after His birth and lived under Jewish law, and who was not yet baptized in the river Jordan. However, as mentioned before, Pharisees and other Sabbath keepers were plotting to kill Jesus for breaking the Sabbath law (Jn. 5:17-18; Mt. 12:9-14; Mk. 3:1-6; Lk. 6:2; 13:10-17; Jn. 9:16). Jesus' Sabbath was much more than the traditional Sabbath as taught by the Jewish law: Jesus honoured the Father as He really is – "*in spirit and in truth*" seven days a week. Regarding the biblical expression "*the Son of man is Lord even of the Sabbath*", Jesus Christ is Lord every day, not just of the seventh day. The Word – Christ Jesus – is Lord over everything; true believers honour God "*in spirit and in truth*" every day.

4. Vow 6

Do you accept the Ten Commandments as still binding upon the Christians; and is it your purpose, by the power of the indwelling Christ, to keep this law, including the forth commandment, which requires the observance of the seventh day of the week as the Sabbath of the Lord?

Vow 6 incorporates belief 18(19) and belief 19(20). Therefore, it is appropriate to quote at least in part belief 18(19).

Belief 18(19) – The Law of God

The great principles of God's law are embodied in the Ten Commandments. They express God's love, will, and purposes concerning human conduct and relationships and are binding upon all people in every age. These precepts are the basis of God's covenant with his people and the standard of God's judgement [...].

Before going into the details of this doctrinal teaching on the law, one should consider the following biblical facts:

- The Ten Commandments, the Tablets of the Covenant, are the "basis" of the covenant made on Mount Sinai (Mount Horeb) between Yahweh and Israel (Ex. 34:27-28; Deut. 9:9-11, 15; 1Kg. 8:21);

- The seventh-day Sabbath is a sign of the covenant established on Mount Sinai (Ex. 31:13, 17; Ezek. 20:12, 20; Deut. 5:15);

- Christians are God's people of the new covenant sealed with the blood of Jesus Christ, the Lamb of God (Mt. 26:27-28; Mk. 14:23-24; Lk. 22:20; 1Cor. 11:23-25). This new covenant is based on Christ's two commandments of love (Mt. 22:36-40; Mk. 12:28-31; Lk. 10:25-27; Rom. 13:9-10; Jn. 13:34; Jn. 15:12, 17; 1Jn. 3:23.

According to vow number 6, baptismal candidate affirms publicly that he accepts the law, the Ten Commandments. In reality, this vow is ambiguous as follows:

1) Baptismal candidate, indirectly, seems to pledge allegiance to the old covenant, as the Ten Commandments are the basis of the covenant made on Mount Sinai and Sabbath is the sign of that covenant. This reasoning is confirmed by the fundamental belief number 18(19), where is stated the following: "These precepts (Ten Commandments) are the basis of God's covenant with his people...";

2) The observance of the seventh day of the week as the Sabbath of the Lord is in opposition to Jesus' statement "*...my Father worketh even until now, and I work*" (Jn. 5:17). The Father and the Son are always working.

231

A Christian cannot be bound to two covenants and two covenant signs. To do this, one must undermine God's new covenant in Christ. Christians are bound to something much better than the Ten Commandments: they are morally bound to Christ's two commandments of love (agape) – the two greatest commandments on which the whole law and the prophets depend on.

Believers under the new covenant have God's laws (commandments) put into their mind and written into their heart (Jer. 31:33; Heb. 8:10); they keep the commandments of God, but they do not keep the sign (seventh-day Sabbath) of the old covenant. Christians do not serve in the old way of the written law, but in the new way of the Spirit. This is done in accordance with the prophets and the teaching of the New Testament (Ps. 95:7-11; Heb. 4:1-11; Is. 1:13; Hos. 2:11; Col. 2:14-17; Jer. 31:31-34; Heb. 8:7-13; 2Cor. 3:6; Rom. 7:6).

As it was mentioned before, the Ten Commandments tolerate certain sins. Therefore, is it morally right for a Christian – the new covenant believer – to be bound to a law that tolerates slavery, polygamy… and so on? Are Christians bound to the "basis" of the old covenant sealed with the blood of animals? If the Ten Commandments are still binding to Christians, does this mean that Christians are allowed to be slaveholders, practice polygamy, divorce, and so forth, as the Ten Commandments and the entire Torah do not prohibit these fleshly desires?

Once again, are Christians bound to the Ten Commandments – the basis of the old covenant? One can answer this question in two ways:

1) Do the Ten Commandments allow or prohibit slavery, polygamy, divorce…? If the Decalogue prohibits these vicious desires, then let Seventh-day Adventists prove it biblically. It is quite evident that Christians are bound to Christ's two commandments of love of the new covenant.

2) The observance of nine commandments is mentioned many times in the New Testament; however, keeping the Sabbath of the fourth commandment is not mentioned.

A reasonable believer should ask himself a different question:

are the <u>Nine Commandments</u> binding on Christians, as the new covenant established on the cross of Golgotha put an end to the old Sinaitic covenant and its sigh, the Sabbath?

God's new covenant is a covenant of the spirit, not of the written law (2Cor. 3:6). This covenant has a sign (seal), the Holy Spirit. The Sabbath of the new covenant sounds like this: "<u>*Come unto me*</u>, *all ye that labor and are heavy laden,* <u>*and I will give you rest*</u>" (Mt. 11:28). However, if a believer considers that it is right and useful to have a day of rest and worship weekly, then let the day of the resurrection of our Lord Jesus Christ be that day!

To be in concordance with the Old Testament law, a believer who is bound to the seventh-day Sabbath should also keep the Sabbath year (see: Lev. 25:1-7). Do Adventists observe the Sabbatical year?

The law is not made for the righteous but for law-breakers. Therefore, if a believer is led by the Spirit, he is not under law (Gal. 5:18). For a Christian, the Ten Commandments represent <u>a reminder</u> of what sin is.

5. Belief 12(13) – The remnant and its mission

The universal Church is composed of all who truly believe in Christ, but in the last days, a time of widespread apostasy, a remnant has been called out to keep the commandments of God and the faith of Jesus. This remnant announces the arrival of the judgment hour, proclaims salvation through Christ, and heralds the approach of His second advent. This proclamation is symbolized by the three angels of Revelation 14; it coincides with the work of judgment in heaven and results in a work of repentance and reform on earth. Every believer is called to have a personal part in this worldwide witness. (Rev. 12:17; 14:6-12; 18:1-4; 2Cor. 5:10; Jude 3, 14; 1Pet. 1:16-19; 2Pet. 3:10-14; Rev. 21:1-14.)

Ellen G. White wrote:
- "As God has shown me in holy vision...we heard the voice of God like many waters, which gave us the day and hour of Jesus'

coming" (*Early Writings, pp.15, 34, 285*).

- (*First Vision 12/1844*) "It was just as impossible for them (those that gave up their faith in the 1844 movement) to get on the path again and go to the city, as all the wicked world which God had rejected. They fell all the way along the path one after another," (Foregoing now deleted), "until we heard the voice of God like many waters, which gave us the day and hour of Jesus' coming. The living saints, 144.000 in number, knew and understood the voice, while the wicked thought it was thunder and an earthquake" (*A Word to the Little Flock, p.14, edition 1847*).

- "[...] I have not the slightest knowledge as to the time spoken by the voice of God. I heard the hour proclaimed, but had no remembrance of that hour after I came out of vision" (*Selected Messages 1, p.298, edition 1889*).

- "To obey the commandments is the only way to obtain His favour" (*Testimonies, vol.2, p.84*).

- "The seal of God is revealed in the observance of the Seventh-day Sabbath" (*Ellen G. White. Testimonies, vol.1, p.117*);

- "Here we find the mark of the beast. The very act of changing the Sabbath into Sunday, on part of the Catholic Church, without any authority from the Bible" (*Ellen G. White. The Mark of the Beast, page 23*).

- "The Sunday Sabbath is purely a child of Papacy. It is the mark of the beast" (*Adventist Review, vol.1, No.2, August, 1850*).

- "The mark of the beast is Sunday-keeping. A law will enforce this upon Seventh-day Adventists. They won't obey. Then they will be outlawed, persecuted, and condemned to death!" (*D.M. Canright, 1914*).

- "The health reform, I was shown, is a part of the 'third angel's message' and is just as closely connected with it as are arm and hand with the body" (*Testimonies vol.1, p.486*).

Belief 12 unveiled would sound like this:

The universal Church is composed of all who truly believe in Christ, but in the last days, a time of widespread apostasy, a remnant – the Millerite movement – has been called to keep the commandments of God and the faith of Jesus. This remnant, the "first-day Adventists", announces the arrival of judgment hour, proclaims salvation through Christ, and heralds the approach of His second advent – on October 22, 1844. To a tiny part of this remnant has been revealed the "sanctuary doctrine" and the "Sabbath" – both revelations confirmed by prophetic visions of Ellen G. White, the Lord's messenger – and it became the Seventh-day Adventists Church. This tiny remnant proclaims the three angels' message of Revelation 14, advocates Sabbath observance, promotes health reform, and denounces all other churches that reject these messages as apostate churches.

The expression "widespread apostasy" stated in belief 12 has a religious significance and is in total opposition with the "remnant", which came into existence around 1844 (more precisely in 1846). This alleged "remnant" has been called to keep the commandments of God and the faith of Jesus. According to the logic of this doctrinal allegation, the vast majority of Christians who do not belong to this "remnant" are apostates – they do not seem to keep God's commandments and the faith of Jesus.

The central issue is that all those who reject the message of this remnant (the Adventist Church) are apostates and carriers of the mark of the beast, thus constitute the widespread apostasy of the last days. Churches that reject the old covenant Sabbath, which the "remnant" identifies as the "seal of God", are apostate churches because they keep Sunday, which the "remnant" identifies as the "mark of the beast." Therefore, all non-Adventists, and all non-Sabbath keeping Christians are apostates thus under God's curse described in the Three Angels' Message of Revelation chapter 14. However, being aware of the consequence of this doctrinal allegation, some Adventists may argue: we do not say that all Christians are apostates, yet, at the same time, they uphold the teaching "Sunday-keeping is the mark of the beast." Being challenged into more investigative conversation, these Adventists often find a subtle ways of dealing with sensitive topics – they avoid direct answers.

These doctrinal teachings, where Ellen White played a prominent role, are deeply rooted in the history of Adventism. Analyzing them, the following remarks cannot escape our attention:

- Christians who took part in the "Millerite Movement" were "apostate believers" because their leader, William Miller, preached the second coming of Christ, not the seventh-day Sabbath – Millerites were Sunday-keepers;

- Martin Luther was an apostate and the entire Protestant movement is an apostasy because these believers were Sunday-keepers;

- Christian martyrs of the first three centuries were apostates and Christianity, the new religion of the Roman Empire which later split into Eastern Orthodoxy and Western Catholicism, has the "mark of the beast." All Sunday-keeping Christians have the mark of the beast;

- Ellen White's writings and other Adventist publications provide considerable material regarding religious persecution within Christianity. However, when it comes to the day of rest, most of those persecuted believers seem to be apostates, as they were Sunday-keepers.

On the other hand, the "remnant" called out to keep the commandments of God and the faith of Jesus must also accept and order their lives in harmony with the following:

1) The "October 22, 1844 Christ" of Crosier's "sanctuary doctrine" promoted by Ellen G. White. **Note:** Somehow, the "Shut door doctrine" was abandoned.

2) Ellen G. White is the "Lord's messenger (prophet)" and her writings as a continuous and authoritative source of truth in the church [Belief 17(18), Vows 8, 11].

As mentioned elsewhere, the contextual expression "called out to keep the commandments of God" is ambiguous. Which commandments? The Ten Commandments – the basis of the old covenant – or the two commandments of Jesus – the basis of God's new covenant – the two greatest commandments on which hangs all the law and the prophets (Mt. 22:36-40; Mk. 12:28-31; Lk. 10:25-27)?

According to the Old Testament law, Israelites had to circumcise their sons on the eighth day after birth – Jesus and the apostle had also been circumcised. To become part of "God's people", thus share in the blessing of the covenant, "*circumcision*" was a mandatory condition (Gen. 17:14); on the other hand, no uncircumcised person was allowed to celebrate the Passover (Ex. 12:47-48). At that time, an uncircumcised person could not possibly be part of God's chosen people thus enjoy Sabbath – the sign of the old covenant. Therefore, to be in harmony with requirements of the law, Adventists should circumcise their sons. In case they do, a logical question should be answered: Abrahamic "*circumcision*" adopted by the Mosaic Law, an essential and mandatory requirement for believers under the Sinaitic covenant, is discriminatory: circumcision is a physical sign of the covenant between Yahweh and men only. What about the women? Is God's kingdom a kingdom for men only? Was Jesus Christ crucified on the cross of Golgotha only for the circumcised?

In this respect, it is pertinent to mention the fact that biblical fulfillment of the verse "*And the Word became flesh, and [h]dwelt among us...*" (Jn. 1:14) was made possible through <u>woman</u>, not through man!

Christians do keep God's commandments and the faith of Jesus. However, they do not give allegiance to Sabbath, the sign of the old covenant sealed with the blood of animal, because they are faithful to God's new covenant sealed with the blood of Jesus Christ, the Lamb of God. Christians give their allegiance to God the Father through Christ and to Christ.

"This remnant announces the arrival of the judgment hour, proclaims salvation through Christ, and heralds the approach of His second advent" [Belief 12(13)].

Such doctrinal allegation is very contradictory. Careful analysis of the history of Adventism unveils the following facts:

Millerites – the First-day Adventists – proclaimed Christ's Second Advent on October 22, 1844, which, as we all know, did not occur;

- Seventh-day Adventists propagate Sabbath observance and the Sanctuary doctrine;

- Ellen White's prophetic visions according to which Jesus Christ would return in 1844 (also in 1845 and 1851) did not come true – a prophetic blunder.

Note: An alternative vow[49] was introduced in 2005, which does not contain a reference to Adventist Church as the remnant church. Candidates may now choose whether to take the traditional vows or the new ones.

This alternative vow consists of three affirmations and seems a direct attack on the traditional vows and the very history of Adventism, as it omits most affirmations of the traditional vows. From the perspective of alternative baptismal vow results the following:

1) Adventist Church is not the remnant church anymore.

2) If Adventist Church is not identified anymore as the "remnant church", does this means that it slides towards the "widespread apostasy"?

3) The gift of prophecy, which refers to Ellen G. White as the Lord's messenger (a prophet), is not one of the identifying marks of this church.

4) The Ten Commandments, including the seventh-day Sabbath, are not binding unto Christians anymore.

5) Could this be a sign that sincere hearts within the Seventh-day Adventist Church are awakening?

On the other hand, this alternative vow proves to be just a cosmetic modification as follows:

1) Does not interfere or change the 27, that is, 28 Adventist fundamental beliefs, as affirmation 2 of this alternative vow – an equivalent of the traditional baptismal vow 11 – requires

of baptismal candidates to pledge to live their life in harmony with Adventist fundamental beliefs.

2) Omits sensitive doctrinal affirmations contained in the traditional vows like:

- Seventh-day Adventist Church is the remnant church;
- The gift of prophecy is an identifying mark of the remnant church;
- The Ten Commandments, including the seventh-day Sabbath, are binding on Christians.

3) Minimizes the exposure of those sensitive doctrinal teachings to criticism.

4) It makes Adventist baptismal ceremony look more compatible biblically.

Was this alternative baptismal vow introduced to the glory of God or is it just a very carefully calculated cosmetic modification? If it is, it can fool only certain people. God's kingdom is not a matter of doctrinal speculation.

If Seventh-day Adventists truly desire to honour God, and if they truly want to be part of the remnant church, then they should get rid of compromised doctrinal teachings. Adventist doctrinal status would be more honourable without the sanctuary doctrine and Ellen G. White. Believers involved in the controversial "Millerite movement" were very sincere and devoted and did not have any doctrines. However, they were naive enough to have more confidence in the so-called human wisdom regarding the interpretation of Daniel 8:14 prophecy than the word of God. Adventist should learn a lesson from the Millerite mistake – they should not embrace it.

Conclusion

The fall of Adam and Eve into sin has affected their fellowship with the Creator and ultimately lead to the separation between God and mankind. God in His Providence has elaborated a plan to re-establish the lost relation with humankind and to bring the entire creation back to its original glory. The Bible, from Genesis to Revelation, is focusing on God's divine plan of salvation of humankind. This was accomplished through the Word, Jesus Christ, who left His heavenly glory, came down to earth and became man. On the cross of Golgotha, by offering Himself as the perfect sacrifice required by the law for redemption of humankind from sin, Jesus Christ fulfilled the law and the prophets. Therefore, announcing of a new prophecy by the so-called new prophets is not in harmony with the Holy Scripture.

In the nineteenth century, as a result of the so-called "freedom of religion", have emerged several ideologically controversial religions. These new religions claim to have direct divine inspiration and the spirit of prophecy; therefore, under such arrogant auspices, propagate a different Gospel.

At the conclusion of this brief exegetical analysis of Adventism, it is a privilege and Christian duty to express my final position regarding Ellen G. White's writings and certain doctrinal allegations of the Seventh-day Adventist Church. It is spiritually offensive to uphold the following:

1) On October 22, 1844, Christ, instead of return to earth as some were expecting, entered into the Most Holy Place of the Heavenly Sanctuary.

2) On October 22, 1844, Christ entered the second and last phase of His atoning ministry, a work of investigative judgment.

3) To be baptized in the name of the Father, and the Son, and

the Holy Spirit, one must accept, among other teachings, the doctrine according to which Ellen G. White is the "Lord's messenger" (a prophet), and her writings are a continuous and authoritative source of truth which provides for the church comfort, guidance, instruction, and correction.

4) Seventh-day Adventist Church is the remnant church of God.

5) Sunday-keeping is the "mark of the beast."

6) Seventh-day Sabbath is the "seal of God."

7) The Sabbath is a symbol of our redemption in Christ;

8) Seventh-day Sabbath, a sign of the covenant between Yahweh and Israel established on Mount Sinai, a memorial of deliverance from Egyptian slavery, is binding on believers under God's new covenant established on the cross of Golgotha.

9) Christ put an end to the old covenant, but did not put an end to Sabbath – the sigh of that covenant.

10) Neglecting the undeniable biblical fact that Jewish religious leader plotted to kill Jesus for transgressing the Sabbath law.

11) The beast with seven heads and ten horns that looks like a "leopard, bear, and lion" represents the alleged revived Western Roman Empire.

12) Seven heads represent seven hills, not "seven mountains."

13) The beast with "two horns like a lamb" represents the Unite States of America.

God is Spirit. His worshipers must worship in spirit and in truth – God seeks such people to worship him. Therefore the Holy Scripture always is to be analyzed "in spirit and in truth." The following selections of Bible verses contain very specific messages. To ignore them means to ignore its source, the Holy Spirit:

Christic and the Sabbath

"*⁹ And he departed thence, and went into their synagogue: ¹⁰ and behold, a man having a withered hand.
And they asked him, saying, Is it lawful to heal on
the sabbath day? that they might accuse him. ¹¹ And
he said unto them, What man shall there be of you,
that shall have one sheep, and if this fall into a pit
on the sabbath day, will he not lay hold on it, and
lift it out? ¹² How much then is a man of more value
than a sheep! Wherefore it is lawful to do good on
the sabbath day. ¹³ Then saith he to the man, Stretch
forth thy hand. And he stretched it forth; and it was
restored whole, as the other. ¹⁴ But <u>the Pharisees
went out, and took counsel against him, how they
might destroy him</u>*" (Mt. 12:9-14).

"*¹ And he entered again into the synagogue; and
there was a man there who had his hand withered.
² And they watched him, whether he would heal him
on the sabbath day; that they might accuse him.
³ And he saith unto the man that had his hand withered, [a]Stand forth. ⁴ And he saith unto them, Is it
lawful on the sabbath day to do good, or to do harm?
to save a life, or to kill? But they held their peace.
⁵ And when he had looked round about on them with
anger, being grieved at the hardening of their heart,
he saith unto the man, Stretch forth thy hand. And
he stretched it forth; and his hand was restored.
⁶ And <u>the Pharisees went out, and straightway with
the Herodians took counsel against him, how they
might destroy him</u>*" Mk. 3:1-6).

"*¹⁰ And he was teaching in one of the synagogues
on the sabbath day. ¹¹ And behold, a woman that
had a spirit of infirmity eighteen years; and she was
bowed together, and could in no wise lift herself up.
¹² And when Jesus saw her, he called her, and said to*

her, *Woman, thou art loosed from thine infirmity.*
*¹³ And he laid his hands upon her: and immediately
she was made straight, and glorified God. ¹⁴ And <u>the
ruler of the synagogue, being moved with indig-
nation because Jesus had healed on the sabbath,
answered and said to the multitude, There are six
days in which men ought to work: in them therefore come and be healed, and not on the day of the
sabbath</u>" (Lk. 13:10-14).*

*"¹⁷ But Jesus answered them, My Father worketh
even until now, and I work. ¹⁸ For this cause therefore <u>the Jews sought the more to kill him, because
he not only brake the sabbath, but also called God
his own Father, making himself equal with God</u>" (Jn.
5:17-18).*

*"¹⁵ Again therefore the Pharisees also asked him
how he received his sight. And he said unto them,
He put clay upon mine eyes, and I washed, and I see.
¹⁶ <u>Some therefore of the Pharisees said, This man is
not from God, because he keepeth not the sabbath</u>.
But others said, How can a man that is a sinner do
such signs? And there was a division among them"
(Jn. 9:15-16).*

*"At that season Jesus went on the sabbath day
through the grainfields; and his disciples were
hungry and began to pluck ears and to eat. ² But <u>the
Pharisees, when they saw it, said unto him, Behold,
thy disciples do that which it is not lawful to do
upon the sabbath</u>" (Mt. 12:1-2; also Mk. 2:23-24; Lk.
6:1-2).*

*"¹⁷ But Jesus answered them, <u>My Father worketh
even until now</u>, and I work" (Mt. 11:28).*

*"²⁸ <u>Come unto me</u>, all ye that labor and are heavy
laden, <u>and I will give you rest</u>" (Mt. 11:28).*

Christ and the Law

"³¹ Behold, <u>the days come, says Yahweh, that I will make a new covenant with the house of Israel, and with the house of Judah</u>: ³² not according to the covenant that I made with their fathers in the day that I took them by the hand to bring them out of the land of Egypt; which my covenant they broke, although I was a husband to them, says Yahweh. ³³ But <u>this is the covenant</u> that I will make with the house of Israel after those days, says Yahweh: <u>I will put my law in their inward parts, and in their heart will I write it</u>; and I will be their God, and they shall be my people" (Jer. 31:31-33).

"⁷ For <u>if that first covenant had been faultless, then would no place have been sought for a second. ⁸ For</u> ^[f] <u>finding fault with them, he saith,</u> ^[g]<u>Behold, the days come, saith the Lord, That I will</u> ^[h]<u>make a new covenant with the house of Israel and with the house of Judah</u>; ⁹ Not according to the covenant that I made with their fathers In the day that I took them by the hand to lead them forth out of the land of Egypt; For they continued not in my covenant, And I regarded them not, saith the Lord. ¹⁰ For <u>this is the covenant</u> that ^[i]I will make with the house of Israel After those days, saith the Lord; <u>I will put my laws into their mind, And on their heart also will I write them</u>: And I will be to them a God, And they shall be to me a people: ¹¹ And they shall not teach every man his fellow-citizen, And every man his brother, saying, Know the Lord: For all shall know me, From the least to the greatest of them. ¹² For I will be merciful to their iniquities, And their sins will I remember no more. ¹³ <u>In that he saith, A new covenant, he hath made the first old. But that which is becoming old and waxeth aged is nigh unto vanishing away</u>" (Heb. 8:7-13).

"¹⁰ but when that which is perfect is come, _that which is in part shall be done away_" (1Cor. 13:10).

"¹⁶ _The law and the prophets were until John_: from that time the [j]gospel of the kingdom of God is preached, and every man entereth violently into it" (Lk. 16:16).

"¹⁷ Now this I say: A covenant confirmed beforehand by God, _the law, which came four hundred and thirty years after_, doth not disannul, so as to make the promise of none effect. ¹⁸ For if the inheritance is of the law, it is no more of promise: but God hath granted it to Abraham by promise. ¹⁹ _What then is the law? It was added because of transgressions, till the seed should come to whom the promise hath been made_; and it was ordained through angels by the hand of a mediator" (Gal. 3:17-19).

"²⁴ So that _the law is become our tutor to bring us unto Christ_, that we might be justified by faith. ²⁵ But _now that faith is come, we are no longer under a tutor_" (Gal. 3:24-25).

"⁶ who also made us sufficient as _ministers of a new covenant; not of the letter, but of the spirit_: for the letter killeth, but the spirit giveth life" (2Cor. 3:6).

"⁶ But now we have been discharged from the law, having died to that wherein we were held; so that _we serve in newness of the spirit, and not in oldness of the letter_" (Rom. 7:6).

"¹ There is therefore now no condemnation to them that are in Christ Jesus. ² For _the law of the Spirit of life in Christ Jesus made me free from the law of sin and of death_. ³ For what the law could not do, [a] in that it was weak through the flesh, God, sending his own Son in the likeness of [b]sinful flesh [c]and for sin, condemned sin in the flesh" (Rom. 8:1-3).

"¹ Brothers, my heart's desire and my prayer to God is for Israel, that they may be saved. ² For I testify about them that <u>they have a zeal for God, but not according to knowledge</u>. ³ For being ignorant of God's righteousness, and seeking to establish their own righteousness, they didn't subject themselves to the righteousness of God. ⁴ For <u>Christ is the fulfillment[a] of the law for righteousness to everyone who believes</u>" (Rom. 10:1-4 WEB).

"¹⁵ <u>having abolished in his flesh the enmity, even the law of commandments contained in ordinances</u>; that he might create in himself of the two one new man, so making peace" (Eph. 2: 15).

"²⁰ And to the Jews I became as a Jew, that I might gain Jews; to them that are under the law, as under the law, not being myself under the law, that I might gain them that are under the law; ²¹ to them that are without law, as without law, <u>not being without law to God, but under law to Christ</u>, that I might gain them that are without law" (1Cor. 9:20-21).

"¹⁸ But if ye are led by the Spirit, <u>ye are not under the law</u>" (Gal. 5:18).

"⁹ as knowing this, that <u>law is not made for a righteous man, but for the lawless and unruly, for the ungodly and sinners, for the unholy and profane</u>, for [c]murderers of fathers and [d]murderers of mothers, for manslayers, ¹⁰ for fornicators, for abusers of themselves with men, for menstealers, for liars, for false swearers, and if there be any other thing contrary to the [e]sound [f]doctrine; ¹¹ according to the [g]gospel of the glory of the blessed God, which was committed to my" (1Tim. 1:9-11).

Christ's Commandments

"36 *Teacher, which is the great commandment in the law?* 37 *And he said unto him,* [n]*Thou shalt love the Lord thy God with all thy heart, and with all thy soul, and with all thy mind.* 38 *This is the great and first commandment.* 39 [o]*And a second like unto it is this,* [p]*Thou shalt love thy neighbor as thyself.* 40 *On these two commandments the whole law hangeth, and the prophets*" (Mt. 22:36-40).

"28 *And one of the scribes came, and heard them questioning together, and knowing that he had answered them well, asked him, What commandment is the first of all?* 29 *Jesus answered, The first is,* [g]*Hear, O Israel;* [h]*The Lord our God, the Lord is one:* 30 *and thou shalt love the Lord thy God* [i]*with all thy heart, and* [j]*with all thy soul, and* [k]*with all thy mind, and* [l]*with all thy strength.* 31 *The second is this,* [m]*Thou shalt love thy neighbor as thyself. There is none other commandment greater than these*" (Mk. 12:28-31).

"25 *And behold, a certain lawyer stood up and made trial of him, saying, Teacher, what shall I do to inherit eternal life?* 26 *And he said unto him, What is written in the law? how readest thou?* 27 *And he answering said,* [h]*Thou shalt love the Lord thy God* [i]*with all thy heart, and with all thy soul, and with all thy strength, and with all thy mind;* [j]*and thy neighbor as thyself.* 28 *And he said unto him, Thou hast answered right: this do, and thou shalt live*" (Lk. 10:25-27).

"9 *For this,* [e]*Thou shalt not commit adultery, Thou shalt not kill, Thou shalt not steal, Thou shalt not covet, and if there be any other commandment, it is summed up in this word, namely, Thou shalt love thy neighbor as thyself.* 10 *Love worketh no ill to his* neighbor: <u>love therefore is the fulfilment of the law</u>" (Rom. 13:9-10).

"³⁴ <u>A new commandment I give unto you, that ye love one another</u>; [o]even as I have loved you, that ye also love one another" (Jn. 13:34; also Jn. 15:12,17; 1Jn. 3:23);

Christians are justified before God through faith in Christ

"¹⁹ Now <u>we know that what things soever the law saith, it speaketh to them that are under the law</u>; that every mouth may be stopped, and all the world may be brought under the judgment of God: ²⁰ because [k]<u>by</u> [l]<u>the works of the law shall no flesh be</u> [m]<u>justified in his sight; for</u> [n]<u>through the law cometh the knowledge of sin</u>. ²¹ But now apart from the law a righteousness of God hath been manifested, being witnessed by the law and the prophets; ²² <u>even the righteousness of God through faith</u> [o]<u>in Jesus Christ unto all</u> [p]<u>them that believe</u>; for there is no distinction; ²³ for all [q]have sinned, and fall short of the glory of God; ²⁴ <u>being justified freely by his grace through the redemption that is in Christ Jesus</u>" (Rom. 3:19-24).

"<u>Being therefore justified</u> [a]<u>by faith,</u> [b]<u>we have peace with God through our Lord Jesus Christ</u>; ² through whom also we have had our access [c]by faith into this grace wherein we stand; and [d]we [e]rejoice in hope of the glory of" (Rom. 5:1-2).

"¹ Brothers, my heart's desire and my prayer to God is for Israel, that they may be saved. ² For I testify about them that they have a zeal for God, but not according to knowledge. ³ For being ignorant of God's righteousness, and seeking to establish their own righteousness, they didn't subject themselves to the righteousness of God. [4] For <u>Christ is the fulfill-ment[a] of the law for righteousness to everyone who believes</u>" (Rom. 10:1-4 WEB).

"[15] We being Jews by nature, and not sinners of the Gentiles, [16] yet <u>knowing that a man is not [l]justified by the works of the law but through faith in Jesus Christ, even we believed on Christ Jesus</u>, that we might be justified by faith in Christ, and not by the works of the law: <u>because by the works of the law shall no flesh be justified</u>" (Gal. 2:15-16).

"[10] For as many as are of the works of the law are under a curse: for it is written, [k]Cursed is every one who continueth not in all things that are written in the book of the law, to do them. [11] <u>Now that no man is justified [l]by the law before God, is evident: for, [m] The righteous shall live by faith</u>" (Gal. 3:10-11).

"[3] For what saith the scripture? [d]And <u>Abraham believed God, and it was reckoned unto him for righ-teousness</u>" (Rom. 4:3).

"[18] [h]Yea, a man will say, Thou hast faith, and I have works: show me thy faith apart from thy works, and <u>I by my works will show thee my faith</u>" (Jas. 2:18).

"[24] Ye see that <u>by works</u> a man is justified, <u>and not only by faith</u>" (Jas. 2:24).

"[26] For as the body apart from the spirit is dead, even <u>so faith apart from works is dead</u>" (Jas. 2:26).

The seal of God

"[13] in whom ye also, having heard the word of the truth, the [i]gospel of your salvation,—in whom, having also believed, <u>ye were sealed with the Holy Spirit of promise</u>" (Eph. 1:13).

"[30] And <u>grieve not the Holy Spirit of God, in whom ye were sealed</u> unto the day of redemption" (Eph. 4:30).

"[21] Now he that establisheth us with you [i]in Christ, and anointed us, is God; [22] [j]<u>who also sealed us, and gave us the earnest of the Spirit in our hearts</u>" (2Cor. 1:21-22).

Sanctification is the work of the Holy Spirit

"[13] But we are bound to give thanks to God always for you, brethren beloved of the Lord, for that God chose you [m]from the beginning unto salvation <u>in sanctification of the Spirit</u> and [n]belief of the truth" (2Thess. 2:13).

"[2] according to the foreknowledge of God the Father, <u>in sanctification of the Spirit</u>, unto obedience and sprinkling of the blood of Jesus Christ: Grace to you and peace be multiplied" (1Pet. 1:2).

"[30] But of him are ye in Christ Jesus, who was made unto us wisdom from God, [q]and righteousness <u>and sanctification</u>, and redemption" (1Cor. 1:30).

"[9] then hath he said, Lo, I am come to do thy will. He taketh away the first, that he may establish the second. [10] [c]By which will <u>we have been sanctified</u> through the offering of the body of Jesus Christ once for all" (Heb. 10:9-10).

"[17] Sanctify them in your truth. Your word is truth. [a]" (Jn. 17:17 WEB).

"[24] [h]God is a Spirit: and they that worship him must worship in spirit and truth" (Jn. 4:24).

Is Sabbath-keeping binding on Christians?

"[13] "Speak also to the children of Israel, saying, '<u>Most certainly you shall keep my Sabbaths: for it is a sign between me</u> and you throughout your generations; that you may know that I am Yahweh who sanctifies you... [16] Therefore the children of Israel shall keep the Sabbath, to observe the Sabbath throughout their generations, for a perpetual covenant. [17] <u>It is a sign between me and the children of Israel</u> forever; for in six days Yahweh made heaven and earth, and on the seventh day he rested, and was refreshed" (Ex. 31:13, 16-17).

"[12] Moreover also <u>I gave them my Sabbaths, to be a sign between me and them</u>, that they might know that I am Yahweh who sanctifies them... [20] and <u>make my Sabbaths holy; and they shall be a sign between me and you</u>, that you may know that I am Yahweh your God" (Ezek. 20:12, 20).

"[15] <u>You shall remember that you were a servant in the land of Egypt</u>, and Yahweh your God brought you out of there by a mighty hand and by an outstretched arm. <u>Therefore Yahweh your God commanded you to</u>

<u>keep the Sabbath day</u>" (Deut. 5:15).

"[13] Bring no more vain offerings. Incense is an abomination to me; new moons, <u>Sabbaths, and convocations: I can't bear with evil assemblies</u>" (Is. 1:13).

"[11] <u>I will also cause all her celebrations to cease</u>: her feasts, her new moons, <u>her Sabbaths, and all her solemn assemblies</u>" (Hos. 2:11).

"[31] Behold, <u>the days come, says Yahweh, that I will make a new covenant with the house of Israel, and with the house of Judah</u>: [32] not according to the covenant that I made with their fathers in the day that I took them by the hand to bring them out of the land of Egypt; which my covenant they broke, although I was a husband to them, says Yahweh. ³³ But <u>this is the covenant</u> that I will make with the house of Israel after those days, <u>says Yahweh: I will put my law in their inward parts, and in their heart will I write it</u>; and I will be their God, and they shall be my people" (Jer. 31:31-33).

"⁷ For <u>if that first covenant had been faultless, then would no place have been sought for a second. ⁸ For</u> [f] <u>finding fault with them, he saith,</u> [g]<u>Behold, the days come, saith the Lord, That I will</u> [h]<u>make a new covenant with the house of Israel and with the house of Judah</u>; ⁹ Not according to the covenant that I made with their fathers In the day that I took them by the hand to lead them forth out of the land of Egypt; For they continued not in my covenant, And I regarded them not, saith the Lord. ¹⁰ For <u>this is the covenant</u> that [i]I will make with the house of Israel After those days, saith the Lord; <u>I will put my laws into their mind, And on their heart also will I write them</u>: And I will be to them a God, And they shall be to me a people: ¹¹ And they shall not teach every man his fellow-citizen, And every man his brother, saying, Know the Lord: For all shall know me, From the least to the greatest of them. ¹² For I will be merciful to their iniquities, And their sins will I remember no more. ¹³ <u>In that he saith, A new covenant, he hath made the first old. But that which is becoming old and waxeth aged is nigh unto vanishing away</u>" (Heb. 8:7-13).

"¹⁶ <u>The law and the prophets were until John</u>: from that time the [j]gospel of the kingdom of God is preached, and every man entereth violently into it" (Lk. 16:16).

"¹⁷ Now this I say: A covenant confirmed beforehand by God, _the law, which came four hundred and thirty years after_, doth not disannul, so as to make the promise of none effect. [18] For if the inheritance is of the law, it is no more of promise: but God hath granted it to Abraham by promise. [19] _What then is the law? It was added because of transgressions, till the seed should come to whom the promise hath been made;_ and it was ordained through angels by the hand of a mediator" (Gal. 3:17-19).

"[24] So that _the law is become our tutor to bring us unto Christ_, that we might be justified by faith. [25] But _now that faith is come, we are no longer under a tutor_" (Gal. 3:24-25).

"[1] There is therefore now no condemnation to them that are in Christ Jesus. [2] For _the law of the Spirit of life in Christ Jesus made me free from the law of sin and of death_. [3] For what the law could not do, [a] in that it was weak through the flesh, God, sending his own Son in the likeness of [b] sinful flesh [c] and for sin, condemned sin in the flesh" (Rom. 8:1-3).

"[6] who also made us sufficient as _ministers of a new covenant; not of the letter, but of the spirit:_ for the letter killeth, but the spirit giveth life" (2Cor. 3:6).

"[6] But now we have been discharged from the law, having died to that wherein we were held; so that _we serve in newness of the spirit, and not in oldness of the letter_" (Rom. 7:6).

"[13] in whom ye also, having heard the word of the truth, the [i] gospel of your salvation,—in whom, having also believed, _ye were sealed with the Holy Spirit of promise_" (Eph. 1:13).

"[30] And _grieve not the Holy Spirit of God, in whom ye were sealed_ unto the day of redemption" (Eph. 4:30).

"[21] Now he that establisheth us with you [i] in Christ,

and anointed us, is God; [22] [j]<u>who also sealed us, and gave us the earnest of the Spirit in our hearts</u>" (2Cor. 1:21-22).

"[14] having blotted out [g]the bond written in ordinances that was against us, which was contrary to us: and he hath taken it out of the way, nailing it to the cross; [15] [h]having despoiled the principalities and the powers, he made a show of them openly, triumphing over them in it. [16] <u>Let no man therefore judge you in meat, or in drink, or in respect of a feast day or a new moon or a sabbath day</u>: [17] which are a shadow of the things to come; but the body is Christ's" (Col. 2:14-17).

"[9] but now that ye have come to know God, or rather to be known by God, how turn ye back again to the weak and beggarly [b]rudiments, whereunto ye desire to be in bondage over again? [10] <u>Ye observe days, and months, and seasons, and years.</u> [11] <u>I am afraid of you, lest by any means I have bestowed labor upon you in vain</u>" (Gal. 4:9-11).

"[27] And he said unto them, <u>The sabbath was made for man, and not man for the sabbath</u>: [28] so that the Son of man is lord even of the sabbath" (Mk. 2:27-28).

"[17] For the law was given through Moses; <u>grace and truth came through Jesus Christ</u>" (Jn. 1:17).

"[14] For sin shall not have dominion over you: for <u>ye are not under law, but under grace</u>" (Rom. 6:14).

"[18] But if ye are led by the Spirit, <u>ye are not under the law</u>" (Gal. 5:18).

"[28] <u>Come unto me</u>, all ye that labor and are heavy laden, <u>and I will give you rest</u>" (Mt. 11:28).

The following prophetic verses cannot be attributed to the Western Roman Empire

"¹ and [a]he stood upon the sand of the sea. And I saw a beast coming up out of the sea, having ten horns and seven heads, and on his horns ten diadems, and upon his heads names of blasphemy. ² And <u>the beast which I saw was like unto a leopard, and his feet were as the feet of a bear, and his mouth as the mouth of a lion</u>: and the dragon gave him his power, and his throne, and great authority" (Rev. 13:1-3).

"⁵ and there was given to him a mouth speaking great things and blasphemies; and <u>there was given to him authority [e]to continue forty and two months</u>" (Rev. 13:5).

"² And the court which is without the [c]temple [d] leave without, and measure it not; for it hath been given unto the [e]nations: and <u>the holy city shall they tread under foot forty and two months</u>" (Rev. 11:2).

"⁷ And when they shall have finished their testimony, <u>the beast that cometh up out of the abyss shall make war with them</u>, and overcome them, and kill them. ⁸ And their [q]<u>dead bodies lie in the street of the great city</u>, which spiritually is called Sodom and Egypt, <u>where also their Lord was crucified</u>" (Rev. 11:7-8).

"³ And he carried me away in the Spirit into a wilderness: and <u>I saw a woman sitting upon a scarlet-colored beast</u>, [a]full of names of blasphemy, <u>having seven heads and ten horns</u>" (Rev. 17:3).

"³So he carried me away in the spirit into the wilderness: <u>and I saw a woman sit upon a scarlet coloured beast</u>, full of names of blasphemy, <u>having seven heads and ten horns</u>" (Rev. 17:3).

"*8 The beast that thou sawest was, and is not; and is about to come up out of the abyss*, [f]*and to go into* perdition. And they that dwell on the earth shall wonder, they whose name hath not been written [g] in the book of life from the foundation of the world, *when they behold the beast, how that he was, and is not, and* [h]*shall come*" (Rev. 17:8).

"*9 Here is the* [i]*mind that hath wisdom. The seven heads are seven mountains*, on which the woman sitteth: *10 and* [j]*they are seven kings; the five are fallen, the one is, the other is not yet come*; and when he cometh, he must continue a little while. *11 And the beast that was, and is not, is himself also an eighth, and is of the seven*; and he goeth into perdition" (Rev. 17:9-11).

"*12 And the ten horns that thou sawest are ten kings, who have received no kingdom as yet*; but they receive authority as kings, with the beast, for one hour" (Rev. 17:12).

"*15 And he saith unto me, The waters which thou sawest, where the harlot sitteth, are peoples, and multitudes, and nations, and tongues*. *16 And the ten horns which thou sawest, and the beast, these shall hate the harlot, and shall make her desolate and naked, and shall eat her flesh, and shall burn her utterly with fire*" (Rev. 17:15-16).

"*20 Rejoice over her*, thou heaven, and ye saints, and ye apostles, and *ye prophets*; for God hath judged your judgment on her" (Rev. 18:20).

"*24 And in her was found the blood of prophets* and of_saints, and of all that have been slain upon the earth" (Rev. 20:24).

Seventh-day Adventists are entangled in a very complex doctrinal compromise that can be perceived only after a thorough analysis of those arrogant doctrinal allegations as follows:

1) Adventists are baptized in the name of the Father, and of the Son, and of the Holy Spirit. However, to be baptized, they must accept the 27(28) Adventist fundamental beliefs with which they were previously acquainted with during baptismal classes. This is confirmed by the baptismal vow (traditional vow 11 or affirmation 2 of the alternative vow introduced in 2005) when baptismal candidate pledges to order his life in harmony with Adventist fundamental beliefs, which include belief 23(24) "Christ's Ministry in the Heavenly Sanctuary." Therefore, they must accept the "October 22, 1844 Christ." Doctrinally, Adventists are being baptized in the name of the Father, and of the Son (the October 22, 1844 Christ), and the Holy Spirit.

2) At baptism, the name "Ellen G. White" is not mentioned. However, as stated previously, baptismal candidate prior to baptismal immersion pledges to order his life in harmony with the 27(28) Adventist fundamental beliefs, which include belief 17(18) "The Gifts of Prophecy." Therefore, doctrinally, Adventists must accept Ellen G. White as the Lord's messenger (a prophet) and her writings as a continuous and authoritative source of truth which provides for the church comfort, guidance, instruction, and correction.

3) According to vow 6, beliefs 18(19) and 19(20) Adventists are bound to the law, the Ten Commandments, which includes the seventh-day Sabbath observance. The Sabbath is presented to Adventist masses as God's perpetual sign of His eternal covenant between Him and His people; however, correct understanding of the word of God is obscured by tendentious interpretations.

Excessive emphasis is placed on Bible verses according to which Sabbath is an everlasting sign of God's everlasting covenant (Ex 31:13, 16-17; Ezek 20:12, 20). However, other verses (Is. 1:13; Hos. 2:11; Heb. 4:1-11) are neglected. The prophet Jeremiah foretold that a day is coming when God will make a new covenant with His people; the prophet Isaiah stated that God is not pleased with sacrifices, Sabbaths, and religious assemblies; the prophet Hosea foretold that God will put an end to Sabbath and all religious festivities of Israel. Therefore, the old covenant and its sign, the seventh-day Sabbath, become terminable, limited by the new covenant that was to come. The expression *"everlasting"* biblically attributed to the Sinaitic (Mosaic) covenant and to the Sabbath, was in effect for generations until God established on the cross of Golgotha a new covenant with His people. The two covenants do not contradict each other; in fact, the old covenant is a precursor of the new covenant; the old one has been replaced by a new and better one! According to the Old Testament law, there are also other practices declared everlasting (daily burned offerings, religious festivals, circumcision…), which do not apply anymore to believers under the new covenant; yet, when it comes to the Sabbath law, Adventists manifest partiality. The allegation that God put an end to the old covenant, but did not put an end to seventh-day Sabbath, the sign of that covenant, reflects a fallacious and tendentious reasoning.

The following Bible topics are being avoided: Christ fulfilled the law; Christ is the end of the law; those who are led by the Spirit are not under the law; Sabbath is a shadow of the things of the future; true rest (Sabbath) is in Spirit – we find that rest in Christ and through Christ; Christians should honour the Lord of the Sabbath, not the Sabbath day; early Christians were gathering for worship and the Lord's Supper (Holy Communion) on the first day of the week – they were not subject to the Sabbath law. Sermons concerning Jewish religious leaders' plot to kill Jesus for breaking the Sabbath law are hardly ever preached; if there are any, those verses are given an interpretation that suits the Seventh-day Adventist doctrines.

The fact that certain believers claim to be bound to the law, the Ten Commandments, which does not prohibit slavery, polygamy, and many other things is saddening. The entire law (Ten Commandments, Torah) and the prophets depend on Jesus' two commandments of love (Mt. 22:36-40). A believer led by the Spirit is not under the law (Gal. 5:18), because the law is for law-breakers (1Tim. 1:9). The law is a reminder of what sin is.

4) Adventists are bound to the law; therefore, doctrinally there is a relative space for God's grace. The new covenant believers are under grace, not under law (Rom. 6:14). Christ has done away with the Levitical priesthood, animal sacrifices, and other Old Testament ordinances. Jesus Christ's Calvary on the cross of Golgotha marks the end of the Sinaitic covenant and its sign, the Sabbath – the cross of Golgotha also marks the beginning of God's new covenant. This new covenant is based on Jesus' two commandments of love (agape). Many sincere Adventist are aware of the fact that certain Adventist doctrinal teachings are questionable, that Seventh-day Adventist Church in many aspects seems rather lukewarm and sad, and that there are moments in their Adventist way of life when agape-love seems scarce. Being marked by legalism concerning the law, Sabbath, and Ellen White's writings a new approach has been elaborated, that of creating a new image – vegetarianism and healthy diet – which does not seem to be a bad idea as long as it does not reach extremes, fanaticism. However, religiously oriented image should be manifested *"in spirit and in truth"*; this requires correction or elimination of controversial doctrinal teachings on the part of the Seventh-day Adventist Church – so far all Adventist fundamental beliefs are still intact.

The sad reality about Seventh-day Adventists is that they are entangled in very controversial doctrinal teachings like: Sunday-keeping is the mark of the beast; Seventh-day Sabbath is the seal of God; Ellen G. White is the Lord's messenger (a prophet) and her writings as a continuous and authoritative source of truth in the church; Seventh-day Adventist Church is the remnant church; the beast with seven heads and ten horns represents the revived Western Roman Empire; the beast with two horns like a lamb represents the USA; the woman (Babylon the Great, the great city) sitting on a scarlet-coloured beast represents Rome (Roman Catholic Church). Seventh-day Adventists are very devoted believers; however, their devotion is partly directed towards man-made doctrines. With a sincere hope that this

Adventist dilemma will be solved, it is pertinent in given case to suggest the following Bible verses:

> "[9] But in vain do they worship me, Teaching as their doctrines the precepts of men" (Mt. 15:9).

> "[35] Look therefore whether the light that is in thee be not darkness" (Lk. 11:35).

> "[17] Sanctify them in your truth. Your word is truth. [a]" (Jn. 17:17 WEB).

A reasonable believer should examine his belief and evaluate it spiritually. An unexamined life is not worth living, and an unexamined religion is not worth believing!

The Gospel of John starts with the following biblical truth:

> "[1] In the beginning was the Word, and the Word was with God, and the Word was God. [2] The same was in the beginning with God. [3] All things were made through him; and without him [a]was not anything made that hath been made. [4] In him was life; and the life was the light of men. [5] And the light shineth in the darkness; and the darkness [b]apprehended it not" (Jn. 1:1-5).

Biblically, the "Word" means "Christ." From a linguistic point of view, the word represents a spoken or written sound or combination of sounds that communicates a meaning, that is, the word is the basic element of communication. Words, written or spoken, are used to express one's feeling, opinion, intellect... The central issue in this context is that God the Creator wants His people, who were made in His image, to be reasonable – God does not want us to live in the shadow of ignorance.

Physically, we rest every day, every time we feel tired, exhausted. God is Spirit; He desires a worship "in spirit and in truth", not through man-made doctrines. Therefore, God the Creator offers His people "eternal" life and "eternal" rest (Sabbath) in Christ and through Christ. The following Bible verses confirm this statement:

"23 But the hour cometh, and now is, when the true worshippers shall worship the Father in spirit and truth: [g]for such doth the Father seek to be his worshippers. 24 [h]God is a Spirit: and they that worship him must worship in spirit and truth" (Jn. 4:23-24).

"17 But Jesus answered them, My Father worketh even until now, and I work" (Jn. 5:17).

"6 Jesus saith unto him, I am the way, and the truth, and the life: no one cometh unto the Father, but [d] by me" (Jn. 14:6).

"28 Come unto me, all ye that labor and are heavy laden, and I will give you rest" (Mt. 11:28).

Some readers might consider this book to be a campaign against the Adventist Church. Absolutely not! As mentioned earlier, Seventh-day Adventists are very devoted believers; however, some of their doctrinal teachings are marked by inconsistency and contradiction. The purpose of this book is to bring to light those controversial doctrinal teachings and combat tendentious interpretations of the prophecy regarding the beasts of Revelation. The book is meant to unveil the hidden and overlooked side of the truth, to break the silence that has been persisting for a long time, and to propose an approach of the word of God *"in spirit and in truth."*

Believers under the new covenant order their life in harmony with the teachings of our Lord Jesus Christ. Sadly, some believers are entangled in erroneous and tendentious interpretations of the Bible; however, the truth is always around to free them.

Bibliography

The Holy Bible, American Standard Version (ASV)

The Holy Bible, World English Bible (WEB)

[1]"Advent." *Wikipedia: The Free Encyclopedia*. Wikimedia Foundation, Inc. 10 June 2016. Web. 4 July 2016. <http://en. wikipedia.org./wiki/Advent>

[2] Signs in Heaven – Truth or Fables. Web. 4 July 2016. <http: // www. truthorfables.com/ Signs_in_ Heaven.htm>

[3] Crosier renounced the "shut door" - Truth or Fables. Web. 4 July 2016. <http://www.truthorfables.com/Crosier_Renounces_ Shut_ Door. htm>

[4] "Edson, Hiram." *Wikipedia: The Free Encyclopedia*. Wikimedia Foundation, Inc. 6 May 2016. Web. 4 July 2016. <http://en. wikipedia.org/wiki/Hiram_Edson>

[5] "Joseph Bates (Adventist)." *Wikipedia: The Free Encyclopedia*. Wikimedia Foundation, Inc. 2 July 2016. Web. 30 June 2016. <http://en.wikipedia.org/wiki/Joseph_Bates_ (Adventist)>

[6] "T. M. Preble." *Wikipedia: The Free Encyclopedia*. Wikimedia Foundation, Inc. 24 May 2016. Web. 4 July 2016. <http://en. wikipedia.org/wiki/T._M._Preble>

[7] "Rachel O. Preston." *Wikipedia: The Free Encyclopedia*. Wikimedia Foundation, Inc. 20 April 2016. Web. 4 July 2016. <http://en. wikipedia.org/wiki/Rachel_Oakes_Preston>

[8] "Seventh-day Adventist Church." *Wikipedia: The Free Encyclopedia*. Wikimedia Foundation, Inc. 4 July 2016. Web. 4 July 2016. <http: //en.wikipedia.org/wiki/Seventh-day_ Adventist_ Church>

9 Early Christians always met on the First day (Sunday) and never ... Web. 4 July 2016. < http://www.bible.ca/H-sunday.htm>

10 Appleton, Helen. What Seventh Day Adventists Believe. Web. 4 July 2016. <http://www.exadventist.com/.../What%20 Seventh%20 Day% 20Adventists%20Believe%20by...>

11 The 3.5 years of the French Revolution - EllenWhiteExposed. com. 4 January 2012. Web. (Not retrieved recently). <http:// www. ellenwhiteexposed.com/gc3.htm>

12 "Dechristianization of France during the France Revolution." *Wikipedia: The Free Encyclopedia*. Wikimedia Foundation, Inc. 29 June 2016. Web. 4 July 2016. <https://en.wikipedia.org.../ Dechristianization_of_France_during_the_French_Revolution>

13 "Reign of Terror." *Wikipedia: The Free Encyclopedia*. Wikimedia Foundation, Inc. 1 July 2016. Web. 4 July 2016. <http://en. wikipedia. org.wiki/Reign_of_Terror>

14 "Declaration of the Rights of Man and of the Citizen." *Wikipedia: The Free Encyclopedia*. Wekimedia Foundation, Inc. 27 June 2016. Web. 4 July 2016. <http://en.wikipedia.org.wiki/ Declaration_ of_ the_Rights_of_Man_and_of_the_Citizen>

15 "Seven hills of Rome." *Wikipedia: The Free Encyclopedia*. Wikimedia Foundation, Inc. 15 June 2016. Web. 4 July 2016. <http://en. wikipedia.org.wiki/Seven_hills_of_Rome>

16 "Seven hills of Istanbul." *Wikipedia: The Free Encyclopedia*. Wikimedia Foundation, Inc. 16 April 2016. Web. 4 July 2016. <http://en.wikipedia.org.wiki/Seven_hills_of_Istanbul>

17 Seven heads and ten horns - Jesus Messiah. Web. 4 July 2016. <http://jesus-messiah.com/prophecy/rev-13.html>

18 "List of cities claimed to be built on seven hills." *Wikipedia: The Free Encyclopedia*. Wikimedia Foundation, Inc. 15 June 2016. Web. 20 April 2015. <http://en.wikipedia.org.wiki/List_ of_cities_ claimed_to_be_built_on_seven_hills>

[19]"Kaaba." Wikipedia: *The Free Encyclopedia*. Wikimedia Foundation, Inc. 24 June 2016. Web. 4 July 2016. <http://en.wikipedia.org/wiki/Kaaba>

[20] "Qibla." Wikipedia: *The Free Encyclopedia*. Wikimedia Foundation, Inc. 31 May 2016. Web. 4 July 2016. <http://en.wikipedia.org/ wiki/Qibla>

[21] "United States Declaration of independence." *Wikipedia: The Free*

Encyclopedia. Wikimedia Foundation, Inc. 12 June 2016. Web. 4 July 2016. <http://en.wikipedia.org/wiki/United_States_Declaration_ of_Independence>

[22] "Islamic calendar." *Wikipedia: The Free Encyclopedia*. Wikimedia Foundation, Inc. 5 July 2016. Web. 6 July 2016. <http://en. wikipedia. org/wiki/Islamic_calendar>

[23] "Seven Laws of Noah." *Wikipedia: The Free Encyclopedia*. Wikimedia Foundation, Inc. 20 June 2016. Web. 4 July 2016. <http://en. wikipedia.org/wiki/Seven_Laws_of_Noah>

[24] "Agape." *Wikipedia: The Free Enciclopedia*. Wikimedia Foundation, Inc. 14 June 2016. Web. 4 July 2016. <http://en.wikipedia.org/ wiki/Agape>

[25] Early Christians always met on the First day (Sunday) and never... Web. 4 July 2016. <http://www.bible.ca/H-sunday.htm>

[26] "Sunday keeping" DID NOT originate in the pagan religion of Mithraism. Web. 4 July 2016. <http://www.bible.ca/7-Mithraism. htm>

[27] Weigall, Arthur: The Paganism of our Christianity - Bible. ca. Web. 4 July 2016. <http://www.bible.ca/trinity/trinity-Weigall.htm>

[28] "Sol Invictus." *Wikipedia: The Free Encyclopedia*. Wikimedia Foundation, Inc. 8 May 2016. Web 4 July 2016. <http://en. wikipedia. org.wiki/Sol_Invictus>

29 The Ellen G. White Website: Prophet? or Plagiarist! - Bible. ca. Web. 4 July 2016. <http://www.bible.ca/7-plagiarism.htm>

30 Prophecy blunders of Ellen G. White. Bible.ca. Web. 4 July 2016. <http://www. bible.ca/7-prophecy-blunders.htm>

31 Ellen G. White Contradicts the Bible Over 50 Times. There is ... - Truth or Fables. Web. 4 July 2016. http://truthorfables.com/ EGW_ Contradicts.htm>

32 Are Ellen G. White's Writings Infallible? - Truth or Fables. Web. 4 July 2016. <http://www.truthorfables.com/EGW_ Writings_Infallible. htm>

33 Ellen G. White eats meat and oysters - Truth or Fables. Web. 4 July 2016. <http://www.truthorfables.com/EGW_Eats_Meat_ Oysters. htm>

34 Ellen G. White's health reforms - Truth or Fables. Web. 4 July 2016. <http://www.truthorfables.com/EGW_Health_ Reform.htm>

35 Ellen G. White bans sports - Truth or Fables. Web. 4 July 2016. <http://www. truthorfables.com/EGW_Bans_Sports.htm>

36 Ellen G. White and Picture Idols - Truth or Fables. Web. 4 July 2016. <http://www.truthorfables.com/EGW_Pictures_ Idols.htm>

37 104 Adventist Pastors fired for rejecting the inspiration of Ellen G. White. Web. 4 July 2016. <http://www.bible.ca/7-white-inp-sired-100-pastors-fired.htm>

38 Ellen G. White found guilty of plagiarism (copying) - Bible. ca. Web. 4 July 2016. <http://www.bible.ca/7-WL-exhibit-de-sire-spirit.htm>

39 Ellen G. White found guilty of plagiarism (copying) - Bible.ca. Web. 4 July 2016. <http://www.bible.ca/7-WL-exhibits-Great-Contro.htm>

[40] Myth #7: Great Controversy delivered by vision – EllenWhiteExposed. com. 4 January 2012. Web. (Not retrieved recently). <http://www. ellenwhiteexposed.com/ myth7.htm>

[41] Plagiarism of Health Writings - EllenWhiteExposed. 4 January 2012. Web. (Not retrieved recently). <http://www. ellenwhiteexposed. com/health2.htm>

[42] EGW's Temporal Lobe Epilepsy - Truth or Fables. Web. 4 July 2016. <http://www.truthorfables.com/EGW%20 Temporal%20Lobe.pdf>

[43] EGW: Royalties and Profits by A Prophet by E. S. Ballenger. Web. 4 July 2016. <http://www.truthorfables.com/EGW_ Royalties. htm>

[44] THE PIRATES OF PRIVILEGE: Walter Rea Rocks the Seventh-day ... December 1984. Web. 4 July 2016. <http:// www.bible.ca/7-pirates-of-privilege. htm>

[45] "The Clear Word." *Wikipedia: The Free Encyclopedia*. Wikimedia Foundation, Inc. 31 March 2016. Web. 4 July 2016. <http://en. wikipedia.org/wiki/The_Clear_Word>

[46] "Five solae." *Wikipedia: The Free Encyclopedia*. Wikimedia Foundation, Inc. 4 July 2016. Web. 4 July 2016. <http://en. wikipedia.org/wiki/Five_solae>

[47] "Baptism." *Wikipedia: The Free Encyclopedia*. Wikimedia Foundation, Inc. 27 June 2016. Web. 4 July 2016. <http://en. wikipedia.org/wiki/ Baptism>

[48] Official creed and Baptismal vows of Seventh-day Adventist ... - Bible.ca. Web. 4 July 2016. <http://www. bible.ca/ cr-SDA.htm>

[49] "Adventist Baptismal Vow." *Wikipedia: The Free Encyclopedia*. Wikimedia Foundation, Inc. 24 January 2016. Web. 4 July 2016. <http://en.wikipedia.org/wiki/Adventist_Baptismal_Vow>

[50] "28 Fundamental Beliefs (Adventist)." Wikipedia: *The Free Encyclopedia*. Wikimedia Foundation, Inc. 15 April 2016. Web. 4 July 2016. <http://en.wikipedia.org/wiki/28_ Fundamenta_ Beliefs_ (Adventist)>

[51] See "Baptized into Ellen G. White" – Truth or Fables. Web. 4 July 2016. <http://www. truthorfables.com/ Baptized_into_ EGW.htm>

[52] "Midnight sun." *Wikipedia: The Free Encyclopedia*. Wikimedia Foundation, Inc. 27 June 2016. Web. 4 July 2016. <http://en. wikipedia.org/wiki/Midnight_sun>